O9-BUB-404

Military
Leadership

FOURTH EDITION

Military
Leadership

In Pursuit of Excellence

EDITED BY

Robert L. Taylor
University of Louisville

AND

William E. Rosenbach
Gettysburg College

WITH A FOREWORD BY
Walter F. Ulmer, Jr.

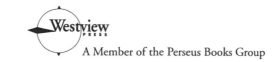
A Member of the Perseus Books Group

All rights reserved. Printed in the United States of America. No part of this publication may be reproduced or transmitted in any form or by any means, electronic or mechanical, including photocopy, recording, or any information storage and retrieval system, without permission in writing from the publisher.

Copyright © 2000 by Westview Press, A Member of the Perseus Books Group

Published in 2000 in the United States of America by Westview Press, 5500 Central Avenue, Boulder, Colorado 80301-2877, and in the United Kingdom by Westview Press, 12 Hid's Copse Road, Cumnor Hill, Oxford OX2 9JJ

Visit us on the World Wide Web at www.westviewpress.com

Library of Congress Cataloging-in-Publication Data
    Military leadership : in pursuit of excellence / edited by Robert L. Taylor, William E. Rosenbach—4th ed.
        p.   cm.
    Includes bibliographical references.
    ISBN 0-8133-6839-1 (pbk.)
    1. Leadership.   2. Command of troops.   I. Taylor, Robert L. (Robert Lewis), 1939– .   II. Rosenbach, William E.   III. Title.
UB210.M553   2000
355.3'3041—dc21   99-048661
                                                                                    CIP

The paper used in this publication meets the requirements of the American National Standard for Permanence of Paper for Printed Library Materials Z39.48-1984.

10   9   8   7   6   5   4   3   2   1

To Lieutenant General Walter Ulmer—
soldier, scholar, LEADER

Contents

Foreword

Because the process of leadership involves basic human needs and aspirations, it can be examined usefully in a wide variety of settings. But a military setting, especially in the armed forces of a democratic society, has the potential for revealing particularly sharp and cogent insights. The military environment seems to provide unique opportunities for learning. Military operations tend to highlight success or failure, confirm courage or hesitation, validate selflessness or ego, assess empathy or callousness, and take measure of the integration of the behavioral and management sciences. Interestingly, a high percentage of leadership studies reported in the mainline literature are related to the military, either by context or author. It is not that leadership in the arts, business, or science is not of ultimate consequence to societal progress. It is simply that these domains do not routinely and vividly expose the bedrock of character. Battles and heroes across the ages of military history are still cited in the textbooks of today because changes in technology and war-fighting doctrine are clearly secondary to unchanging human nature.

These collected articles do justice to the full spectrum of leadership interests. There is plenty for scholar and practitioner alike, as there was in previous editions of this book. Since none of us has completed the entire leadership curriculum, there is something here for everybody. How nice it would be if everyone knew for sure which parts of the text were personally most applicable. Continuing the adult learning process, particularly among accomplished people, remains a formidable challenge. It is especially difficult with leadership, since it deals with the most fundamental and sensitive aspects of our nature. It is becoming ever more clear that good leadership in organizations can be sustained only through the efforts of leaders at all organizational levels. What is also clear is that, as George Orwell would put it, "All leaders are important, but some leaders are more important than others!" Only in a few scholarly dialogues are there still questions about whether or not senior leaders really count. They count particularly as they design and influence systems within the organization. They also conspicuously set standards by their own behavior, a fact more apparent to subordinates than to principals. More than a few leaders become unaware of the impact of their behavior after they move up to high positions. Books such as this one can stimulate self-assessment, always more of a chore than critiquing other people's efforts. In looking at our own and at others' experience, we tend to explore *what happened* and neglect the issue of *why did it happen that way?*

Improving our leadership competencies may be noticeably difficult as we start this new century in "interesting times": an era filled with new excitement, new opportunities, and little time for contemplation or renewal. Leaders in all venues will face a severe test of their competence and commitment. Military leaders may well find themselves at the vortex of the geopolitical, social, and technological factors that we have heard about as characteristic of the new century. Again, we have convincing evidence from at least three decades of quantitative data and 2,000 years of anecdotal information that leaders play a key role in organizational productivity. However, whether or not our institutions, including the military, take leadership seriously enough is an open question. As Kouzes notes in his article, "Despite our cry for more effective leadership I've become convinced that we are quite satisfied to do without it." In the same vein, Potter, Rosenbach, and Pittman note that ". . . the ways that organizations measure performance do not always include every aspect of leadership." It might not be too dramatic to conclude that we may be approaching a watershed regarding our ability to apply effectively and routinely the principles of individual and organizational leadership in the military—and elsewhere. According to Lehman and to Hasty and Weber, among others, we have not done as well as we should have over the last decade. That local leadership can make an exciting difference is spelled out again in the LaBarre article. With a few variations here and there, the basic leadership theories are firmly in hand. It is the practice—the application of theory—that remains disjointed. Since we know leadership can make a difference, why do we not demand that effective leadership techniques be used and evaluated at all levels? There are four recurring themes among the many rich concepts in this book that can help us answer that question.

Four specific elements of leadership application are among those needing prompt attention. The first of the elements is the high expectation of the workforce for a stimulating, rational, and supportive work environment. The second is the tendency of leaders in a stressful, competitive situation to fall back on positional rather than motivational influence to get the immediate results organizations prize so highly. The third element is the inherent, often unresolved stress among competing loyalties that confronts all leaders in organizations. The fourth is the recent technological magic that stuffs mountains of raw data into every crevice of the organization. Each of these elements is addressed in useful form, from different perspectives, by the articles in this book.

Computer programmers, laboratory technicians, airline pilots, teachers, and soldiers, among others, have come to expect a reasonable work envi-

ronment. This is a logical, healthy outcome from an increasingly more educated and sophisticated citizenry. When members of the civilian workforce
are discontented they move to another company, another university, another laboratory. When members of the armed forces are similarly discour-
aged they often move to another career. Too many are now moving to that
other career. That move is made easier since current opportunities in our
society for adventure, travel, equal opportunity for success, and altruistic
service can be found outside as well as within the military. The pay outside
is often better and the nights away from family fewer. Additional resources
in terms of dollars for training and repair parts are part of the formula for a
more satisfying work environment. Leadership that is more uniformly insightful, thoughtful, and courageous is an even larger part of that formula.
Yet our analyses of institutional problems rarely discuss leadership performance—particularly at higher levels—as a factor. (Perceived problems with
strategic leadership are of course regularly, mostly constructively, mentioned by individuals at the tactical level!)

Several dissatisfied career members of our armed forces have mentioned
that "It's just not fun anymore!" Fun? Since when should service in the
armed forces be "fun"? In the context of their complaints, the answer is
"Always had been—always should be." The mere occupational model, a
simple transaction of pay for service, will never produce a combat-ready
force, or a peacekeeping-ready force for that matter. This "fun" of course
does not mean freedom from responsibility or hardship. It means adventure, challenge, companionship, mutual trust, and a broad sense of satisfaction. It means having a clear mission and resources to accomplish the mission without peculiar bureaucratic encumbrances. It means being able to
train to standards and to be proud of excellence. As the Navy captain was
quoted in the article by Hasty and Weber, "Give good junior officers opportunities to have fun in a culture willing to confront problems and take care
of its own, and they will stay." "Fun" provides an essential tonic for the
armed forces. It is almost entirely a product of leadership, both local and
strategic.

The fact that immediate gratification, prompt results, and uncomplicated
plots are hallmarks of our modern times is relevant. In the tactical mode of
assaulting a hill this determination for quick victory may be crucial. But
most leader decisions are not driven by a clear short-term objective that ap-
proves any kind of action just to get today's job done. There is almost always time for motivation and inspiration that will sustain enthusiasm beyond the next hill. The competent leader thinks of the requirements for
tomorrow's battle. But battlefield or conference room, the urge to demonstrate results, and resort unnecessarily to positional power, is strong among
those who rise to the higher leadership positions. The authoritarian mode is

even more automatic when organizational stress is high and fear of failure abounds. The basis for these reactions and fears may be deeply biological or psychological. Whatever their sources they are incapacitating. They need to be remedied by the kind of solid leadership initiatives described in the pages ahead. Because there are at least as many supportive organizational climates as dysfunctional ones within our armed forces, we have proof therefore that good leadership, the only variable in the equation, can make a profound difference even in challenging times. What a pity that somehow the lesson still does not echo clearly everywhere.

That conflicts exist among competing positive values is not news. All professions confront ethical dilemmas between laudable principles: to make the new wonder drug available before the clinical trials are complete; to tap the phone line of an innocent to capture a criminal. The DeRemer article introduces directly that most perplexing value conflict of competing loyalties. The problem of responding promptly to the boss when the boss *may* be wrong or ill advised or self-serving is ageless. It is also not amenable to a neat solution. Additionally, it is exacerbated by the competitive nature of the dynamic leaders who, thankfully, populate the military. As Mark Cantrell puts it, "Just as the subordinate is duty bound to voice dissent, the senior leader should consider himself obliged to listen if time allows." The crucial obligation to be candid, to have the courage to be candid, is closely tied to the dilemma of conflicting loyalties.

"Command by e-mail" is a newly perceived phenomenon. It is surely an unintended consequence. What commander in his right mind substitutes electrons for a visit to the front? Yet the intrusive, impersonal electron is sprinting through the processors and onto the screens of the multitude in many an organization. High speed, multi-directional communication is obviously a lifesaver in many circumstances. Yet the possibilities for disturbing the natural order, for facilitating micro-management, for developing reporting and assessment systems which undermine mutual trust, are enormous.

Recent studies of the perceptions and attitudes of members of America's armed forces of all ranks show a solid respect for basic military values. While the socialization process is more difficult with some recruits and officer candidates than it might have been thirty years ago, there is by every measure a strong base of the right stuff among military personnel, active and reserve. A basic willingness to sacrifice for mission accomplishment, a recognition that the armed forces must insist on unique standards of behavior on and off duty, and an expectation for tough discipline are still around in good measure. This is as it must be because the likely environment for twenty-first century military operations will demand those qualities and more. The "more" will center about the need for agility, versatility, and strong cohesion in our operational units. Agility, versatility, and cohesion depend absolutely on the quality of leadership we provide to the good people who continue to populate the remarkable, heroic institution that is the American military establishment. The next couple decades may decide whether or not we really appreciate what leadership is all about.

Lt. Gen. (Ret.) Walter F. Ulmer, Jr.
Former President and CEO
Center for Creative Leadership

Preface

As the international political situation has changed over the past fifteen years, we have seen substantial changes in the military. In each of the three prior editions, we developed a collection of articles and essays that reflected the military at that time. This is our objective again in this fourth edition.

With the increasing ambiguity and complexity of political, social, and technological issues, we find that there continues to be a need to study leadership. The tenets of leadership have not necessarily changed. However, the context is drastically changing, and the way leaders behave is changing all the time. For this edition, we searched the literature and discovered that nearly 150 articles and essays had been written on military leadership since roughly 1995. In examining those works, we found that the classic articles remain a solid base for understanding leadership in the military. At the same time, we found several new pieces that clearly articulate the changing environments and their impact on military leadership today.

We believe, still, that no one book or text can provide a checklist of teachable skills that will ensure that the reader will be effective as a leader. Leadership is a process of human interactions and behaviors with an infinite number of personalities and situations. We continue to conclude that there is *no one right answer*.

Much of the contemporary literature discusses the mixed roles of the military: humanitarian peacekeeper, combat-readiness, flexible and adaptable, and managed with an eye toward efficiency. Budgets are reduced as the "Cold War" becomes a historical term. Yet military missions continue to emerge in diverse parts of the world. Today it is Kosovo. Recently, missions have been conducted in the Middle East, the Caribbean, Africa, and Eastern Europe. Much of this has involved the active participation of NATO through the use of international forces. Thus, the complexities are increased with multicultural and multinational forces under a single command. The impact has been pronounced, and so the search for a philosophy and an understanding of leadership increases.

In Part I, we provide a set of articles that creates the historical context for military leadership as well as some reflections on how contemporary events are modifying the traditional concepts. Our objective here is to identify the unique aspects of military leadership as well as the universal constructs associated with leadership in general. The comparisons and contrasts should be helpful.

Because the leader is so closely associated with the organization, we address climate, culture, and influence in Part II. Because we deal so much with change these days, the impact on organizational climate is significant. Whether it is social change or new technologies, the leader must adapt. The leader as role model defines the climate. Individual and group responsibilities are affected by our awareness of who we are and the impact we have on our followers.

Thus, in Part III, we deal with the personal challenge of military leadership. Simply stated, the dynamic behavioral interactions between leader and follower are the essence of military leadership. Appreciating effective leadership comes from understanding effective followership. Both concepts are worth pursuing. The situation is important, just as the personality of the followers influences the ability of the leader to command.

We conclude by addressing the current environment in Part IV. As the role of the military has changed, the people involved are different. Their expectations do not match those of the past, and the social context of the military continues to evolve. We see that enlightened leaders can succeed, but their victories reflect an understanding of those who follow as well as the environment in which they operate. As we move into the twenty-first century, there is much to reflect upon and even more to do.

Our goal is to make you think about those things that are special about military leadership. At the same time, we want the reader to explore the issues that will impact effective leadership for the future. The variety of perspectives is designed to capture nearly every bias one might have as a student of leadership. Our joy has been in our continuing study of military leadership in the hopes that our perspectives will influence the training and development of the leaders of the future.

Our commitment to this book is a continuing loyalty to the men and women with whom we served as well as those who serve today. We know that our leadership is now a retrospective. Our association with military people today suggests that the answers to understanding effective leadership are within those men and women, and our objective is to assist military leaders in developing their own effectiveness.

We are able to continue this series because of outstanding colleagues and friends. Our heartfelt thanks to Captains Rob Weber and Derek Hasty of the United States Army for their research on this volume as well as their commitment to sharing their views of leadership today. Cindy McDonald and Laura Ahrens gave unselfishly of their time to provide us superior administrative support. As always, Marda Numann kept us organized and on track by making sure that everything was done *right*. Leo Wiegman of

Westview Press and his staff demonstrate that quality editorial support makes a difference. Finally, we know that without the time and support given by those with whom we live, Colleen Rosenbach and Linda Shapiro, the friendship and book we share would not be possible.

Robert L. Taylor and William E. Rosenbach

PART 1

Military Leadership— Perspectives

Leadership is intangible, and therefore no weapon ever designed can replace it.
—Gen. Omar Bradley,
Command and General Staff College,
May 16, 1967

There continues to be a quest for understanding leadership. Historians search for clues that will help us understand how leaders are defined and what they do. Much of their work centers on the military and its leaders throughout the ages. And although politics and religion provide chronicles describing great leaders, the search continues. For the past several decades, the study of business leadership has added much to our understanding of the concept. Despite what has been learned, the military continues to focus on the need for leadership development. Despite changes in the political, social, and technological environments, we find that the modern historical perspectives as well as contemporary research provide an excellent background for those wishing to understand what is unique about military leadership.

Understanding Leadership

Each individual develops an idea of leadership, and there are as many definitions and descriptions of the term as there are people who write and speak about it. Most agree that leadership is an influence process with defined relationships between leaders and followers. Getting things done through others implies a process where people work together to achieve shared goals and aspirations.

The first thing that differentiates leaders from others is that they have a *vision* for the future. Leaders have an ability to "see" and place matters in perspective. Such vision is not made up of daydreams but rather the goals of an organization and its people. The vision becomes the focus for the leader's and followers' commitment, drive, and energy. Followers often feel

1

a sense of energy and excitement simply by being associated with their leader.

However, successful leadership entails more than just having a vision and being committed to it. The vision must be shared, and thus the leader must be skilled in *communicating*. This is a sensitive art, and the most effective leaders are able to not only communicate their own vision but also to work with followers to co-create a vision. The result is that *all* share the vision as their own. Should something happen to the leader, the vision remains powerful in the hearts and minds of the followers; goals and objectives are pursued in a way that reflects that they are "ours."

Motivating people to work together to fulfill the vision is an exciting challenge. We hear a great deal today about teams and team-building. The leader does not drive teams. Effective leaders create an environment in which people motivate themselves. Leaders empower others, share authority, and provide the wherewithal for committed followers to accomplish the mission. The vision is translated into action because everyone wants to succeed. Motivation is a collective energy, allowing people to achieve personal as well as organizational goals.

Leaders must be prepared to take charge when needed; *timing* is everything. Too often people are placed in leadership roles without being prepared. The predictable result is failure. Failure also ensues when a leader prepares incessantly but does not recognize when it is time to act. The latter situation relates to the concept of *risk*; some are unwilling to take action that may result in success or failure. With self-knowledge and self-confidence, leaders can assess the situation and determine the time and place for action in the best interests of the organization and its people.

There is no effective leadership without *trust*. Leaders are dependent upon trust as a bond between them and their followers. This bond is a two-way process. Leaders must demonstration their trust in followers through delegation and empowerment. The leader enables followers to be worthy of that trust by ensuring adequate training, constant communication, and clearly defined goals. At the same time, followers depend upon the leader to be trustworthy—honest, consistent, equitable, and humane. Of all the modern organizations, there is none so dependent on the bonds of trust as the military.

Military Leadership

The study of leadership is laced with paradox. Individuals who possess all of the important characteristics and qualities of effective leaders don't necessarily succeed, and if they do, their efforts often result in great harm or tragedy to others. Moreover, leaders and followers often find themselves using unethical means to achieve worthy ends and vice versa. An individual who is a successful leader in one situation may fail in other situations even though he or she employs the same capacity, skill, and style. Other individuals (although not very many) are able to successfully lead in a variety of different settings. This brings up the question of whether leaders are born or made. Although there is general agreement that leadership can be learned, it is certainly true that some find it much easier to learn the qualities of successful leadership.

Can leadership be taught? That is the wrong question. A more relevant question is: Can leadership be learned? The answer is a resounding "Yes!" The potential for good leadership is widely dispersed in our society, not limited to a privileged few. Learning about leadership means learning to recognize bad leadership as well as good. Learning about leadership involves understanding the dynamic relationship between the leader and followers; recognizing the differing contexts and situations of the leadership landscape; and understanding the importance of the behavioral sciences, biography, the classics, economics, history, logic, and related disciplines that provide the perspective so important to leadership effectiveness. Individuals committed to improving their leadership effectiveness will take advantage of opportunities to improve their skills as speakers, debaters, negotiators, problem-clarifiers, and advocates. We agree with John Gardner that it is what you learn after you know it all that really matters.

There are significant differences in military, business, political, religious, and social organizations. Each calculates a "bottom line" in a unique way. Nonetheless, there are commonalties in organizational leadership, and the military has provided models that have been adopted by other organizations. At this point in our history, the dynamic changes taking place in our technological, international, and psychosocial environments are having a profound effect on the military. Developments in communications and technology have created a world in which the boundaries are less clear than ever before, and it is increasingly important that the military share what it has learned about leadership.

We do not believe that definitions of "military leadership" and "leadership" are important at this point. Rather, we invite you to clear away your preconceptions and biases. Read these chapters with an eye toward creating a framework in which you can understand the construct of leadership. Rather than searching for answers, examine your beliefs and values and resist adopting what others say or do. We have selected what we find are the best historical perspectives of military leadership and conclude the section with a view to the future. Think about who you are, what your situation is, and the needs of your unit. Leadership will come into focus, and it may or may not be what you originally thought.

From Then to Now

In "Leadership" (Chapter 1), Gen. Matthew Ridgway acknowledges that leadership is probably a combination of art and science. He thinks that there is far more art than science involved. He describes the chief ingredients of leadership as character, courage, and competence. His advice for developing leadership is to read history and biography, work hard, be humble, and be oneself. Ridgway's inability to specifically define activities or events that create success helps demonstrate why many keep returning to the concept of leadership as an art.

Gen. S.L.A. Marshall writes in "Leaders and Leadership" (Chapter 2) that great military leaders of the past possessed a certain set of qualities. These were inner qualities rather than outward marks of greatness. Relatively few leaders were acclaimed for leadership in their early years. Marshall's thesis is that most successful leaders are molded by the influences around them and that they have the average person's faults and vices. Leaders have a common desire for substantial recognition (ego) and the will to earn it fairly. Too often, people with great inner strength hold in contempt those less well endowed by nature than them and, hence, fail as leaders. He cites courage, humor, presence, and integrity as the ingredients for successful military leadership.

Brig. Gen. Huba Wass de Czece effectively summarizes leadership in four key functions in "A Comprehensive View of Leadership" (Chapter 3). First is the providing and instilling of purpose. The effective leader must have a clear idea of how the unit or organization fits into the larger scheme. Second is effective direction. Through information-gathering, analysis, decisionmaking, giving orders, and monitoring outcomes, the effective leader establishes context for action. Third, the effective leader provides motivation; followers act at all levels with mutual trust and respect. Effectiveness depends upon the leader's values and ethics as well. Finally, the leader focuses on sustaining continued effectiveness. Long-term development of the unit or organization is essential; leaders should think of the group as if they lead an organism, not a machine. He then suggests that there are differences in levels of leadership, with junior officers leading by example and the more senior officers influencing through the shaping of values, policies, and eventually organizational culture.

In "Leadership: Views from Readers" (Chapter 4) we provide the feedback to Gen. Wass de Czece's piece, which, in our opinion, is the mark of a provocative presentation. To assist you in understanding the breadth and depth of leadership perceptions, we selected representative letters that can help you to finalize a concept of leadership.

As we look to the military of the future, Marshall Sashkin and William E. Rosenbach propose "A New Vision of Leadership" (Chapter 5). They suggest that there has been a paradigm shift in leadership theory and practice. They review the evolution of the concepts in transactional and transformational leadership and examine three empirically derived models. First is Bernard Bass's Transactional/Transformational Leadership theory and his and Avolio's Multi-Factor Leadership questionnaire. Second, they review James Kouzes and Barry Z. Posner's model of transformational leadership and their Leadership Practices Inventory. Finally, they examine Sashkin's Visionary Leadership theory and the Leadership Profile developed by Sashkin and Rosenbach. They offer explanations of the apparent paradoxes in leadership as well as a criticism of the concept of transformational leadership. Our purpose here is to present a framework for you, the reader, to craft the future context of military leadership.

1

Leadership

Gen. Matthew B. Ridgway

In discussing the subject of leadership, I am struck by two diametrically opposite concepts. One conceives leadership as an exact science capable of being understood and practiced by anyone. This view is ably developed by Colonel Sherman L. Kiser, US Army, Retired, in his book, *The American Concept of Leadership*. An opposite concept holds that "no amount of learning will make a man a leader unless he has the natural qualities of one." This latter view was that of General Sir Archibald P. Wavell, and is expounded in his published lectures in *Generals and Generalship*. One concept treats leadership as a science; the other as an art.

I incline strongly to the Wavell concept. While recognizing that there are many principles, or truths, pertaining to the exercise of leadership, and while firmly believing that powers of leadership can be greatly increased in any individual through knowledge of these principles and practice in their application, I still think the variables of human nature combined with those of combat, and to a lesser degree with those in peacetime training, make the exercise of leadership far more of an art than a science.

There is, of course, a great deal of bad leadership as well as of good. It, too, deserves study so that its pitfalls may be avoided. But in general, I believe bad leadership is the result either of violation of basic principles, or the lack or failure to develop one or more of the qualities of good leadership. In any event, I want to speak now of the good type of military leadership with some specific reference later to combat leadership of large units—the division, corps, and army.

The chief ingredients of leadership, as I have known it to be exercised by those whose careers I have studied, or under whose command I was privi-

Reprinted by permission from *Military Review*, 46:10 (October 1966), pp. 40–49.

leged to serve, are three. I call them the three C's—character, courage, and competence.

Character is the bedrock on which the whole edifice of leadership rests. It is the prime element for which every profession, every corporation, every industry searches in evaluating a member of its organization. With it, the full worth of an individual can be developed. Without it—particularly in the military profession—failure in peace, disaster in war, or, at best, mediocrity in both will result.

Types of Character

We often use this word "character" carelessly. There are those of notoriously evil character, as well as those of an exemplary one. Yet in its usual acceptation it stands for those magnificent traits which placed George Washington first among his countrymen and, in fact, made him the Father of his Country—the unanimous choice for our first Presidency. It stands for the time-honored code of the officer corps. It stands for self-discipline, loyalty, readiness to accept responsibility, and willingness to admit mistakes. It stands for selflessness, modesty, humility, willingness to sacrifice when necessary, and, in my opinion, for faith in God. Let me illustrate.

During a critical phase of the Battle of the Bulge, when I commanded the 18th Airborne Corps, another corps commander just entering the fight next to me remarked: "I'm glad to have you on my flank. It's character that counts." I had long known him, and I knew what he meant. I replied: "That goes for me, too." There was no amplification. None was necessary. Each knew the other would stick however great the pressure; would extend help before it was asked, if he could; and would tell the truth, seek no self-glory, and everlastingly keep his word. Such feeling breeds confidence and success.

Self-Discipline

Only those who have disciplined themselves can exact disciplined performance from others. When the chips are down, when privation mounts and the casualty rate rises, when the crisis is at hand, which commander, I ask, receives the better response? Is it the one who has failed to share the rough going with his troops, who is rarely seen in the zone of aimed fire, and who expects much and gives little? Or is it the one whose every thought is for the welfare of his men, consistent with the accomplishment of his mission; who does not ask them to do what he has not already done and stands ready to do again when necessary; who with his men has shared short rations, the physical discomforts and rigors of campaign, and will be found at the crises of action where the issues are to be decided?

I know your answer: self-disciplined, self-controlled, and so in control of others, no matter how tough the going—Washington at the Battle of Long Island and at Valley Forge; Grant at Shiloh; Mackenzie of the 4th Cavalry in his epic raid; the junior officer pursuing hostile Indians in subzero weather on our western plains, closing up at dark for a dawn attack, with no fires permitted and only cold rations, if any, before H-hour—much the same many times in Korea, I might add, and I am sure under equally arduous conditions in Vietnam today; the young ship commander named Kennedy, his patrol torpedo boat sunk in action, his crew safely on the beach, then swimming out in shark-infested waters to try to intercept a friendly destroyer and rescue his men.

The world's annals and our own are studded with the names of such men, of all services and all grades. Always ready to assume responsibilities, they could always assign them to others and know they would be willingly accepted. True to themselves and to their conscience, their men sense they will be true to them, giving them full credit, and frankly admitting mistakes and accepting responsibility when they themselves are to blame.

General Washington wrote to Congress from Valley Forge:

> . . . without arrogance or the smallest deviation from truth, it may be said that no history now extant, can furnish an instance of an Army's suffering such uncommon hardships as ours have done, and bearing them with the same patience and fortitude. To see men without clothes to clothe their nakedness, without blankets to lie on, without shoes, by which their marches might be traced by the blood from their feet, and almost as often without provisions as with; marching through frost and snow, and at Christmas taking up their winter quarters within a day's march of the enemy, without a house or hut to cover them till they could be built, and submitting to it without a murmur, is a mark of patience and obedience which in my opinion can scarce be paralleled.

And what Washington did not say—a mark of his own unexcelled leadership.

An eyewitness report of Lee after Pickett's failure stated:

> His face did not show the slightest disappointment, care or annoyance, and he addressed to every soldier he met a few words of encouragement; "All will come right in the end, we'll talk it over afterwards," And to a Brigade Commander speaking angrily of the heavy losses of his men: "Never mind, General, all this has been my fault. It is I who have lost this fight, and you must help me out of it the best way you can."

For leadership through willingness to admit mistakes and instantly to accept responsibility, I think, history can offer few examples to surpass this.

Willingness to Sacrifice

Archibald Rutledge once wrote that there can be no real love without a willingness to sacrifice. Tuck this away in your inner minds. It may pay off in some crisis coming to you in the years now hidden beyond the horizon. Do you love your country and its flag? Do you love the branch in which you are serving, the men with whom you will be privileged to share service and to command? If you do, then you will be prepared to sacrifice for them, if your responsibilities or the situation so demands. The commander of Torpedo Squadron 8 at Midway; the four army chaplains on the torpedoed *SS Dorchester* off Iceland in predawn darkness in February 1942; the many aircraft commanders who have ordered "abandon ship," then stuck over-long to the controls to insure that their last man was out.

Courage, the second "C," could well be treated as a trait of character, as, indeed, it is. Yet it deserves, I believe, a separate category, for I know of not one recipient of history's accolade for battle leadership of enduring fame who was not known for great gallantry.

Physical and Moral Courage

There are two kinds of courage, physical and moral, and he who would be a true leader must have both. Both are products of the character-forming process, of the development of self-control, self-discipline, physical endurance, of knowledge of one's job and, therefore, of confidence. These qualities minimize fear and maximize sound judgment under pressure and—with some of that indispensable stuff called luck—often bring success from seemingly hopeless situations.

Putting aside impulsive acts of reckless bravery, both kinds of courage bespeak an untroubled conscience, a mind at peace with God. An example is Colonel John H. Glenn who was asked after his first rocket flight if he had been worried, and who replied: "I am trying to live the best I can. My peace had been made with my Maker for a number of years, so I had no particular worries."

Examples of physical courage are neither confined to combat nor limited to a stouthearted few, but are common throughout the world among men and women of every color, creed, race, and age, in peace as well as in war. However, examples of moral courage are less well known. They can be considered as proof of true greatness of soul. Where the individual has not measured up, he has generally failed fortune's bid to fame.

To me such incidents most frequently found in war are those where the career of the leader is at stake, and where his actions or decisions will determine the saving or slaughter of many of his men. History is full of these cases. The lure of glory, the fear of being thought afraid, of losing personal power and prestige, the mistaken idea that blind obedience to orders has no alternative—all have been followed by tragic losses of lives with little or no gain.

History often glosses over the countless thousands of lives which have been fruitlessly sacrificed to the pull of power, prestige, and publicity. Haig's Flanders Campaign in 1917 is a conspicuous example. Here, 100,000 men were sacrificed for the gain of 1,000 yards of almost bottomless morass.

It is easy to gamble with other peoples' money, and sometimes easier still with other men's lives, particularly when your own is in no great danger. You remember the commanders' conference prior to one of the big offensives of World War I, when a corps commander—whose command post was miles behind the front—spoke out during a lull in the meeting, saying: "I'd give 10,000 men to take that hill." And a liaison officer from a frontline infantry unit remarked to a brother officer standing beside him in the back of the room: "Generous, isn't he?"

Opposition to Orders

The military services deal harshly, as they should, with failure to carry out orders in battle. The commander present on the scene is entitled to full, instant, and enthusiastic execution of orders by subordinates. Yet when faced with different situations from those anticipated, as well as in the transition from plans to orders, there sometimes comes the challenge to one's conscience, the compelling urge to oppose foolhardy operations before it is too late, before the orders are issued and lives are needlessly thrown away.

Or the leader may be faced with the decision: Shall I take the responsibility of discarding the original mission? Shall I take the initiative and strive for success along different lines? He will have to put those questions to his conscience. "Blind obedience," said Napoleon Bonaparte, "is due only to a superior present on the spot at the moment of action." I concur.

I still support a statement of mine of some years ago:

It has long seemed to me that the hard decisions are not the ones you make in the heat of battle. Far harder to make are those involved in speaking your mind about some harebrained scheme which proposes to commit troops to action under conditions where failure seems almost certain, and the only results will be the needless sacrifice of priceless lives. When all is said and done, the most precious asset any nation has is its youth, and for a battle commander ever to condone the unnecessary sacrifice of his men is inexcusable. In any action you must balance the inevitable cost in lives against the objectives you seek to attain. Unless the results to be expected can reasonably justify the estimated loss of life the action involves, then for my part I want none of it.

General George C. Marshall, one of the noblest men who has worn an American uniform since Washington, once said of decisions of this kind: "It is hard to get men to do this, for this is when you lay your career, perhaps your commission, on the line."

Twice in my personal experience as a division commander I felt compelled to protest against tactical decisions that were about to be assigned to my 82d Airborne Division.

The first occasion was the planned drop on Rome in September 1943. I have recounted the incident in some detail in my book, *Soldier*. Recently, however, published memoirs of German generals then present in the Rome area have confirmed my views. One passage from the account of that incident illustrates the point I wish to make: "When the time comes that I must meet my Maker, the source of most humble pride to me will not be accomplishments in battle, but the fact that I was guided to make the decision to oppose this plan, at the risk of my career, right up to the Theater Commander."

The drop was not ordered.

The second experience was a proposed attack by the 82d across the Volturno River where the Germans had brought the Allied advance to a halt. The sector chosen involved getting across an unfordable river and, then, after an advance of roughly 1,000 yards across open flat terrain, the attack and seizure of a line of hills, curving away from the river on one flank, then like a bow curving back almost to the stream again on the other flank of the zone of attack, so that the assaulting troops would be under concentrated fire from the front and both flanks.

While the proposal to use the 82d was a high compliment—since it was the weakest numerically, and much the most lightly armed of any of the divisions in the 5th Army—I could only view the proposed operation as a suicide mission that would result in the loss of most of the assaulting troops and, then, with small chance of success. I could not accept such a mission without protest. But first I decided to discuss the plan with General Lucien K. Truscott, Commanding General, US 3d Infantry Division, a field commander conspicuous for competence and gallantry, and an old friend. He said he wouldn't touch it with a 40-foot pole, even with his heavier division. So I spoke my mind, first to the corps commander, under whom the operation was to be mounted—and I recall I used the word "fantastic"—and, finally, to the army commander. The plan was canceled.

In action and out, there is often a thin dividing line between recklessness, boldness, and caution. Even later study of battle records may fail to erase that line, for it is next to impossible to reconstruct the exact picture as it was thrown on the screen of the commander's brain at any particular crisis of combat. Yet experience, your own and that of others which you have absorbed, together with common sense, will be your best guides, and with good luck will see you through.

Physical Fitness

Physical fitness comes under competence, the third of my three basic ingredients of leadership. It plays a great part. My own earlier training at Fort Leavenworth, Fort Benning, Fort Sam Houston with the 2d Division, with the 33d Infantry in the Panama area, and with the airborne paid off in battle—first as a division, then as a corps, and, finally, as an army commander. Because of strenuous and unremitting physical training, I was able to keep up with the best of my troops in the hottest sectors and the toughest terrain and climate.

Let me mention briefly what I think the standards should be for commanders of large units. The division commander should have the physical endurance, stamina, and reserves of his best infantry battalion commanders, because that is where he belongs—with them—a good part of the time; the corps commander, those of his infantry regimental commanders; and the army commander just about the same.

And remember this, since no one can predict today when you may be thrown into combat, perhaps within hours of deplaning in an overseas theater—as happened to thousands in Korea, and as I have no doubt to many in Vietnam—you will have no time to get in shape. You must be in shape all the time.

There is another element in battlefield leadership which I want to mention and illustrate. It is a cardinal responsibility of a commander to foresee insofar as possible where and when crises affecting his command are likely to occur. It starts with his initial estimate of the situation—a continuing mental process from the moment of entering the combat zone until his unit is pulled out of the line. Ask yourself these questions. What are the enemy capabilities? What shall I do, or what could I do, if he should exercise that one of his capabilities which would be most dangerous to me, or most likely to interfere with the accomplishment of my mission?

Personal Presence

As commander of a division or smaller unit, there will rarely be more than one crisis, one really critical situation facing you at any one time. The commander belongs right at that spot, not at some rear command post. He should be there before the crisis erupts, if possible. If it is not possible, then he should get there as soon as he can after it develops. Once there, then by personal observation of terrain, enemy fires, reactions, and attitudes of his own commanders on the spot—by his eyes, ears, brain, nose, and his sixth sense—he gets the best possible picture of what is happening and can best exercise his troop leadership and the full authority of his command. He can start help of every kind to his hard-pressed subordinates. He can urge higher commanders to provide additional fire support, artillery, air, other infantry weapons, and, in the future, perhaps, nuclear strikes.

No other means will provide the commander with what his personal perceptions can provide, if he is present at the critical time and place. He can personally intervene, if he thinks that necessary, but only to the extent that such intervention will be helpful and not interfere with his subordinates. He is in a position to make instant decisions, to defend, withdraw, attack, exploit, or pursue.

If, at this time, he is at some rear command post, he will have to rely on reports from others, and time will be lost, perhaps just those precious moments which spell the difference between success and failure. Notwithstanding the console capabilities of future television in combat, I still believe what I have said is true. In any event, keep this time factor ever in mind. It is the one irretrievable, inextensible, priceless element in war.

Relief of Commanders

The occasion for the relief of commanders may regrettably arise. If it does, there are three points to consider: Is your decision based on personal knowledge and observation, or on secondhand information? What will the effect be on the command concerned? Are you relieving a commander whose men think highly of him—even with affection—regardless of professional competence? And, finally, have you a better man available?

Every man is entitled to go into battle with the best chance of survival your forethought as a leader can provide. What best helps you discharge this responsibility? Sharing things with your men; to be always in the toughest spots; always where the crisis is, or seems most likely to develop; always thinking of what help you can give your commanders who are executing your orders; doing your utmost to see that the best in rations, shelter, first aid, and evacuation facilities are available; being generous with praise, swift and fair with punishment when you have the facts, intolerant of demonstrated failure in leadership on which lives depend, yet making full allowances for human weaknesses and the stresses and strains of battle on individuals.

Know Your Men

Know your men, and be constantly on the alert for potential leaders—you never know how soon you may need them. During my two years in command of the 82d Airborne Division in World War II, I was in close and daily touch with every regimental and most battalion commanders. Before acceding to command of the division, and while I was General Omar N. Bradley's assistant division commander, I had learned to call by name every infantry officer in the division.

Later, by frequent exchange of views with the infantry regimental commanders and the divisional artillery commander, I knew in advance whom they had earmarked for battalion command. I do not recall any instance where I thought the regimental commander had not picked the right man. The payoff came in Normandy. I went in with 12 infantry battalion commanders—four regiments—and I had 14 new ones when we came out, for some battalions lost as many as three commanders during the 33 days we were in that fight.

The qualities of a leader are not limited to commanders. The requirements for leadership are just as essential in the staff officer, and in some respects more exacting, since he does not have that ultimate authority which can be used when necessary and must rely even more than his commander on his own strength of character, his tact and persuasion in carrying out his duties.

Between the commander and his chief of staff in a division or larger unit there should be thorough mutual respect, understanding, and confidence with no official secrets between them. Together they form a single dual personality, and the instructions issuing from the chief of staff must have the same weight and authority as those of the commander himself.

But this does not mean that a commander who delegates such authority to his chief of staff can allow his chief to isolate him from the rest of his staff. If that happens, the commander will soon find himself out of touch, and the chief of staff will be running the unit.

There is a fine balance here. The chiefs of staff sections should know that they always have access to their commander. He should see them and visit their sections with sufficient frequency to understand their problems, to let them know he appreciates their efforts, and that he stands ready to help where he can.

Inform Subordinates

Closely akin to the relationship with staff officers is keeping in close personal touch with your principal subordinate commanders—in the division, with your brigade and separate battalion commanders; in the corps, with your division commanders, their chiefs of staff, and as many of the commanders of attached corps units as you can; and in the army, with corps and division commanders and their chiefs of staff. There is always time for these visits; administrative work can be done at night. By day you belong with your troops.

Keep them informed of your thinking and plans. When you have the concept of an operation first in mind, consult your principal commanders without delay and get their reactions. No matter how sound a tactical plan may be, the chances of successful execution will be greatly increased if you have first secured the willing acceptance by commanders responsible for execution of the missions you plan to assign them. Insure that they receive notice of your decision and the principal details of your plan as approved in ample time to permit them and their subordinates to make their necessary reconnaissances and issue their orders.

These are some of the reasons why I hold that leadership is not a science, but an art. It conceives an ideal, states it as an objective, and then seeks actively and earnestly to attain it, everlastingly persevering, because the records of war are full of successes coming to those leaders who stuck it out just a little longer than their opponents.

Some suggestions for leadership are:

- Read widely and wisely all the history and biography possible. Soak up all the personal experiences you can of battle-tested brother officers. This broadens your understanding of an art of which you can never hope to know all.
- Study thoughtfully the records of past successful leaders and adapt their methods to yours.
- Work hard to keep fit. That little extra stamina may some day pull you out of some deep holes.
- Work hard, in your own way, at being tops at your job.
- Keep the three C's—character, courage, and competence—always before your mind, and with faith in God, be yourself.
- Remember there are many others on your team, and be inwardly humble. Every man's life is equally precious, although all are at the disposal of our country, and the contribution each makes in battle is of equal potential value.

2

Leaders and Leadership

Gen. S.L.A. Marshall

In that gallery of great Americans whose names are conspicuously identified with the prospering of the national arms in peace and war, there are almost as many types as there are men.

There were a certain few qualities they had to possess in common or their names would never have become known beyond the county line.

But these were inner qualities, often deeply buried, rather than outward marks of greatness that men recognized immediately upon beholding them.

Some almost missed the roll call, either because in early life their weaknesses were more apparent than their strengths, or because of an outward seeming of insignificance, which at first fooled their contemporaries.

In the minority are the few who seemed marked for greatness almost from the cradle, and were acclaimed for leadership while still of tender years.

Winfield Scott, a brigadier in the War of 1812 when brigadiers were few and Chief of Staff when the Civil War began, is a unique figure in the national history.

George Washington, Adjutant of the State of Virginia at 21, is one other military infant prodigy who never later belied his early fame.

The majority in the gallery are not like these. No two of them are strikingly alike in mien and manner. Their personalities are as different, for the most part, as their names. Their characters also ran the length of the spectrum, or nearly, if we are talking of moral habit rather than of conscientious performance of military duty. Some drank their whiskey neat and frequently; others loathed it and took a harsh line with any subordinate who used it.

Reprinted by permission from *The Armed Forces Officer* (Washington, D.C.: Government Printing Office, 1975), pp. 47–57.

One of the greatest generals in American history, celebrated for his fighting scarcely more than for his tippling, would walk from the room if any man tried to tell an off-color story in his presence. One of the most celebrated and successful of our World War II admirals endeared himself to millions of men in all ranks by his trick of gathering his chief subordinates together just before battle, issuing his orders sternly and surely, and then relaxing long enough to tell them his latest parlor story, knowing that finally it would trickle down through the whole command.

In Korea, one infantry division commander was a skilled banjo player. Up at the front, he formed a small orchestra of enlisted men and fitted into it. Between fire fights, they played for troops. The men loved him for it. Later, he became one of the Army's ranking generals and was named to one of its top posts. His name: Arthur G. Trudeau.

Among the warriors in this gallery are men who would bet a month's pay on a horse race. There are duelists and brawlers, athletes and aesthetes, men who lived almost saintly lives and scholars who lived more for learning than for fame.

Some tended to be so over-reclusive that they almost missed recognition; others were hail-fellow-well-met in any company.

Their methods of work reflected these extreme variations in personal type, as did the means they used to draw other men to them, thereby setting a foundation for real success.

Part of their number commanded mainly through the sheer force of ideas; others owed their leadership more to the magnetism of dynamic personality.

In the very few there was the spark of genius. All things seemed to come right with them at all times. Fate was kind, the openings occurred, and they were prepared to take advantage of them.

But the greater number moved up the hill one slow step at a time, not always sure of their footing, buffeted by mischance, owning no exalted opinion of their own merits, reacting to discouragement much as other men do, but finally accumulating power as they learned how to organize the work of other men.

While a young lieutenant, Admiral Sims became so incensed when the United States would not take his word on a voucher that he offered to resign.

General Grant signally failed to organize his life as an individual before a turn of the wheel gave him his chance to organize the military power of the United States in war.

General Sherman, who commanded the Army for almost 15 years, was considered by many of his close friends to be a fit subject for confinement as a mental case just before the Civil War.

General Meade, one of the calmest and most devoted of men in his family relationships, lacked confidence in his own merits and was very abusive of his associates during battle.

Admiral Farragut, whose tenderness as an individual was demonstrated during the 16 years in which he personally nursed an invalid wife, was so independent in his professional thought and action that both in and out of the Navy he was discredited as a "climber." He got into wretched quarrels with his superiors mainly because he felt his assignments afforded him no distinction. The Civil War gave him his opportunity.

General Winfield Scott, as firm a commander as any in our history, plagued the Army with his petty bickering over rank, seniority, and precedent.

Being human, they had their points of personal weakness. A newly appointed ensign or second lieutenant also has chinks in his armor, and sometimes views them in such false proportion that he doubts his own potential for high responsibility.

There is not one perfect life in the gallery of the great. All were molded by the mortal influences surrounding them. They reacted in their own feelings, and toward other men, according to the rise and fall of their personal fortunes. They sought help where it could be found. When disappointed, they chilled like anyone else. But along with their professional talents, they possessed in common a desire for substantial recognition, accompanied by the will to earn it fairly, or else the Nation would never have heard their names.

All in all it is a much mixed gallery. If we were to pass it in review and then inspect it carefully, it would still be impossible to say: "This is the composite of character. This is the prototype of military success. Model upon it and you have the pinnacle within reach."

The same thing would no doubt hold true of a majority of the better men who commanded ships, squadrons, regiments, and companies under these commanders, and at their own level were as superior in leadership as the relatively few who rose to national prominence because of the achievements of the general body.

The same rule will apply tomorrow. Those who come forward to fill these places, and to command them with equal or greater authority and competence, will not be plaster saints, laden with all human virtue, spotless in character, and fit to be anointed with a superman legend by some future Parson Weems. They will be men with ambition and a strong belief in the United States and the goodness of a free society. They will have some of the average man's faults and maybe a few of his vices. But certainly they will possess the qualities of courage, creative intelligence, and physical robustness in more than average measure.

What we know of our great leaders in the current age should discourage the idea that only a genius may scale the heights. Trained observers have noted in their personalities and careers many of the plain characteristics each man feels in himself and mistakenly regards as a bar to preferment.

Drew Middleton, the American correspondent, wrote of General Carl "Tooey" Spaatz: "This man, who may be a heroic figure to our grandchildren, is essentially an unheroic figure to his contemporaries. He is, in fact, such a friendly, human person that observers tend to minimize his stature as a war leader. He is not temperamental. He makes no rousing speeches, writes no inspirational orders. Spaatz, in issuing orders for a major operation involving 1,500 airplanes, is about as inspiring as a groceryman ordering another five cases of canned peas."

An interviewer who called on General Ira C. Eaker when he was leading the 8th Air Force against Germany found "a strikingly soft-spoken, sober, compact man who has the mild manner of a conservative minister and the judicial outlook of a member of the Supreme Court. But he is always about two steps ahead of everybody on the score, and there is a quiet, inexorable logic about everything he does." Of his own choice, Eaker would have separated from military service after World War I. He wanted to be a lawyer, and he also toyed with the idea of running a country newspaper. In his off hours, he wrote books on aviation for junior readers. On the side, he studied civil law and found it "valuable mental training."

On the eve of the Guadalcanal landing, General A. A. Vandegrift's final order to his command ended with the stirring and now celebrated phrase "God favors the bold and strong of heart." Yet in the afterglow of later years, the Nation read a character sketch of him that included this: "He is so polite and so soft-spoken that he is continually disappointing the people whom he meets. They find him lacking in the fire-eating traits they like to expect of all marines, and they find it difficult to believe that such a mild-mannered man could really have led and won the bloody fight." When another officer spoke warmly of Vandegrift's coolness under fire, his "grace under pressure," to quote Hemingway's phrase, he replied "I shouldn't be given any credit. I'm built that way."

The point is beautifully taken. Too often the man with great inner strength holds in contempt those less well endowed by nature than himself.

Brilliance of intellect and high achievement in scholarship are an advantage, though in the end they have little or no payoff if character and courage are lacking. Thousands of officers who served in Vietnam, some dubious about the wisdom of the national policy, questioning whether the tight rein on operations made military sense, still believed that "My country right or wrong" is the only course possible for one who has taken the oath.

No, brain trusting and whiz kidding are not what it takes. Of 105 major generals who served in World War I, 56 had failed to score above the middle of their class in mathematics. Of 275 in World War II, 158, or 58 percent, were in the middle group or among the dubs in the same subject. General William C. Westmoreland, who commanded in Vietnam and was later

Army Chief of Staff, had punched practically none of the buttons. As for military schooling, for over 30 years after graduating from West Point, he attended only Cooks and Bakers School and the Airborne School. One of his outstanding subordinates, a two-star general, respected and loved by all who served under him, had joined the service at the age of 15 out of reform school to straighten himself out. By sweat and study, he won his sergeant's stripes at 18 and his commission at 21. He made his resolve and stayed with it, which was the main thing. The solution of every problem, every achievement is, as Justice Holmes said, a bird on the wing; and he added, one must have one's whole will on one's eye on that bird. One cannot be thinking of one's image, or one's place in history—only of that bird.

While there are no perfect men, there are those who become relatively perfect leaders of men because something in their makeup brings out in strength the highest virtues of all who follow them. That is the way of human nature. Minor shortcomings do not impair the loyalty or growth of the follower who has found someone whose strengths he deems worth emulating. On the other hand, to recognize merit, you must yourself have it. The act of recognizing the worthwhile traits in another person is both the test and the making of character. The man who scorns all others and thinks no one else worth following parades his own inferiority before the world. He puts his own character into bankruptcy just as surely as does that other sad sack of whom Thomas Carlyle wrote: "To recognize false merit, and crown it as true, because a long trail runs after it, is the saddest operation under the sun."

Sherman, Logan, Rawlins, and the many others hitched their wagons to Grant's star because they saw in him a man who had a way with other men, and who commanded them not less by personal courage than by patient work in their interest. Had Grant spent time brooding over his own civilian failures, he would have been struck with a disorderly camp and would never have gotten out of Illinois. He was not dismayed by his own shortcomings. Later he said: "I doubt that any of my officers ever discovered that I hadn't bothered to study tactics."

The nobility of the private life and influence of General Robert E. Lee and the grandeur of his military character are known to every American school boy. His peerless gifts as a battle leader have won the tribute of celebrated soldiers and historians throughout the world. Likewise, the deep religiosity of his great lieutenant, Stonewall Jackson, the fiery zeal and almost evangelical power with which he lifted the hearts of all men who followed him, are hallmarks of character that are vividly present in whatever context his name happens to be mentioned.

If we turn for a somewhat closer look at Grant, it is because he, more than any other American soldier, left us a full, clear narrative of his own growth, and of the inner thoughts and doubts pertaining to himself which attended his life experience. There was a great deal of the average man in Grant. He was beset by human failings. He could not look impressive. He had no sense of destiny. In his great hours, it was sweat, rather than inspiration, dogged perseverance, rather than the aura of power, that made the hour great.

Average though he was in many things, there was nothing average about the strong way in which he took hold, applying massive common sense to the complex problems of the field. That is why he is worth close regard. His virtues as a military leader were of the simpler sort that plain men may understand and hope to emulate. He was direct in manner. He never intrigued. His speech was homely. He was approachable. His mind never deviated from the object. Though a stubborn man, he was always willing to listen to his subordinates. He never adhered to a plan obstinately, but nothing could induce him to forsake the idea behind the plan.

History has left us a clear view of how he attained to greatness in leadership by holding steadfastly to a few main principles.

At Belmont, his first small action, he showed nothing to indicate that he was competent as a tactician and strategist. But the closing scene reveals him as the last man to leave the field of action, risking his life to see that none of his men had been left behind.

At Fort Donelson, where he had initiated an amphibious campaign of highly original daring, he was not on the battlefield when his army was suddenly attacked. He arrived to find his right wing crushed and his whole force on the verge of defeat. He blamed no one. Without more than a fleeting hesitation, he said quietly to his chief subordinates: "Gentlemen, the position on the right must be retaken." Then he mounted his horse and galloped along the line shouting to his men: "Fill your cartridge cases quick; the enemy is trying to escape and he must not be permitted to do so." Control and order were immediately reestablished by his presence.

At Shiloh the same thing happened, only this time it was worse; the whole Union Army was on the verge of rout. Grant, hobbling on crutches from a recent leg injury, met the mob of panic-stricken stragglers as he left the boat at Pittsburgh Landing. Calling on them to turn back, he mounted and rode toward the battle, shouting encouragement and giving orders to all he met. Confidence flowed from him back into an already beaten Army, and in this way a field nearly lost was soon regained, with decisive help provided by Buell's Army.

The last and best picture of Grant is on the evening after he had taken his first beating from General Lee in the campaign against Richmond. He was new with the Army of the Potomac. His predecessors, after being whipped by Lee, had invariably retreated to a safe distance. But this time, as the defeated army took the road of retreat out of the Wilderness, its columns got only as far as the Chancellorsville House crossroad. There the soldiers saw a squat, bearded man sitting horseback, and drawing on a cigar. As the head of each regiment came abreast of him, he silently motioned it to take the right-hand fork—back toward Lee's flank and deeper than ever into the Wilderness. That night, for the first time, the Army sensed an electric change in the air over Virginia. It had a man.

"I intend to fight it out on this line" is more revealing of the one supreme quality that put the seal on all of U.S. Grant's great gifts for military leading than everything else that the historians have written of him. He was the essence of the spirit that moderns call "seeing the show through." He was sensitive to a fault in his early years, and carried to his tomb a dislike for military uniform, caused by his being made the butt of ridicule the first time he ever donned a soldier suit. As a junior officer in the Mexican War, he sensed no particular aptitude in himself. But he had participated in every engagement possible for a member of his regiment, and had executed every small duty well, with particular attention to conserving the lives of his men. This was the school and the course that later enabled him to march to Richmond, when men's lives had to be spent for the good of the Nation.

In more recent times, one of the great statesmen and soldiers of the United States, Henry L. Stimson, has added his witness to the value of this force in all enterprise: "I know the withering effect of limited commitments and I know the regenerative effect of full action." Though he was speaking particularly of the larger affairs of war and national policy, his words apply with full weight to the personal life. The truth seen only halfway is missed wholly; the thing done only halfway had best not be attempted at all. Men can't be fooled on this score. They will know every time when the arrow falls short for lack of a worthwhile effort. And when that happens, confidence in the leader is corroded, even among those who themselves were unwilling to try.

There have been great and distinguished leaders in our military Services at all levels who had no particular gifts for administration and little for organizing the detail of decisive action either within battle or without. They excelled because of a superior ability to make use of the brains and command the loyalty of well-chosen subordinates. Their particular function was to judge the goal according to their resources and audacity, and then to hold the team steady until the goal was gained. So doing, they complemented the power of the faithful lieutenants who might have put them in the shade in any IQ test. Wrote Grant: "I never knew what to do with a paper except to put it in a side pocket or pass it to a clerk who understood it better than I did." There was nothing unfair or irregular about this; it was as it should be. All military achievement develops out of unity of action. The laurel goes to the man whose powers can most surely be directed toward the end purposes of organization. The winning of battles is the product of the winning of men. That aptitude is not an endowment of formal education, though the man who has led a football team, a class, a fraternity, or a debating society is the stronger for the experience he has gained. It is not unusual for those who have excelled in scholarship to despise those who have excelled merely in sympathetic understanding of the human race. But in the military Services, though there are niches for the pedant, character is at all times at least as vital as intellect, and the main rewards go to him who can make other men feel toughened as well as elevated.

- Quiet resolution.
- The hardihood to take risks.
- The will to take full responsibility for decision.
- The readiness to share its rewards with subordinates.
- An equal readiness to take the blame when things go adversely.
- The nerve to survive storm and disappointment and to face toward each new day with the scoresheet wiped clean, neither dwelling on one's successes nor accepting discouragement from one's failures.

In these things lie a great part of the essence of leadership, for they are the constituents of that kind of moral courage that has enabled one man to draw many others to him in any age.

It is good, also, to look the part, not only because of its effect on others, but because, from out of the effort made to look it, one may in time come to be it. One of the kindliest and most penetrating philosophers of our age, Abbe Ernest Dimnet, has assured us that this is true. He says that by trying to look and act like a socially distinguished person, one may in fact attain to the inner disposition of a gentleman. That, almost needless to say, is the real mark of the officer who takes great pains about the manner of his dress and address, for as Walt Whitman said: "All changes of appearances without a change in that which underlies appearances are without avail." All depends upon the spirit in which one makes the effort. By his own account, U.S. Grant, as a West Point cadet, was more stirred by the commanding appearance of General Winfield Scott than by any man he had ever seen, including the President. He wrote that at that moment there flashed across his mind the thought that some day he would stand in Scott's place. Grant was unkempt of dress. His physical endowments were such that he could never achieve the commanding air of Scott. But he left us his witness that Scott's military bearing helped kindle his own desire for command, even though he knew that he could not be like Scott. Much is said in favor of modesty as an asset in leadership. It is remarked that the man who wishes to hold the respect of others will mention himself not more frequently than a born aristocrat mentions his ancestor. However, the point can be labored too hard. Some of the ablest of the Nation's military commanders have been anything but shrinking violets; we have had now and then a hero who could boast with such gusto that this very characteristic somehow endeared him to his men. But that would be a dangerous tack for all save the most exceptional individual. Instead of speaking of modesty as a charm that will win all hearts, thereby risking that through excessive modesty a man will become tiresome to others and rated as too timid for high responsibility, it would be better to dwell upon the importance of being natural, which means neither concealing nor making a vulgar display of one's ideals and motives, but acting directly according to his dictates.

This leads to another point. In several of the most celebrated commentaries written by higher commanders on the nature of generalship, the statement is made rather carelessly that to be capable of great military leadership a man must be something of an actor. If that were unqualifiedly true, then it would be a desirable technique likewise for any junior officer; he, too, should learn how to wear a false face and play a part that cloaks his real self. The hollowness of the idea is proved by the lives of such men as Robert E. Lee, W. T. Sherman, George C. Marshall, Omar N. Bradley, Carl A. Spaatz, William H. Simpson, Chester A. Nimitz, Harold K. Johnson, Matthew B. Ridgway, Lew Walt, Creighton W. Abrams, and John S. McCain, Jr., to mention only a few. As commanders, they were all as natural as children, though some had great natural reserve, and others were warm and much more outgoing. They expressed themselves straightforwardly rather than by artful striving for effect. There was no studied attempt to appear only in a certain light. To use the common word for it, their people did not regard them as "characters." This naturalness had much to do with their hold on other men.

Such a result will always come. He who concentrates on the object at hand has little need to worry about the impression he is making on others. Even though they detect the chinks in the armor, they will know that the armor will hold.

On the other hand, a sense of the dramatic values, coupled with the intelligence to play upon them skillfully, is an invaluable quality in any military leader. Though there was nothing of the "actor" in Grant, he understood the value of pointing things up. To put a bold or inspiring emphasis where it belongs is not stagecraft but an integral part of the military fine art of communicating. System that is only system is injurious to the mind and spirit of any normal person. One can play a superior part well and maintain prestige and dignity, without being under the compulsion to think, speak, and act in a monotone. In fact, when any military commander becomes over-inhibited along these lines because of the illusion that this is the way to build a reputation for strength, he but doubles the necessity for his subordinates to act at all times like human beings rather than robots.

Coupled with self-control, consideration and thoughtfulness will carry a man far. Men will warm toward a leader when they come to believe that all the energy he stores up by living somewhat within himself is at their service. But when they feel that this is not the case, and that his reserve is simply the outward sign of a spiritual miserliness and concentration on purely personal goals, no amount of restraint will ever win their favor. This is as true of him who commands a whole Service as of the leader of a squad.

To speak of the importance of a sense of humor would be futile, if it were not that what cramps so many men isn't that they are by nature humorless as that they are hesitant to exercise what humor they possess. Within the military profession, this is as unwise as to let the muscles go soft or to spare the mind the strain of original thinking. Great humor has always been in the military tradition. The need of it is nowhere more delicately expressed than in Kipling's lines:

> My son was killed while laughing at some jest,
> I would I knew
> What it was, and it might serve me in a time
> When jests are few

Marcus Aurelius, Rome's soldier philosopher, spoke of his love for the man who "could be humorous in an agreeable way." No reader of Grant's *Memoirs* (one of the few truly great autobiographies ever written by a soldier) could fail to be impressed by his light touch. A delicate sense of the incongruous seems to have pervaded him; he is at his whimsical best when he sees himself in a ridiculous light. Lord Kitchener, one of the grimmest warriors ever to serve the British Empire, warmed to the man who made him the butt of a practical joke. There is the unforgettable picture of Admiral Beatty at Jutland. The *Indefatigable* had disappeared beneath the waves. The *Queen Mary* had exploded. The *Lion* was in flames. Then word came that the *Princess Royal* was blown up. Said Beatty to his Flag Captain, "Chatfield, there seems to be something wrong with our – ships today. Turn two points nearer the enemy." Admiral Nimitz, surveying the terrible landscape of the Kwajalein battlefield for the first time, said gravely to his staff: "It's the worst devastation I've ever seen except for that last Texas picnic in Honolulu." There is a characteristic anecdote of General Patton. He had just been worsted by higher headquarters in an argument over strategy. So he sat talking to his own staff about it, his dog curled up beside him. Suddenly he said to the animal "The trouble with you, too, Willy, is that you don't understand the big picture." General Eisenhower, probably more than any other modern American commander, had the art of winning with his humor. He would have qualified under the English essayist Sydney Smith's definition: "The meaning of an extraordinary man is that he is eight men in one man; that he has as much wit as if he had no sense, and as much sense as if he had no wit; that his conduct is as judicious as if he were the dullest of human beings, and his imagination as brilliant as if he were irretrievably ruined."

In Korea, just before the first battle of Pork Chop Hill began, Lt. Thomas V. Harrold heard a loud wailing from the Communist trench and asked his company its meaning.

"They're prayer singing," said an interpreter. "They're getting ready to die."

Said Harrold: "Then I guess we ought to be singing too."

And not a bad idea. The 1st Marine Division, fighting its way back from the Chosin Reservoir in December 1950, was embattled amid the snows from the moment the column struck its camp at Hagaru. By midnight, after heavy loss through the day, it had bivouacked at Kotori, still surrounded, still far from the sea. Maj. Gen. Oliver P. Smith was alone in his tent. It was his bad moment. The task ahead seemed hopeless. Suddenly he heard music. Outside some truckers were singing the Marine Hymn. "All doubt left me," said Smith. "I knew then we had it made."

Concerning leadership within the terms here set forth, the final thought is that there is a radical difference between training and combat conditions.

In training the commander may be arbitrary, demanding, and a hard disciplinarian. But so long as his sense of fair play in handling his men becomes evident to them, and provided they become aware that what he is doing is making them more efficient than their competition, they will approve him, if grudgingly, stay loyal to him, and even possibly come to believe in his lucky star.

They are more likely to do it, however, if he takes a fatherly interest in their personal welfare. But that feeling doesn't have to come naturally to a man for him to win the respect of troops. If he knows his business, they're on his team.

When it comes to combat, something new is added. Even if they have previously looked on him as a father and believed absolutely that being with him is their best assurance of successful survival, should he then show himself to be timid and too cautious about his own safety, he will lose hold of them no less absolutely. His lieutenant, who up till then under training conditions has been regarded as a mean creature or a sniveler, but on the field suddenly reveals himself as a man of high courage, can take moral leadership of the company away from him, and do it in one day.

On the field there is no substitute for courage, no other binding influence toward unity of action. Troops will excuse almost any stupidity; excessive timidity is simply unforgivable. This was the epitome of Captain Queeg's failure in *The Caine Mutiny*. Screwball that he was, and an oppressor of men, his other vices would have been tolerable had he, under fire, proved himself somewhat better than a coward.

3

A Comprehensive
View of Leadership

Brig. Gen. Huba Wass de Czece

Every Army leader, active or retired, should be considered knowledgeable on the subject of leadership. This is only natural since this has been the essence of the military profession. I have learned much from the views of others and have developed my own way of thinking about leadership and how to talk to younger leaders about it.

Before one can understand and write about what leaders ought to *be*, *know* and *do* (and that is a good way to talk about leadership), one ought to be clear about what leaders are for in a more fundamental sense. What are the critical leadership functions performed by Army officers as they lead small and large units within an Army preparing for, deterring and conducting war on behalf of a free society? How are these functions performed differently as one proceeds up the scale from sergeant to general? How do *being, knowing* and *doing* change at each level and how do we prepare our leaders to advance? The purpose of this article is to propose a systematic way to ask and answer those questions and to thus learn more about the science and art of leadership.

There is general agreement that leadership is the art of influencing others to take action toward a goal, and that military leadership is the art of influencing soldiers in units to accomplish unit missions. It is also generally understood that small-unit leaders rely on direct-influence processes while senior leaders rely more on indirect processes in proportion to their seniority. This is a slim framework for understanding the leadership function—why we *have* leaders.

Reprinted by permission from *Military Review*, 72:8 (August 1992), pp. 21–29.

What are the key leadership functions that must be performed to produce truly effective military organizations? Effective organizations have clearly defined purposes, respond to direction, are composed of people motivated to pursue organizational purposes along clearly identified paths and have programs that sustain their effectiveness over time. Organizations without these critical characteristics are not effective. Leaders provide purpose. They also establish direction, generate motivation and sustain effectiveness. They really do more, but they cannot do less. Thus effectiveness can be reduced to four leadership functions—providing purpose, establishing direction, generating motivation for unit actions and sustaining the effectiveness of the unit for future tasks (providing for continuity and constant improvement of the organization). All other functions are really subfunctions of these four; they facilitate the accomplishment of one or more of these four primary functions. For instance, setting the proper unit values may facilitate all four, but the reason for having the proper values is not that they are an end in and of themselves but they are a means to an ultimate end—a unit that can be led to accomplish its intended aims with greater effectiveness.

Four Primary Functions of Effective Military Leadership

Although the four primary functions of effective leadership are interdependent, we discuss purpose first because effective directing, motivating and sustaining require a focus or aim. We discuss directing next because it is composed of the actions the leader takes to guide the unit in the direction of purpose. Motivating follows this because it comprises the actions the leader takes to impel individuals within the unit to follow the directing guidance. We discuss sustaining effectiveness last because it is primarily an activity with long-range payoffs.

Provide and instill purpose.   The effective leader must be an effective link in the chain of command. The leader must possess a broad vision to guide the organization drawing meaning or purpose from this vision for unit activity. The leader must have a clear idea of how the organization fits into a larger scheme—why they are doing what they are doing. The leader imparts a sense of purpose on subordinates and instills a sense of purpose in soldiers, aligning unit missions, goals and objectives within broader schemes and purposes.

To shape the vision, the effective leader may draw upon many sources:

- Beginning with the oath of office to defend and support the Constitution, or even higher moral and spiritual imperatives.

- Draw on institutional and national values, goals and aspirations to formulate the concept of purpose he articulates to subordinates.

A leader's commander and the next higher headquarters will transmit their articulation of purpose both directly and indirectly. In combat, this may be directly and clearly expressed (paragraphs 1b., 2 and 3 of the operations order he receives). A leader may have to read between the lines of their words or actions to clearly understand the commander's intent (or the vision from which they derive purpose). This is called "restating the mission" and "identifying the implied tasks." A leader must remain aware of events beyond those involving the unit. In reality, this may require filling gaps in the picture of purpose by deductive or inductive logic.

However arriving at the conception of purpose, the effective leader passes on a coherent picture of how the unit mission fits into the "big picture." Imparting a sense of importance of the tasks to be accomplished and how success or failure of the unit mission will affect the world beyond the unit. In combat, events will not unfold as planned, assumptions may prove to be wrong and assigned tasks may not be appropriate. Knowing the purpose of the unit mission helps subordinates judge what new tasks would be more appropriate. Understanding the purpose of unit missions (the "intent of higher commanders") aids them in coordinating their unit's actions with those of others and leads to overall harmony in execution and economy of effort toward common goals. It provides a frame of reference for independent thought and decision making by subordinates to solve unanticipated problems, which are best resolved and acted on rapidly.

As one proceeds from squad to the highest strategic levels, the leader must become more active in clarifying and transmitting purpose as it becomes more conceptual, longer range and ephemeral. At the highest levels, there may be a great deal of latitude in shaping, articulating and refining purpose. And higher values such as the oath of office and moral and spiritual imperatives, while important at all levels, play a more significant role because less specific guidance is provided. At squad level, it may be simply to know, pass on and imbue squad members with a simple idea such as "We must take out that bunker because it is holding up the platoon or company advance," or "We will train hard because we want to be the best squad in the company."

At all levels, it is the duty of leaders to clarify the purpose of their missions by asking appropriate questions, if time permits, and to inform subordinates appropriately. (It is also well known that there is a motivational side benefit of letting soldiers know the purpose of their sacrifices—the more important the purpose, the greater the motivational benefit.) The key benefit of providing and instilling purpose is to ensure that what is to be done is accomplished so as to fit into a higher scheme. This is the mechanism that aids synchronization in an environment where initiative is highly valued.

Providing direction. Effective leaders provide unambiguous direction and guidance for action. They have a clear vision of what must be done, what is necessary to get the job done and how to proceed. They clearly articulate and assign objectives, missions and goals to subordinates. In addition to such direct guidance, they also provide indirect guidance. They promote values; set standards for accomplishment of tasks; enforce discipline; establish standard operating procedures; ensure the training of soldiers and units in appropriate doctrine, methods and techniques; and establish policies and regulations. At the highest levels, military leaders also may be responsible for development of doctrine, methods and techniques in some or all areas.

Providing direction effectively requires command and control skills, processes and functions—information gathering, analysis, decision making, issuing instructions or orders performing appropriate supervision and monitoring the effectiveness of the resulting actions. Effective leadership in combat is measured in terms of the speed and effectiveness of this cycle (often called the decision cycle) relative to that of the enemy.

As leadership advances from the squad to the highest levels, the function of providing direction becomes more complex. Setting and communicating standards, promoting values, enforcing discipline, establishing methods and procedures, and command and control processes become more dependent on systems and organizational functionaries than on direct interpersonal relations. Management, the control of things and the coordination and sequencing of events, while applicable at all levels, becomes an important tool in providing direction at senior levels of leadership. It is in this sense that it relates to leadership.

Effective senior leaders know that even the act of gathering information about the activities of subordinates may cause a reorientation of those activities. They take this into account in designing systems that will gather information purposefully. They ask for meaningful reports and develop unobtrusive ways to find out what they need to know without unintentionally reorienting the focus of subordinate activity.

Providing motivation. Effective leaders provide motivation—they harness the willingness of subordinates to work toward common goals, missions, objectives and tasks. All combat is, in the end, a test of will, both of soldiers and leaders. In combat, leaders must motivate soldiers to do difficult things in trying circumstances. In peacetime, motivation to perform tasks well is important. In combat, it can be decisive. Marshal Maurice de Saxe, writing in the 18th century, pointed out that "a soldier's courage must be reborn daily," and Ardant du Picq, writing in the 19th, remarked that "you can reach into the well of courage only so many times before the well runs dry."

It is common knowledge that motivation promoted by rewards is more effective in generating commitment than motivation promoted by punishments. Providing positive motivation should be the aim of all leaders, but negative sanctions are also important for delineating the limits of acceptable behavior. Effective leaders elicit willing compliance and devote a considerable effort to obtaining it.

Means and methods for motivating soldiers differ at various levels. At all levels of authority, mutual trust and confidence are key, but styles may differ.

The moral force that impels subordinates to action at all levels is rooted in mutual trust and respect. This in turn stems from a record of association and a reputation for ethical behavior and sound decision making. Values, or held beliefs, when appropriate and shared in the unit, are important motivators. "This unit can't be beat" and "This unit doesn't leave its dead on the battlefield" are examples. Ethics are standards of behavior in relation to values. Mutual trust and respect derive in part from perceptions of ethical behavior and in part from a record of success. Mutual trust and respect also derive from "taking care of the troops." When troops know that their efforts will not be wasted on unnecessary tasks; that the leader recognizes the value and quality of their labors and is doing the best to meet their needs within the constraints imposed; is concerned about them as human beings; listens to their grievances; and respects subordinates and builds their self-esteem; they will give their full measure of support. All of these factors combine to provide the leader the moral force he needs to motivate in stressful situations in combat, or anytime.

American soldiers have always fought well when they feel they are in a good outfit and trust their leaders. At the lowest levels, direct daily face-to-face appeals to values, insistence on standards and a record of fairness, self-discipline, competence, displays of example, courage and resourcefulness are the most effective motivators. At times, especially in combat, resorting to intimidation may be necessary, but intimidation never elicits a full measure of commitment. At the highest levels, personal displays of courageous example, self-discipline, fairness, competence and force of personality (in both a positive and negative sense) are occasionally necessary and effective, but a more complex system of authority, mutual trust and confidence must be established.

At the higher levels, soldiers learn to trust the collective leadership of "higher headquarters" when that leadership is reliable and demonstrably sound. A trusted and respected senior leader will have difficulty overcoming the deleterious efforts of a fumbling staff. Senior leaders ensure a positive command climate because they understand that they must influence soldiers through layers of their subordinate leaders. They cultivate positive leadership among their immediate subordinates and resort to face-to-face persuasion to bolster will as the occasion warrants (but usually with subordinate commanders and staffs).

While discipline is primarily a direction-providing tool, in the sense that a disciplined soldier or unit does what is expected even when the "boss" is absent, maintaining discipline also plays a motivational role. A disciplined unit is responsive. One of its internalized values is "We always do what's right," and what is "right" is following the direction of the leader toward the purpose to be achieved.

Commanders at all levels establish or administer formal systems of rewards and punishments. Traditionally, on the positive side, this has been in the form of pay and benefits, promotions, decorations, skill badges, service ribbons, symbols of unit recognition and time off. On the negative side have been judicial and nonjudicial punishments ranging from extra training to the gallows, as well as release from the service and so forth. They use the provisions of military regulations and the Uniform Code of Military Justice to administer punishments. In order to motivate effectively, these systems must be seen to be fair by those they seek to motivate.

Commanders at higher levels have a more powerful, more important and perhaps more difficult role in establishing and maintaining a just system of formal rewards and punishments. They have a more powerful role in that they have more latitude and authority. The importance of their role stems from the impact they have in this powerful tool to motivate positively through an effective system, and the potential damage they can cause with an ineffective system. Their role is difficult because they have to work through many people who administer the system.

As mentioned earlier, soldiers who understand why an action is necessary and worthy of their sacrifices will fight more fiercely or work harder toward unit goals and missions. This function of informing and educating also becomes more complex with seniority of position. At more senior levels, it involves command information programs of great complexity and subtlety.

Sustaining continued effectiveness.   The final function of military leadership is different in that it orients to the future. Providing purpose, direction and motivation has immediate payoffs, but leaders must also ensure the continuity, health and further development of the organization. It is difficult to find one word to describe this function; the closest would be sustainment—sustaining the effectiveness of the organization over time. This implies continuity in a Darwinian rather than a static sense—the ability to remain a viable organism through adaptation as conditions change. It implies health in that all elements of an organism remain sound and function as intended. It implies further development in that leaders should never be satisfied with the current levels of proficiency and always seek to improve in areas which are weakest. Leaders should think of organizations they head as organisms and not as machines. Machines have no built-in recuperative powers, and they perform best when new. They wear out with use. This is not the case with organisms and organizations. Organisms can learn, adapt, grow, become more effective and stronger. They can also unlearn, maladapt, shrink, become less effective and weaker. And they can die. An organism cannot be stressed near maximum capacity for too long a time before it becomes less capable, but an organism can peak well above normal levels of effectiveness for short periods. Effective military leaders recognize these characteristics of military organizations and lead them accordingly.

Some have said that the most effective leaders provide for their succession. Others have said that they develop "high-performing" units. They do both and more. The good squad leader cross-trains the new man on the machine gun, teaches the machine gunner to be a team leader and coaches the team leaders. This squad leader trains the squad to be a cohesive and highly adaptive organism; looks for ways to take the pressure off when no expenditure of effort is required and ensures that squad members get needed rest when possible. When a tough chore is to be performed, the squad peaks for it.

Leaders at higher levels do essentially the same. The higher the level, the more systematic and institutionalized the process becomes. Senior leaders must prepare for attrition of key personnel, the introduction of more modern weapons and a myriad of environmental changes affecting the health and effectiveness of their command. In performing current tasks, they must consider future tasks. In combat, they may mortgage the future for a vital present mission or hold back to save strength and peak for a more vital task to come. They train their soldiers and leaders in peacetime and during lulls in battle. They build or rebuild morale or physical strength. They build teamwork between units of different branches and develop "high performing" staffs. The essential elements of this function are present at all levels, but at the most senior levels these efforts are formalized and highly organized. In the long term, tending to this function is as important as providing purpose, direction and motivation.

Effective military leadership requires that four key functions be performed well to influence soldiers and units to successfully accomplish tasks and missions over time. To be successful, military leaders must:

- Provide purpose and meaning for unit activity—fitting the specific mission into a broader framework of guidance derived from higher purpose, direction, motivation and sustaining sensings.
- Establish direction and guidance for the actions of subordinates leading to mission accomplishment.

- Generate or instill in his subordinates the will, or motivation, to perform assigned missions well.
- Sustain the effectiveness of his organization over time—provide for the continuity, improvement and future effectiveness of the organization.

The effectiveness of large military organizations depends on the performance of all of these functions up and down the chain of command. Although these functions are performed at every link in the chain, they are performed differently at each level. While there is room for variations in style (or the way functions are performed), there is little room for variations in values and ethical standards or in the understanding of doctrinal fundamentals. These and the purpose function at each level provide the glue that binds smaller organizations together to form larger ones—to make them one organism.

Differences in levels of leadership.   Intuition tells us that there may be distinct differences in the way the purpose, direction, motivation and organizational sustainment functions are performed, and what leaders must *be*, *know* and *do* to perform them at different levels. What follows is an intuitive sketch of some key distinctions by level based on 28 years of fallible experience and some historical reading over that time.

Junior noncommissioned officers (NCOs) who serve as squad leaders and team leaders and their equivalents practice "do as I do" leadership almost exclusively. For them, "showing" is as important as "telling." In combat, "do as I do" leaders are at or near the front of their organizations to direct and to motivate effectively. They derive purpose from company-level goals, missions and values. They embody the warrior ethic of their branch and specialty and reflect the values inculcated in them by more senior NCOs. They provide direction by leading from the front, by establishing and enforcing squad standards and values, by demonstrating "how to do it." They enforce discipline directly and on the spot. They motivate by example and by the respect they have earned within the squad. They work to achieve a cohesive, "high-performing" squad. They care for and about their men. They provide for continuity by identifying talent among the younger soldiers and by providing for their own succession from among them. They cross-train soldiers to perform more than one task in the squad, and perform necessary individual training.

Senior NCOs (platoon sergeants, master sergeants, first sergeants and sergeants major) also practice "do as I do" leadership, often not as directly, but they do more. They are primarily responsible for junior NCO development. They execute policies, supervise activities and advise officers in the performance of all of their purpose, direction, motivation and organizational sustainment functions. They are the repository of organizational values.

Company grade officers also practice "do as I do" leadership. They lead literally and directly, face-to-face. (Some headquarters company commanders with close to 300 men performing disparate functions over a wide area may not fit this mold; they face a challenge similar to the next higher level.) They act as important value setters; making short-term policies, setting short-term goals and executing short-range tactical schemes. They make a given organization function. Their longer-range policies and goals are interpretations of higher-level ones and their plans are very dependent upon plans and priorities set above their level. They are expected to display initiative and continuity in the short-term execution of tasks.

Junior field grade officers alternate between indirect and "do as I do" leadership. They are the first level of real value shapers. They are responsible for company grade officer development. They make longer-term policies and set longer-term goals. They execute short-range combined arms tactical schemes. They make a task force with nonorganic parts function.

Indirect leadership is characterized by some physical detachment due to time and space. These leaders must work harder to maintain intellectual and spiritual attachment. Every leader beyond the lowest levels must understand that time and space limits those in the organization whom the leader can touch personally. And this implies a decision as to whom within the organization, to how many and how far he can spread his personal influence. The leader must choose carefully, for there are pitfalls to spreading too thin as well as to staying too near the headquarters. One can visualize this as a series of concentric circles. There is a pitfall in bypassing a circle or two and trying to reach all the way down to deal with the soldier in the ranks too often. This affects the mutual trust within a chain of command. It is best to reach out by degrees and occasionally "test the waters" beyond the three rings any leader can influence effectively. Some may be better at reaching out farther. Each leader should know this "range" and stay within it.

Senior field grade and junior general officers practice mostly indirect leadership. They are important value shapers and are responsible for junior field grade development. They shape command climates in the Army. They are long-term policy makers and goal setters. They execute complex combined arms tactical schemes. They create task forces, shape organizations and make large, complex organizations function.

Senior general officers practice indirect leadership except on rare occasion and with a small segment of their subordinates. They lead other general officers and senior field grade officers in direct ways and work hard to shape consensus among their peers. They are the very long-range institutional value shapers. They are responsible for the development of field grade and junior general officers. They shape the command climate on Army posts, within major commands and within the Army for long periods of time. They make policies and set goals that have impact many years beyond their tenure. They are responsible for the execution of complex operational and strategic schemes. They create organizations and set long-range trends. They shape institutions and make long-term important decisions frequently based on intuition because easily recognizable tradeoffs are not apparent.

There are differences other than those identified in this short sketch, and they should be identified and studied. Study may reveal that this intuitive grouping of ranks is not the best. Whatever grouping is used, a matrix can be developed. This could be useful for developing effective leaders because we could then identify what the *be*, *know* and *do* requirements are for each level.

There is much written on the subject of leadership. U.S. Army Field Manual (FM) 22-100, *Military Leadership* and FM 22-103, *Leadership and Command at Senior Levels*, are the best leadership manuals we have had. The historical record is full of useful material as are more recent studies by behavioral scientists. But until we undertake an orderly and scientific study of the functions of leadership and understand more fully what leaders must be, know and do at each level to effectively perform those functions in peace and war, we will only be partly informed.

4

Leadership: Views from Readers

Leadership:
A Dependent's View

Green rows of mud-covered men silently marching past my front yard; sergeants and officers excitedly "talking shop" in my quarters' living room; and the solemn, respectful, changes of command that I have attended— each has given me the opportunity to see what leaders can and should be. As a dependent, I've seen the kind of commanders who watch their drenched, red-clayed soldiers slide up and down ravines while they sit in a dry, clean jeep. But growing up through countless Hails and Farewells, I've talked to leaders who stress participating in training, not just observing. These are the commanders for whom coldness and fatigue may threaten, yet cannot hinder, a mission from being accomplished. The leader who is known for thinking ahead, for inspirational actions, for always remaining flexible, and focusing on the important is the leader I can strive to become.

—Ms. Kerith Dana Dubik, Fort Leavenworth, Kansas

Thomas "Stonewall" Jackson

Leadership's concepts are epitomized in General "Stonewall" Jackson. He personifies 10 of FM 22-100's 11 attributes of good leadership. He sought self-improvement, was proficient at the art, responsible and soundly decisive; he led by example, cared for his troops, developed subordinates, ensured task completion, trained his team, and used his unit according to its capabilities. By using these sound principles long before they were set down formally, his units performed feats far in excess of what other commanders extracted from their men. His flanking maneuver at Chancellorsville is the historical forerunner of General H. Norman Schwarzkopf's "Hail Mary."

—Major Warner D. Farr, USA, Brooks AFB, Texas

Reprinted by permission from *Military Review*, 72:8 (August 1992), pp. 53–62.

The Ability to
Articulate a Vision

Leadership does not seem to follow any type of template, each "Great Captain" achieving greatness on his own merits based on the challenges encountered. But the truly great leaders seem to have similar characteristics. All have a vision, and more important, the ability to articulate that vision to their soldiers. They have a sense of selflessness, always ensuring they maintained this perspective, no matter to how high an office they had ascended. Part of this selflessness involved taking the jobs that were not always the most popular, or the most "career enhancing." The great leaders were also unique in that they took the time to train and develop subordinates, usually in their own mold, and had a great love for our country, the plain old flag-waving type of patriotism.

—Major Eduardo Martinez Jr., USA, Fort Leavenworth, Kansas

R.E. Lee:
Example of Personal Integrity

Robert E. Lee was a great captain. His brilliance and audacity on the battlefield inspired his men. Yet it was his personal integrity—his moral fortitude—that gave his soldiers unity, identity, purpose and loyalty. It enabled them to go beyond their physical limitations. General Lee became the center about which everything revolved within the Army of Northern Virginia, center of gravity for an army.

—Chaplain (CPT) Robert N. Neske, USA, Fort Leavenworth, Kansas

Furthermore:

To me leadership is the art of wisdom, intelligence and decisiveness to handle a crisis situation, turn it around, and get it under control or solve the problem that it represents. Examples of this would be General Matthew Ridgway in the Korean War and General Ulysses Grant in the American Civil War.

Jimmy Doolittle is my idea of a "great captain" because he served in both the Army and the Air Force. He also showed the proper balance of vision, intelligence and decisiveness in his handling of air power in the years of World War II.

—Charles Trudell, West Carrollton, Ohio

Words on Leadership

Realization: recognize the present.

Vision: know where organization ought to go.

Prescience: anticipate needs.

Involvement: participate,
- teach: train and educate,
- learn: commit to self-improvement,
- practice: "practice, practice, practice."

Incisiveness: dig for details and truth; mediocrity fails.

Linkage: inter-relationship of events; go beyond the obvious.

Responsibility: keep subordinates and superiors informed, on time, and out of trouble.

Thick skin: withstand trivial and professional denigration.

Dignity: exercise your vocabulary, but avoid "profane" and "vulgar" language.
- compliment people, say "thank you" and mean it,
- do not "touch" people—may be perceived as patronizing and presumptuous,
- treat people fairly, with respect and honor.

Reward: recognize good and bad, appropriately.

Courage: physical, moral and professional; "do the right thing."

—Major Eben H. Trevino Jr., USAF, MacDill AFB, Florida

Leadership:
Sergeant's Business

The great captain I am going to talk about is my Command Sergeant Major, Johnnie Riley. Although Riley is not well known, he has the three qualities that make a great captain—he is a thinker, a motivator and most important a warrior. During the two years I have known him, I have consistently been in awe of his tactical acumen, his rapport with the soldiers and his overall knowledge of the Army. An example of his tactical brilliance was his input into the plan for our 80-mile air assault into Iraq. His recommendations were sound. In hearing that Riley was in a defensive position during a brigade field training exercise, the division's assistant division commander for operations said Riley was such a combat multiplier that it was like having another platoon in that position. Perhaps the essence of Riley's philosophy on being a soldier can best be described by this quote: "People say that war is hell, well if that's true it is our duty as soldiers to put out the fires and kill the devil."

—LTC Frank R. Hancock, USA, Fort Campbell, Kentucky

The Virtues of Followership

I believe that in order for one to be a successful leader, he must first understand and appreciate what it takes to be a good follower. The successful leader must experience what it is like to be on the receiving end of commands. He must gain this experience so that he can comprehend the strength that his own actions and words will one day have upon others. This appreciation is essential because he understands what it takes to inspire and motivate just as he realizes what rewards they appreciate for a job well done.

—Cadet Allen T. Thiessen, US Military Academy

How to Be an
Effective Leader

I was very proud the day my dad pinned my second lieutenant's bars on me; he was a colonel in the mature years of a distinguished career. His guidance on leadership summed up what he had practiced all his life:

"Keep your troops out of the sun and don't BS the old man."

Dad summed up a lot of books with those 13 pithy words, which have guided me ever since: take care of your soldiers and they will take care of you and your mission; tell it like it is, even when it hurts; uncompromising integrity in all you do.

—Colonel John B. Haseman, USA, US Embassy, Indonesia

Ike and the
Limits of Intuition

Field Manual 22-103 states that leadership vision "can be an intuitive sensing." There is no question that Eisenhower "sensed" the right moment to launch Operation *Overlord*. Whether he sensed it intuitively is subject to question. He did, however, have all of his commanders present when he made his decision, including his meteorologist. Had any one commander been adamant or had even seriously taken exception, for whatever reason, the chances are that the invasion of Normandy would not have taken place on June 6th, and no amount of "intuition" on Eisenhower's part could have cajoled the members of the coalition into going along with him. Intuition has definite limitations in decision making. Eisenhower was aware of the limits and relied heavily upon his staff to help him with his decision.

—David Craig, New Orleans, Louisiana

Intangible Inspiration

Leadership is that intangible quality which inspires subordinates to follow with assurance and confidence when hardship and danger are present. Leadership is therefore of the utmost importance to soldiers at all levels since success depends wholly upon the leader's ability to control and direct. In fact, it may be said that the effectiveness of our Army depends more upon the quality of its leadership than any other factor. Inferior numbers and inferior material, coupled with superior leadership may always be counted upon to win against superior numbers, superior material and inferior leadership.

—Colonel Dennis P. Vasey, USA (Retired), Naples, Florida

Stuck in Transmit?

We lead people, we manage programs.
We all lead people sometimes, so are we good at it?
Can we change our leadership style, or were we cast in final form?
Should we adopt some clever leadership style, or should we be ourselves?
If we lead by fear, do we get the top effort?
If we lead with a firm human touch, do the hearts and minds follow?
Do we lead alone, or do we seek advice from all levels?
Do we learn each day how to be a better leader, or are we stuck in transmit?

—Colonel David K. Burke, USAF, Fort Leavenworth, Kansas

A Great Captain at Vera Cruz

Winfield Scott, bold but not brash, epitomes the phrase "Great Captain." His Vera Cruz campaign shows these characteristics. Designing his own landing craft and doctrine, he led the Army's first large-scale amphibious invasion. Outnumbered, he boldly advanced on Mexico City without a supply line. With his small professional army, he outmaneuvered his adversary on three battlefields with minimal losses. After a march of 200 mountainous miles, he captured Mexico City, thus winning the war.

—LTC Timothy T. Tilson, USA, Wauwatosa, Wisconsin

The Techniques of Leadership

Leadership techniques are not concrete, nor guaranteed to be successful. Being able to adjust to changing situations and using the available resources are traits that a successful leader must exhibit. Successful leadership integrates consideration for subordinates and goal planning.

—Cadet Marshall Arthur McKay, US Military Academy

For the Troops

Leadership is an intangible concept, exercised in many ways, dependent on many factors. Some, including personal charisma, are beyond one's control. Others, such as use of troop leading procedures (TLP), are within one's control. In my opinion the key element in leadership is personal commitment to one's troops and involvement in their activities. The commander who is on the scene participating in training (or combat) will know his troops and their problems and sees in person what must be done. His presence motivates them and his presence at the site of critical action may in itself determine the outcome.

—Brigadier General Peter W. Clegg, USA, Fort Devens, Massachusetts

Bottom Line Orientation

In most organizations, there are few people at the top, a bunch in the middle, and a large number at the bottom. The bottom is where products are made, and where services are delivered. This work defines not just the worker's purpose, but the organization's purpose. The trenches is where the organization happens—the true "bottom line."

The real purpose of leadership is to reduce the uncertainty of those at the next echelon below, until, finally, when the decision making of the chain-of-command finally meets with the energy of the worker, there is, ideally, no uncertainty in the minds of either party.

Too often, the people in the trenches have unmet information needs, even at the moment when human energy is finally applied to the actual doing. This is not ignorance; it is uncertainty. Bottom-line uncertainties reflect failures on the part of leaders, at all levels, to provide workers with timely, accurate, coherent information.

The next time you see an organization chart, look at the trenches. You'll realize that the levels and the positions above the trenches, all the way up to and including the chief executive officer, are of no value whatsoever unless they somehow serve the information needs of people down there on . . . the bottom line.

—LTC Mike McGee, USA, Washington, D.C.

"I Propose to Fight on This Line . . . "

As general in chief of the Union armies, Grant conducted multiple campaigns over half a continent, commanding over 500,000 troops in 21 army corps. Grant spoke little and listened well. Self-reliant, he was calm amid excitement, patient, sure in judgment and foresight, and not depressed by reverses or unduly elated by success. He was tenacious and could discipline himself and others. Tireless in action he once personally wrote 42 important dispatches in one day. Fearless in battle, he had empathy for his soldiers. Setting an austere example in the field, he provided the steadfast command and control around which everything else turned. His magnanimity to Lee at Appomattox saved the country from prolonged guerrilla warfare. He was all the Union Army wanted, a leader.

—LTC Thomas D. Morgan, USA (Retired), Leavenworth, Kansas

The Leadership Paycheck

In my previous assignment as an ROTC instructor, we had a cadet in our battalion who thought that leadership was like a contest. Show up with the shiniest boots and win the prize. Become a fair-haired boy of a few superiors and rest on your hands.

Nothing could be further from the truth. Unfortunately, too many of us in leadership positions forget (in fact some never learn to begin with) that leadership of men and women is really a paycheck—it has to be earned every day. More important, the check is signed by our troops, not by our superiors. Our troops are the ones who grant us the privilege of leading them. They alone decide whether or not we've earned our "pay."

—Major Joseph W. T. Pugh, USA, Fort Bliss, Texas

Communicating Success

Before one can discover the essential qualities of a successful leader, he first has to communicate his definition of success to his audience. Although there are many ways to assess the success of a leader, the most resourceful is to measure the success of his unit in accomplishing given tasks. Regardless of whether the leader epitomizes one's concept of a great leader or not, a leader whose unit is successful is successful as well.

—Cadet Landy Donnell Dunham, US Military Academy

The Hallmark of a Leader

By definition, leadership is the art of influencing others to accomplish the mission. To paraphrase Napoleon, the great leader is not the one who can lead men. The great leader is the one the men will follow. This is truer today than it ever was, owing in large part to the intelligence of today's soldiers. Any officer or NCO can give orders, and the troops will have no choice but to obey. To be a leader, however, means understanding your soldiers and what makes them tick. A leader is one who can make the tough choices, who will roll up his sleeves and "get dirty" when he's short-handed.

—SFC Terence L. Johnson, USA, Fort Leavenworth, Kansas

Killer Angel

Joshua Lawrence Chamberlain is a great captain whose example few can match but all can follow. He voluntarily answered the call to serve; self-motivated himself to study the profession of arms; accepted mentoring by his commander; trained his soldiers for combat with available time; continually inspired his soldiers through his personal example, even when wounded; was tested at Fredericksburg; innovated at Gettysburg; took up his unit colors and moved forward at Petersburg; marched to the sound of the guns at Five Forks; respected his enemy's capabilities and honor; continued to serve his state and country after leaving the Army.

—Captain Edward S. Loomis, USA, Fort Polk, Louisiana

What Are the Essential Qualities of a Successful Leader?

There are those who fail, those who survive, and those who succeed. Any man charged with the leadership of others who is lacking integrity, morality, honesty, and concern is doomed to fail. Any leader possessing these qualities at a minimum has at least established a platform to succeed. Finally, there are those who seem to rise above the platform. That leader is the one who has the courage, foresight, and persistence to ask: Why? A successful leader will question the status quo. A response of "It has always been that way" will not satisfy a leader seeking improvement. That leader recognizes that nothing is perfect and everything needs improving. He views the old adage "If it ain't broke, don't fix it" as an excuse for complacency. The strive for excellence is, and will always be the determining factor between the successful and the survivor.

—Captain Phil Deaton, USA, White Sands Missile Range, New Mexico

The Basics of Leadership

I believe all successful leaders have one fundamental quality that stands out—the quality of human understanding. All soldiers need to know that they are more important than a weapon system. With all of our new technological advances and the downsizing of the Army, the soldier remains the key ingredient for success. Too often the needs of the soldier are subordinate to the needs of the Army. When a soldier knows that he has a chain of command that really cares and listens, his attitude and performance is magnified. "Leaders work with people and feelings."

—Captain Joseph C. Lopez, USA, APO AE 09630

Successful Leaders Develop
Successful Subordinates

Successful leaders develop confidence and aggressive, independent action in their subordinates. They take a moment after a brutal after-action review to express continued confidence in a subordinate who has made a mistake while attempting to faithfully achieve the commander's intent. The successful leader does not sanction poor judgment; he reaffirms aggressive initiative on the part of junior leaders. In the darkest moments of an NTC rotation, a future leader's aggressive spirit can be formed or broken by a single word.

—CPT Frederick C. Hellwig, USA, Columbia, South Carolina

Improvisation

Successful leadership has many facets to it. A leader must know the fundamentals of leadership, but must also be able to improvise. Answers to most leadership puzzles will never be found in a book because the people involved will change constantly, causing new puzzles. A successful leader must be able to understand people and human nature. Leaders need to know the limits and capabilities of those they lead to maximize their potential. Being able to adapt to changing situations quickly and effectively has always been the hallmark of the more successful leaders.

—2LT Lawrence E. Collins Jr., USA, DeKalb, Illinois

For Want of a Nail

A former commander of mine used the metaphor of leadership as the process of making a good horseshoe. He began by noting that you need a skilled blacksmith, a hammer, a heated strip of metal and an anvil to make a good horseshoe.

The blacksmith in this case is any leader from general officer to section leader. The leader must be proficient and should have a vision of what goals the unit has set out to accomplish. The hammer is one of many tools available to us as leaders. It's equivalent to position, authority, knowledge or the ability to make things happen. The metal is the unit and soldiers. In almost every situation, soldiers want to do well. They're malleable metal ready to take shape under the direction of the leader. The anvil is the key item of equipment. Without it you can bang away at the metal and get the sparks and sound of a blacksmith, but the finished product will look nothing like the horseshoe. You need the firm evaluative base of an anvil to make things go right.

—Major Stephen P. Walsh, USA, Mt. Clemens, Michigan

Words of Wisdom

In his search to be a great leader, the young centurion sought out the Republic's veteran warrior. Looking up from his labor, the sage spoke:

> "I know not what beats beneath your tunic, but what I saw in a leader
>   from foot soldiers to proconsul is thus:
> One who makes drill bloodless combat and combat bloody drill . . .
> One who disciplines the offense and not the offenders . . .
> One whose heart is with the Legion and whose loyalty is to the Republic
>   . . .
> One who seeks the companionship of the long march and not the privi-
>   lege of position . . .
> One whose commission is assigned from above and confirmed from
>   below . . .
> One who knows the self and, therefore, is true to all . . .
> One who seeks to serve and not to be served . . .
> This is the one who leads best of all."
>   —LTC Jeffrey L. Spara, USA, Syracuse, New York

Getting There

Leaders are first and foremost individuals of character. Although Army leadership doctrine does not neglect this attribute—and even places it first in the Be, Know, Do trinity—practice places Be far behind Know and, especially, Do. Army practice looks at leadership as an algorithm: in such-and-such a situation, do the following and you too will be a leader. It's all a question of technique. We have missed the leadership boat. We talk about history while encouraging our officers to spend their spare time earning business administration degrees. We publish lists of professional books but reward reading military fantasy novels. The first orients on Do; the second kills time. The Chief of Staff encourages us to grow leaders of character, and Harry Summers suggests future readiness will emerge from education. Without an institutional change, we won't get there from here.

                        —Major Steve G. Capps, Fort Leavenworth, Kansas

Leadership—Old Testament Style

Nehemiah was an Old Testament leader who was able to translate commander's intent into mission accomplishment and the Old Testament book bearing his name is perhaps the first written manual on effective leadership. He clearly epitomized the four values—courage, candor, commitment, and competence—that leaders should possess. As cup bearer to King Artaxerxes, Nehemiah showed considerable courage by asking for an extended TDY to rebuild Jerusalem's walls. He demonstrated candor by requesting specific assistance. Despite active opposition, Nehemiah remained unwavering in his commitment to the mission. Nehemiah's proficiency in communications, planning, reconnaissance, and decision making attest to his competence. His adherence to the four "Cs" resulted in the rebuilding of the walls in only 52 days.

—LTC Russell V. Olson Jr., USA, Fort Leavenworth, Kansas

From the Napoleonic Era

Marshall Louis Nicholas Davout, of Napoleon's Army, possessed three qualities that are the hallmark of a great leader—character, competence and caring. Marshall Davout believed in honesty, loyalty and courage. Even though men made fun of his devout Christian beliefs, no one ever doubted Davout's purity of character. Davout's competence on the battlefield saved Napoleon from defeat at Austerlitz. Davout's concern for his soldiers was evident to them. The soldiers, who didn't like their commander personally could look around and see that he kept them supplied better than any other unit in the French Army. Marshall Davout's reward for his leadership ability was the respect and obedience of his men.

—Cadet Veronica D. Robertson, US Military Academy

Leadership and Modern Technology

The complexity of the integrated battlefield and application of technology to complete mission objectives as demonstrated during Operation *Desert Storm* suggests that leaders should possess the ability to identify individuals, irrespective of rank, who possess relevant knowledge, skills, and attitudes and to effectively and efficiently utilize these individuals to complete assigned missions. This essential quality if possessed and applied by leaders will provide participating soldiers with enhanced self esteem and the pride of accomplishment. Consequently unit esprit de corps and combat readiness may be enhanced through the demonstrated recognition of and reliance on individual capabilities.

—1LT Doug Rokke, USA, Rantoll, Illinois

The Right Leader at the Right Place

Writing on Sir Garnet Joseph Wolsely, Archibald Forbes says, "The heaven-born soldier is he who achieves startling success with apparently inadequate means." Only good leadership turns defeat into victory. Good leaders set personal standards that harden individual and unit resolve and take risks because they trust subordinates to do the right thing at every level of command. Great Captains have the flexibility of mind to seize every initiative the enemy allows them and have the physical and mental toughness to stand firm on their decisions. Thus, leadership is the right mix at the right time of trust, flexibility, and firmness.

The "Great Captain" who epitomizes my definition of leadership was Field Marshall Sir William Slim, commander of Allied Land Forces in South East Asia, perhaps the toughest and least resourced World War II front. His commoner roots, his experience teaching the poor before he became a soldier and his service in the colonial army taught him to value the humanity of those he led regardless of race or class. From his World War II experience and his wounds at Gallipoli, Slim learned the importance of not wasting soldiers lives. A rare blend of improvisation and determination, he did not repeat the same mistakes. He was a leader who knew his trade, had great rapport with the men he led, and had the physical and mental resilience to turn a hopeless defeat in India into a remarkable victory over the Japanese in Burma.

—Colonel Joseph T. Cox, USA, US Military Academy

The Human Quality

The best leaders, in all walks of life, are honest and humane. As a noncom once remarked to me "You don't lead men into battle by telling them you're taking them to the Post Exchange." And as General Schwarzkopf observed: men don't die for abstract ideals like "Mom and apple pie" but for the buddies at their side. A leader's most important job is to inspire—by being trustworthy and protecting the lives of his men.

—Mrs. D. J. Collier, China Grove, North Carolina

Caring Is Key

The ability to care, guide, and teach are essential components for successful leadership. Weaving these components into a solid foundation, a leader makes subordinates better people. The first component, caring, creates a trusting relationship between leader and follower. Both parties show the other empathy, compassion, and understanding. This caring gives the leader the ability to guide subordinates to self-improvement by providing guidelines and perspectives. Teaching, the final component, strengthens the caring and guiding foundation. Leaders teach subordinates through positive role models and examples. Working together, these three components make successful leaders by creating better subordinates.

—Cadet Heidi Strubbe, US Military Academy

Qualities of Leaders

The three most essential qualities of a successful leader are competence, courage, and wisdom. Competence is essential because a leader must know what he or she is doing. Without competence, the followers will not have confidence in him or her. Courage is essential because a leader must keep trying when the followers want to give up. Without courage, a leader cannot push his or her followers in tough times, which is when they most need a leader. Wisdom is essential because a leader must know how to react to circumstances. Without wisdom, a leader will make wrong decisions.

—Cadet Steven Park, US Military Academy

Leadership as Instinct

Leadership is not an art nor a technique, but an instinct occurring at a precise moment in time. A moment which might be critical on a smoke-filled battlefield or important to a boardroom problem-solving process. It exists just below the level of consciousness yet essential to its environment. Its absence creates a void which is often filled by a randomness of undefined and unguided efforts. The leader sees clearly at the critical moment and acts to focus available energies to seize that moment and turn it to its conclusion. The study of this instinct creates an art and the imitation of its characteristics defines the technique.

—Major John W. Lemza, USA, Fort Lee, Virginia

5

A New Vision of Leadership

Marshall Sashkin and William E. Rosenbach

Looking through the history of the study of leadership, we find that the earliest coherent thrust centered on an approach now referred to as the "Great Man" or "Great Person" theory. For a full generation, leadership scholars concentrated on identifying the traits associated with great leadership. At first it seemed obvious; are not great leaders exceptionally intelligent, unusually energetic, far above the norm in their ability to speak to followers, and so on? However, when these "obvious" propositions were subjected to test, they all proved false. Yes, leaders were found to be a bit more intelligent than the average, but not much more. And yes, they were more energetic and dynamic—but not significantly so. True, they were better-than-average public speakers, but again their overall advantage was not very great. And so it went: Each of these and other leadership myths evaporated under the glare of scientific scrutiny.

What followed was a focus on the behavior of leaders. If the key was not *who* they were, perhaps the crux of leadership could be found in *what* they did. In fact, researchers were able to identify two crucial types of leader behavior: behavior centered on task accomplishments and behavior directed toward interpersonal relations. Their peers typically reported individuals who consistently exhibited high levels of both of these types of behavior as leaders. Those who engaged in a high level of task-related activity but only an average level of relationship-centered behavior were sometimes still designated leaders. Those who engaged only in a high level of relationship behavior were rarely designated leaders by their peers. Finally, those who did

This chapter can also be found in *Contemporary Issues in Leadership*, 4th ed. (Boulder: Westview Press, 1998).

little in the way of either task- or relationship-centered activity were never seen as leaders.

Perhaps, then, the essence of effective leadership is engaging in high levels of both task-oriented and relationship-centered activity. To test this possibility, researchers trained factory foremen in the two types of behavior and put them back on the job. For a while things did seem to improve, but the effects were short-lived. After only a few weeks the foremen went back to their old behaviors; performance and productivity also returned to their prior levels. Although further research showed that even sustained high levels of the new behaviors had limited long-term effects on employees' performance, productivity, or satisfaction, the leadership-training programs developed in the early 1960s are still popular. Serious students of leadership, however, soon recognized the need to look further for answers to the riddle of effective leadership.

Some took a new path, suggesting that leadership effectiveness might require different combinations of task and relationship behavior in different situations. Theoretically, the most effective combination would depend upon certain situational factors, such as the nature of the task or the ability level of employees reporting to a certain supervisor. Another somewhat different path was to combine the situational hypothesis with some variations of the personal characteristics approach. Like earlier attempts, however, these efforts to explain effective leadership met with limited results. The puzzle remained unsolved.

Earlier in this century, Chester Barnard commented that leadership "has been the subject of an extraordinary amount of dogmatically stated nonsense." More recently, Joseph Rost observed that leadership as good management is what the "twentieth-century school of leadership" is all about. Rost argues for the development of a whole new paradigm of leadership that includes the dynamic interplay between leaders and followers. Later on, we will have more to say about Rost's interesting and important ideas. But first we will examine the ground-breaking work of political scientist and historian James MacGregor Burns who has had the most influence on leadership research and theory over the past fifteen years.

Burns's work served to reacquaint scholars with a critical distinction first raised by the famous German sociologist Max Weber—the difference between economic and noneconomic sources of authority. This important distinction was one basis for Weber's discussion of charisma and charismatic leadership. Burns amplified and focused this issue, using examples such as Gandhi and Roosevelt, illustrations that made the distinction between *leaders* and *managers* so striking that it could not be ignored. The work of Burns led to the development of several new approaches to the study of what many now refer to as "transformational" leadership. That term is now widely used to contrast this "new leadership" with the old "transactional" leadership (or *management*) approach.

The transactional approach is based on economic and quasi-economic transactions between leaders and followers and appeals to followers' self-interest. In contrast, the new transformational approaches appeal to followers beyond their self-interest and incorporate the idea that leadership involves what Weber called noneconomic sources of authority or influence. In his widely acclaimed 1978 book *Leadership*, Burns defined transformational leadership as occurring when one or more persons engage with others in such a way that leaders and followers raise one another to higher levels of motivation and morality. In other words, both leader and followers—as well as the social system in which they function—are transformed.

Explorations in the New Paradigm

Burns's early work was crucial for the establishment of the new transformational paradigm, but he did not carry forward his concept by developing a clear theory or any direct measures. It was left to others, inspired by his original work, to build on it by defining theory and creating measures. The first and one of the most important of these follow-up efforts was initiated by Bernard M. Bass. Bass had long been recognized as a serious leadership researcher and scholar and had taken responsibility for updating and preparing new editions of Ralph Stogdill's classic *Handbook of Leadership*. Perhaps Bass's immense breadth of background knowledge led him to try to turn Burns's new concept into a more rigorous and measurable theory.

Leadership and Performance
Beyond Expectations

Bass's first contribution was to identify a serious error in Burns's work. Burns thought transactional (managerial) and transformational leadership were the end points of a continuum. This belief resembled an error made many years earlier by traditional leadership researchers, who thought that "relationship orientation" and "task orientation" were end points of one leadership dimension. They soon found, however, that they were really two independent dimensions, that a person could exhibit one, the other, both, or neither. Bass realized that transactional leadership is simply different from, not inconsistent with, transformational leadership. A person might exhibit just one, the other, both, or neither.

Bass demonstrated this point by creating a measuring tool, the Multifactor Leadership Questionnaire (MLQ). The MLQ is filled out by a leader as well as by others who report on that person. This variety of perspectives gives what is called a "360 degree" picture of the leader. The MLQ was developed by getting several hundred people to give descriptions of leaders and leadership, by identifying specific actions and characteristics contained in those descriptions, and by then translating those behaviors and characteristics into specific questions. These questions were put into a single, long questionnaire that was administered to hundreds more people. Their answers were then analyzed using factor analysis, a statistical technique that groups together all the questions that seem to fit with one another, producing a relatively small set of categories. This process helps clarify the underlying meaning of the specific questions.

Bass refined the MLQ repeatedly by revising the questions and administering them to new groups of people. Ultimately, he concluded that the questionnaire was able to measure the two forms of leadership and, within each, to identify several more specific categories.

With respect to the old transactional, or managerial, side of leadership, Bass found three subcategories very much like some of those identified by earlier researchers.

Laissez-faire—This component refers to a tendency for the leader to abdicate responsibility toward his or her followers, who are left to their own devices. Laissez-faire leadership really indicates an absence of leadership.

Contingent reward—Often called reward-and-punishment or simply carrot-and-stick leadership, this approach means that the leader rewards followers for attaining performance levels the leader had specified. Performance-contingent strategies are by no means completely ineffective; in general, they are associated with both the performance and satisfaction of followers.

Management by exception—This type of transactional leadership involves managers taking action only when there is evidence of something not going according to plan. There are two types of MBE: *active* and *passive*. The former describes a leader who looks for deviations from established procedure and takes action when irregularities are identified. The passive form describes a tendency to intervene only when specific problems arise because established procedures are not being followed.

The MLQ also taps four specific aspects of transformational leadership. Each of these is different from the forms of transactional leadership just described, because there is no tit-for-tat, no reward (or punishment) from the leader in exchange for followers' efforts.

Charisma—For Bass and, in a statistical sense, for the MLQ, this is the most important dimension assessed by the instrument. Followers see leaders as charismatic when the leader provides emotional arousal— that is, a sense of mission, vision, excitement, and pride. This feeling is typically associated with respect and trust of the leader.

Inspiration—Transformational leaders who inspire their followers set high expectations, use symbols to focus efforts, express important purposes in simple ways, and are specifically concerned with communicating a vision to followers.

Individualized consideration—This aspect of transformational leadership is similar to the old notion of relationship behavior. Individualized consideration means that the leader gives personal attention to followers. The leader builds a personal, considerate relationship with each individual, focusing on that person's needs. Leaders who show individualized consideration toward followers also help followers learn and develop by encouraging personal responsibility. In the process, the leader exhibits trust and respect, which followers then come to feel toward the leader.

Intellectual stimulation—Transformational leaders often provide followers with a flow of new ideas, challenging followers to rethink old ways of doing things. In one sense, this aspect of transformational leadership is related to the older form of task-focused managerial (transactional) leadership, because the focus is on the actual content of the work. The difference is that instead of giving structure and directions, transformational leaders stimulate followers to develop their own task structure and figure out problems on their own.

Bass developed these dimensions of leadership to identify specific categories and types of transactional and transformational leadership behavior. The MLQ could then be used as a coaching and development tool, not just to aid in research or to assess individuals' potential in order to hire or promote the person most likely to succeed. Bass and his associates have made substantial contributions in this regard, developing training programs for navy officers and school superintendents, among other groups, based on this approach to transformational leadership and the MLQ.

However, we believe that the MLQ and Bass's theory have some important deficiencies. Although Bass argues that the MLQ is a measure of *behavior*, when one looks at the actual questions it becomes evident that the most important transformational leadership dimension, charisma, is measured by attitudinal questions, not by leader actions. This approach is actually quite sensible, because charisma is the *result* of transformational leadership rather than its *cause*. Max Weber was the first to use the term *charisma* to describe leaders. There was something special about them that he didn't understand, so he used the ancient Greek word meaning "gift of the gods." That seemed the only available explanation.

We now know that charisma is neither magical nor mysterious. It is simply the feeling that most people have about another person when that person behaves toward them in certain ways. (Later, we will look at some of the specific behaviors associated with charisma.) The chief flaw in Bass's approach is his continued acceptance of charisma as some mysterious quality of the leader. It is true that people often attribute certain special characteristics to leaders because of the way those leaders behave and the feelings they arouse. However, this doesn't really tell us anything about either the personal qualities or behaviors leaders display that produce charismatic effects. To understand transformational leadership we must explore, identify, and measure both the specific actions and the personal characteristics of leaders.

Although Bass's work has been very important in helping to clarify and make concrete Burns's ideas, it ignores some important aspects of transformational leadership that are rooted in the *personal characteristics* of individual leaders. Nor does Bass address the *culture* of the organization.

However, before looking at characteristics of leaders or organizational culture, we need to examine transformational behavior more closely. We will draw on the empirical and behavior-focused work of two other leadership researchers, James M. Kouzes and Barry Z. Posner.

Five Behavioral Dimensions of Leadership

Not long after Bass began theorizing about transformational leadership, researchers on the other side of the country took up the same general problem. Kouzes and Posner were also affected by Burns's work; however, rather than having people describe great leaders and then using those descriptions to construct a questionnaire, they asked managers to write detailed memoirs of their own greatest, most positive leadership experience. These "personal best" cases, some of which ran on for ten pages or more, were analyzed to identify common threads. Only then did the researchers begin to construct questions about leadership behavior.

Kouzes and Posner, like Bass, developed a very long list of questions. They asked hundreds of managers to answer these questions, describing exceptional leaders they had known personally (instead of concentrating on great leaders in history as did Bass). Like Bass, Kouzes and Posner examined the results using factor analysis. They identified five clear factors, all describable in terms of reasonably concrete behaviors. Ultimately (and again like Bass) Kouzes and Posner constructed a questionnaire to measure transformational leadership: the Leadership Practices Inventory (LPI).

The LPI has five scales, one for each of the five types of leadership behavior. We will briefly define each.

Challenging the process—This means searching for opportunities and experimenting, even taking sensible risks, to improve the organization.

Inspiring a shared vision—This sounds a lot like Bass's category, but it is focused less on inspiration per se and more on what leaders actually do to construct future visions and to build follower support for the vision.

Enabling others to act—Leaders make it possible for followers to take action by fostering collaboration (as opposed to competition) and supporting followers in their personal development.

Modeling the way—Leaders set examples by their own behaviors. They also help followers focus on step-by-step accomplishments of large-scale goals, making those goals seem more realistic and attainable.

Encouraging the heart—Leaders recognize followers' contributions and find ways to celebrate their achievements.

The five practices of exemplary leadership identified by Kouzes and Posner are, in our view, much more specific and behaviorally focused than the transformational leadership dimensions developed by Bass. We don't mean that Bass's dimensions or his MLQ are not useful: His ideas were crucial for moving beyond Burns's groundbreaking concepts, and the MLQ can be a valuable tool for executive development. Still, Kouzes and Posner have taken a big step beyond Bass toward a much clearer behavioral explanation of transformational leadership. Yet even this work is not the final word. There's more to transformational leadership than behavioral practices.

The Visionary Leader

At about the same time Bass and Kouzes and Posner were working on their models of transformational leadership, Marshall Sashkin was constructing the first draft of his Leader Behavior Questionnaire (LBQ). Sashkin originally based the LBQ on the work of Warren Bennis, who studied ninety exceptional leaders. Bennis looked for some common factors, some things that would explain just what these leaders did that made them so successful. He identified several commonalties that he called, at various times, "competencies," "behaviors," and "strategies." Sashkin took five of those behavior categories and developed a questionnaire based on them. The categories were:

Clarity—Sashkin's first category of transformational leadership behavior involves focusing the attention of others on key ideas, the most important aspects of the leader's vision. In practice, this means (for example) coming up with metaphors and analogies that make clear and vivid what might otherwise be abstract ideas.

Communication—The second behavior is more general, dealing with skills such as active listening and giving and receiving feedback effectively. These actions ensure clarity of communication.

Consistency—Leaders establish trust by taking actions that are consistent both over time and with what the leader says. Trust, of course, exists in the minds and hearts of followers and is not an obvious aspect of leader behavior. But consistency over time and between words and actions produces trust in followers.

Caring—The fourth behavior is demonstrating respect and concern for people. Psychologist Carl Rogers called this behavior "unconditional positive regard." By this he meant caring about and respecting another person regardless of one's feelings or judgments about that person's actions. Caring is shown not just by "big" actions such as ensuring job security but also by many everyday actions, such as remembering people's birthdays or even something as basic as learning and using their names.

Creating opportunities—Bennis originally associated this behavior with risk taking and risk avoidance, but the underlying issue is more complicated. Transformational leaders do empower followers by allowing them to accept challenges—taking on and "owning" a new project, for example. But transformational leaders also are careful to plan ahead and not to ask more of followers than they know the followers are capable of. Followers might honestly feel a sense of risk in accepting a challenge, but a transformational leader does all that is possible to ensure that any risk is relatively low, that with the right resources and (if necessary) help the follower can and will be successful.

The similarity between these categories and the five leadership practices identified by Kouzes and Posner are striking; in some cases even the words are the same. Sashkin used the categories identified by Bennis to create a questionnaire with a scale for each category and five questions on each scale. Then, like Kouzes and Posner, he collected data and used factor analysis to show that the five dimensions are replicated in people's real experience.

However, there is an interesting difference between the approach taken by Kouzes and Posner and that taken by Sashkin. Kouzes and Posner started by capturing significant experiences and, from those experiences, generated questions that identified their five practices. Sashkin, however, came from the opposite direction, developing measures of the five behaviors on the basis of Bennis's concepts and then validating his measure by analyzing reports of significant experiences. The fact that these two independent research efforts, coming from different directions, wound up in essentially the same place gives us confidence that these researchers are on to something, that the behaviors they've identified are real and important.

In the course of his study of leadership, Sashkin concluded that there had to be more to transformational leadership than just the five behaviors. He identified three specific personal characteristics that mark the differences among exceptional transformational leaders, average leaders, transactional leaders (managers), and nonleaders. None of these characteristics is a *trait* in the strictest sense, because all of them are learnable and changeable. Sashkin developed questionnaire scales to assess the extent to which leaders act on the basis of each of these three characteristics. The three scales were then added to the LBQ.

The first and perhaps most basic characteristic is self-confidence. Psychologists call this "self-efficacy" or "internal control." It is, in essence, the belief that one controls one's own fate. The second characteristic concerns the need for power and the way that need is manifested. Getting things done in organizations depends on one's power and influence and how that power is used. Finally, exceptional leaders have vision, but that vision is not an aspect of charisma or inspiration or some trait like creativity. Vision is based on the ability to think through what's happening, to determine causes, and to identify how complicated chains of cause and effect actually work. Only then can a person begin to figure out how to bring about the outcomes he or she wants. We will briefly describe the nature of each of these three personal characteristics.

Self-confidence.   The great American writer Mark Twain probably said it best: "If you think you can . . . or think you *can't* .. . you're probably right." Often we defeat ourselves before we start. Sometimes it's almost intentional. In the comic strip *Calvin and Hobbes*, Calvin, a precocious seven year-old, asks his best friend, a stuffed tiger named Hobbes, whether he believes the stars control our fate. "Naw," says Hobbes. "Oh, I do," replies Calvin. "Life's a lot more fun when you're not responsible for your actions." However, by denying control, Calvin denies all of the vast possibilities of leadership. How can someone who has no faith in himself or herself become a leader of others?

Self-confidence or self-efficacy is a prerequisite to leadership. And it is not a trait. Self-efficacy is learned. Did you ever hear someone scold a child by saying, "Johnny, that's not how you do it! Can't you do anything right?!" Well, every time that happens, Johnny learns that he cannot control his fate. That's not a good lesson for success, let alone leadership. Parents and teachers must help children learn that they can control their own fate. But it's never too late; even adults can learn, and that's one of the most important jobs of leaders—teaching followers that they *can* do things for themselves. This is the first paradox of leadership: To become a leader, one must believe in one's own ability to achieve results for one's self, but the *real* job of a leader is not doing it but teaching others that *they* can do it.

Power. Harvard psychologist David McClelland has studied human motivation for about half a century. Early on he came to believe that three motives, or needs, play particularly important roles: the need to achieve, the need for power and control, and the need for friendship and human interaction. McClelland thought of needs not as fixed or inborn traits but rather as habits that people develop in the course of their lives. His particular focus for many years was on the need to achieve, which he believed might relate to business success. He thought it might be possible to actually "teach" people to need achievement, which should make it more likely for them to actually attain their goals.

In an important real-world experiment, McClelland found that small business entrepreneurs could learn to "need" achievement and that this enhanced their business success. But when he looked at managers in organizations, he found that the need for *power*, not achievement, was most strongly associated with success. Organizations are set up because there is work to do that can't be done by just one person, that requires people to work together to achieve goals. The process is controlled by the exercise of power and influence. Managers who have an extremely high need to achieve tend to burn out; they get frustrated about things not getting done and try to do everything themselves. But that's not really possible; one gets things done, in large organizations, by using influence and relying on others.

McClelland went on to observe that some managers with a high need for power appeared to be quite effective, while others were very ineffective. Looking more closely at this second group, McClelland characterized them as using power primarily to benefit themselves—to get status, to get "perks," and even just to get others to obey them and be subservient. In contrast, the effective managers used power to empower others, to delegate and to legitimate employees' taking charge and taking real responsibility for accomplishments.

People who use power to manipulate others to serve their own self-centered ends are often seen as charismatic. In fact, that's often how such leaders dupe others into doing as they, the leaders, wish. This helps explain why one must be careful about measures of charisma, such as that contained in Bass's MLQ, and about reasonable-sounding theories that glorify charismatic leadership. In the United States people tend to associate charisma with admirable leaders such as Franklin Roosevelt and John Kennedy. But in Europe charisma is often identified with tyrants such as Napoleon and Hitler. Roosevelt and Kennedy certainly used charisma, but they did not use it to control followers by promising that the followers could become more like *them* (i.e., the leaders) by obeying the leader's every command. Instead, these and other great leaders who might be cited as positive models, people such as Gandhi or Churchill, appealed to what Abraham Lincoln called "the better angels of our nature." These are simply the basic values about what is right, what is good, what should be done, and what should be avoided that guide us toward positive long-run goals.

Nontransformational leaders who use charisma to get what they want appeal primarily to the self-serving side of human nature. They say (in effect), "If you do as I wish you'll be like me and have all the wonderful things I have." Psychologists call this an appeal to narcissism, or self-love. Of course, such leaders are really lying—their narcissistic appeals are designed only to get followers to do as the leader wants. Their charisma is artifice, a result of behaviors that they have carefully learned and rehearsed for the specific purpose of manipulating followers.

In contrast, transformational leaders seek power not for self-aggrandizement but in order to share it. They empower others to take an active role in carrying out the value-based mission or vision defined by the leader. That vision is based on what the organization and followers need, not what the leader wants personally. Thus, transformational leaders appeal to followers' *values*, emphasizing that certain important values serve as the common basis for our ideals and goals.

This brings us to the second paradox of leadership: While it may seem that charismatic and transformational leaders are complete opposites, the power need is common to both. Thus the paradox: The same power need that gives us a Gandhi can also produce a Hitler. Those who have worked closely with even an exceptional transformational leader have probably seen in that person at least a touch of the self-serving tyrant. Again, the paradox: The source is the same—the power need—but how that need is channeled makes all the difference.

Vision.   The term *vision* is commonly applied to leadership. Many speak of leaders' vision and the importance of constructing a vision. Few observers, however, are able to explain exactly what vision means. Some seem to think it means that leaders come up with an image of an ideal future condition and then explain it to others and convince them to do what's necessary to attain the vision. But visionary leaders don't simply think up a vision and sell it to followers. If it is more than just a slick sales pitch, the long-term ideal that leaders come up with will always derive (at least in part) from followers' ideas.

Developing a vision doesn't mean dreaming. It means thinking, and thinking hard. That's what the groundbreaking work of social psychologist Elliott Jaques tells us. After years of study, Jaques concluded that when organizations are working well, they have leaders who possess the perspective necessary to deal with problems of the degree of complexity common to their particular hierarchical level.

Most organizations, Jaques found, need no more than six levels of hierarchy. But they also need people at each level who can think about chains of cause and effect and see how things work. At the higher levels these leaders must figure out how several causal chains affect one another over relatively long periods of time and must decide what to do to achieve desired outcomes. Jaques calls this ability "cognitive power," the ability to think in complex ways. Cognitive power isn't the same thing as intelligence, nor is it a fixed, unchangeable trait. Successful leaders *learn* to use cognitive power effectively. What's the time span over which you are comfortable in planning? A few months? A year? Two years? What's the longest-term project you are working on right now? That should tell you something about the time-span limits you're comfortable with.

Transformational leaders transform organizations by first using their cognitive power to understand complex causal chains and then acting to design outcomes that will benefit the organization and advance the leader's vision. But transformational leadership is much more than that. While a substantial degree of cognitive power is required in order for top-level leaders to be effective, such effectiveness results as much from the leader's success in developing followers' cognitive abilities as from the exercise of his or her own. A transformational leader with the degree of cognitive power required for a top-level position makes important long-term strategic decisions. But how much do these decisions affect what actually goes on in the organization on a daily, weekly, monthly, and yearly basis? It is the thought and action of managers and employees at lower levels that most affect current and short-term future operations. The finest long-term plan and the wisest long-range actions will surely fail if those who must act today and tomorrow are not capable of doing so. Thus, it is more important for top-level leaders with great cognitive power or vision to help followers expand and improve on their *own* vision than it is for leaders to simply exercise their cognitive power. This is the third paradox of leadership.

Personal characteristics. The personal characteristics of effective leaders are somewhat different from what traditional "trait" theories of leadership addressed. These characteristics are not obvious as the foundations of leadership, yet that's exactly what they are. More important, these foundations are not something people are born with; they are developed. At least to some extent, that development can be planned and carried out over one's life and career. Indeed, transformational leaders teach followers to develop these characteristics for themselves, rather than simply using their own capabilities to do things *for* followers.

Incorporating the three personal characteristics into his Visionary Leadership Theory (VLT), Sashkin modified his LBQ to include a total of eight scales—the five original scales developed to assess certain types of leader behavior, along with three new scales designed to examine how the three specific characteristics important for transformational leadership show up in leaders' actions. But there was still more to the transformational leadership equation. Behavior is a function of the person and the situation or context. What about that context? Sashkin addressed this question by looking at organizational culture in terms of the situational context of transformational leadership.

The Leader's Role in Shaping the Organization's Culture

Edgar H. Schein has said that the only important thing leaders do may well be constructing culture. They somehow help define and inculcate certain shared values and beliefs among organizational members. Values define what is right or wrong, good or bad; beliefs define what people expect to happen as a consequence of their actions. The values and beliefs shared by people in an organization are the essence of that organization's culture.

The elements of organizational culture are not just selected by chance or at random. They deal with the most important and fundamental issues faced by people in organizations. These issues include *adaptation*—how people deal with external forces and the need to change; *goal achievement*—the nature of organizational goals, how they are defined, and their importance; *coordination*—how people work together to get the job done; and *the strength of shared values and beliefs*—that is, the degree to which people in the organization generally agree that these values and beliefs are important and should guide their actions. We will briefly consider each issue and the values and beliefs relevant to that issue.

Adaptation.   Consider two specific beliefs about change and adaptation. The first goes like this: "We really just have to go along with outside forces; what we do can't really make much difference." Such a belief has some pretty clear implications for action—or inaction. After all, why bother? Contrast this outlook with the belief, "We can control our own destiny." The former belief may be more accurate in an objective sense. However, it also pretty much ensures that nothing will be done and that what is done will not, in fact, make a difference, because no one expects it to. Even if the second belief is not as accurate, it certainly helps make it more likely that action will be taken. And perhaps that action will have a positive effect, especially because people expect it to.

These beliefs dealing with change and adaptation are actually the organizational analog of self-efficacy, the belief that one's destiny is a matter of self-control. Therefore, it is crucial that leaders teach followers self-efficacy. Only then is it likely that the organization will develop the sort of culture that makes successful adaptation to change more likely.

Goal achievement. "Every person, every department, has its own goals; the organization is best served by competition among them." Does that sound like a typical organizational value? Unfortunately it is; it's unfortunate because organizations are not well served by such a value. Contrast it with this one: "We are all here to serve our customer by identifying and meeting the customer's needs, whatever they may be." That value says a lot about how goals are defined and what goal achievement is all about. And, unlike the first value, this one really does benefit the organization.

The issue of goals relates to the leader's need for power and how that need can be played out—to benefit the organization by empowering others, or to benefit only the individual through narcissistic self-aggrandizement. Leaders' empowerment of others is so important because it models the value of achievement in a larger, organizational sense, not just for their own benefit or the benefit of their department.

Coordination. Many organizations seem to operate on the maxim, "Every person for him- or herself; we all compete to be best." But this is not a very functional value when the very essence of organization is to perform tasks that require the coordinated work of several individuals and groups. In contrast, the value "We all must work together" is a much better expression of the reality of organization. Only when people work together effectively can an organization prosper.

We spoke of vision or cognitive power as the means by which leaders think through complicated cause-and-effect chains and decide how to create desirable outcomes. This process entails looking at the organization as a system and thinking about how it fits together, which happens, of course, through the coordinated efforts of organization members. Leaders, then, must help followers develop their cognitive power, their own vision so that followers are able to coordinate their efforts effectively.

Shared values and beliefs. In some organizations one hears people say, "Everyone has the right to his or her own philosophy." Although that might seem to be a sound democratic ideal, it makes poor organizational sense. Such a principle destroys the potentially positive effect of the three issue-focused beliefs and values just identified. If everyone can buy into or reject them at will, how can these values and beliefs be expected to have any consistent impact? "Everyone here is expected to adhere to a common core of values and beliefs" is itself a value that strengthens a positive, functional approach toward adapting, achieving goals, and coordinating efforts. Of course, such a value would make alternative beliefs and values even more dysfunctional. That's why "cultural strength," the degree to which values are shared among the members of an organization, is a poor predictor of organizational effectiveness.

But How?

All this may seem reasonable, especially because it is relatively easy to see how the personal characteristics required for effective leadership relate to the fundamental aspects of organizational culture. Still, we must ask how leaders construct cultures—that is, how they go about defining and inculcating values and beliefs. There are many ways that leaders do this, but three general approaches are of special importance and impact. First, leaders develop a clear, simple, value-based philosophy, a statement of organizational purpose or mission that everyone understands. This task is anything but simple. A philosophy does not spring fully formed from the brow of the leader. Leaders must use their cognitive power to assess the organization's context, its environment, and the key factors in that environment; they must solicit input from others; and they must convince top level executives that all this is possible.

Second, leaders empower others to define organizational *policies* and develop *programs* that are explicitly based on the values and beliefs contained in the philosophy that in fact put those values and beliefs into organizational action. For example, hiring and promotion policies should take into account values consistent with those in the organization's philosophy as well as applicants' knowledge and skill. Reward systems and bonus programs must be based on the values of cooperation and innovative action instead of on competition over a limited pool of resources.

Finally, leaders inculcate values and beliefs through their own individual behaviors, their personal *practices*. Leaders model organizational values and beliefs by living by them constantly and consistently. That is why the leadership behaviors we described earlier are extremely important. Many people think of these behaviors as tools with which leaders explain their vision to followers and convince them to carry out that vision. Although this is not totally untrue, the far more significant reason these behaviors are important is that leaders use them to demonstrate and illustrate the values and beliefs on which their visions are founded. That's why transformational leadership takes so much time and effort—and why transformational leaders must be good managers with strong management skills. These leaders use everyday managerial activities—a committee meeting, for example—as opportunities to inculcate values. In a meeting the leader may guide a decisionmaking process while making it clear that final authority and responsibility rests with the group. By so doing, the leader takes what might otherwise be a bureaucratic process and instills the value of empowerment into it. Whenever possible, leaders "overlay" value-inculcating actions on ordinary bureaucratic management activities. Without a sound base of management skills, this would not be possible.

The Leadership Profile

Thus, Sashkin's Visionary Leadership Theory brings us full circle, from the easiest-to-observe behaviors to a deeper understanding of the personal source of visionary leadership to the more subtle and fundamental expression of leadership through culture building. Ultimately, VLT leads to the recognition that transformational leaders' own personal behaviors play a large part in shaping organizational culture. This comprehensive theory goes beyond behavior to incorporate personal characteristics. Even more, it includes the organizational context of transformational leadership—that is, culture building. It is the only analysis of leadership that attends to all three factors—behavior, personal characteristics, and the organizational context—thus paying heed to the basic equation of behavior as a function of person and environment.

The latest work by Sashkin and Rosenbach incorporates an assessment of transactional as well as transformational leadership within a revised questionnaire instrument, The Leadership Profile (TLP). The first two LBQ scales both measured aspects of communication, so they were combined into a single scale, *communication leadership*. The last two scales were measures of the leader's culture building efforts and were also combined to form a single scale labeled *principled leadership* because it is by defining and inculcating values and beliefs – principles – that leaders must build culture. This allowed the construction of two new transactional leadership scales, *capable management* and *reward equity*.

With the development and validation of this new assessment, VLT incorporates a complete approach to leadership, including the baseline of sound management, identifying the specific behavioral dimensions of transformational leaders, and extending to the personal characteristics of transformational leaders. With the complete theory in mind, we are prepared to examine our most basic assumption: that there really is such a thing as transformational leadership.

Is There Really Such a Thing as Transformational Leadership?

We began by trying to define what most of those now involved in studying transformational leadership refer to as a "paradigm shift." A paradigm is a way of thinking, a frame of reference. Sometimes—generally not very often—we are forced to change the way we look at and think about things. When this happens it's most often because of some major change in scientific knowledge. When Copernicus, for example, concluded that the sun, not the earth, was the center of the solar system, he caused a radical scientific paradigm shift. Similarly, the proposal that what we had thought of as leadership is really something rather different—management/supervision—forced many researchers to take a step back and rethink their basic assumptions about leadership in organizations. Others concluded that this "discovery" was nothing more than a wrong-headed assertion, that a full understanding of leadership could still be had in the context of the existing paradigm.

The existing paradigm, of course, is based on the notion of transactions or exchanges: Leaders provide followers with rewards for doing as the leader wishes or administer punishments if the wishes are not heeded. In the 1950s various social scientists, George Homans (a sociologist) and Edwin Hollander (a social psychologist) in particular, developed detailed models of "social exchange." These models show how people exchange not just money for doing a job but also "sentiments." A person might, for example, exchange friendship for certain favors. This sounds a bit crass, and the fact is that whenever such exchanges become obvious they automatically lose their value. No one would consciously say, "I'll be your buddy if you'll drive me to work." But that's exactly what people do all the time without explicitly saying so.

The examples above are purposely simplistic and extreme for the sake of clarity. The social exchange model is really more subtle and complex than we have made it appear. Still, it may seem at first glance that transformational leadership is obviously more than an exchange of work for money and certainly goes beyond an exchange of sentiments, such as commitment and caring from the leader in exchange for followers' acceptance of the leader's agenda. Edwin Hollander has recently suggested that there is an exchange, an exchange that goes beyond money or sentiments. In exchange for their willingness to carry out the leader's vision, followers receive intangible but very real and useful rewards, such as a new, clear, and practical understanding of how to design and carry out projects that require interdepartmental coordination Thus, exchange can take at least three forms. At its simplest, leader-follower exchange involves concrete rewards for actions. In its simple social version, leader-follower exchange consists of sentiments for actions, friendship for favors. But in what may be its most sophisticated form, leader-follower exchange balances followers' committed actions against the intangible but practically useful insights and understandings they receive from leaders.

Is it possible, then, that what we have called transformational leadership could be reinterpreted within the traditional paradigm of transaction and exchange? We are not convinced. Our objection is based on the essence and nature of transformation. Leaders transform organizations, but they also transform followers, a process that involves much more than simply exchanging useful insights for followers' actions.

Transformational leadership, then, is more than a form of transactional leadership in which the transactions are subtle and intangible. But that doesn't mean that Hollander's extended social exchange model can be dismissed. It's easy to say that simple observation of a transformational leader in action yields no sign of social exchange, but it would be foolish to reject the social exchange model on that basis, because if social exchange is actually operating, that is exactly how it would have to appear. Remember, when a social exchange process is obvious, it tends to lose its utility; most people reject the thought of an exchange that involves "buying" feelings. Anyone actually involved in the transformational "exchange" would be expected to deny that such an exchange existed.

Our disagreement with the social exchange approach is not based on the notion that there is an "obvious" difference between transactional and transformational leadership. Rather, our view is based on evidence—the evidence provided by Bass's research. Remember, Bass was able to define and measure several aspects of transactional leadership and to show that these were clearly independent of the dimensions of transformational leadership. If there were really no difference—if these were all simply transactions, with some just more open than others—it's hard to imagine that Bass would have been able to show such a clear separation. Some of our own recent research adds support to Bass's work by showing that two very different approaches to measuring transformational dimensions yield consistent results.

We believe that the conceptual distinctions we have made provide clear theoretical support for our view. Transformational leadership is used to construct a value-based culture. But it requires the context of transactional leadership, the everyday bureaucratic and managerial activities that form the "text," with values and culture the "subtext." It is clear to us that these are very different activities and processes. Transactional leadership—management—is the "paper" on which transformational leaders define values and describe organizational cultures. Without management there could be no leadership. Thus, both are important—but they are different.

Current "Transformational" Leadership Approaches as Wolves in Sheep's Clothing

Some may argue that there is no such thing as transformational leadership or that it is simply a form of charisma; others insist that current transformational theory is still ill defined. One scholar, Joseph Rost, feels that a paradigm shift has not yet occurred; he views the present transformational leadership theories as merely providing an *opportunity* for a transition. What is especially lacking in current transformational theories, according to Rost, is a full and complex consideration of the role of followership. Leadership, he argues, involves more than leaders getting followers to carry out leaders' wishes. A distinction between leaders and followers is crucial, but the concept of follower must, according to Rost, take on a new meaning. Followers must be seen as active, not passive, and as themselves engaging in leadership, not just in followership. We agree with Rost that leadership involves more than leaders getting followers to carry out leaders' wishes; that is, motivating followers as does a transactional or charismatic leader.

Rost has emphasized that both leaders and followers make important contributions. Although we agree with Rost that there must be mutual contributions, we disagree on the *nature* of those contributions. Rost appears to us to say or suggest that leaders' and followers' contributions are similar in nature. We, however, believe that leaders' essential contributions are quite different from the contributions of followers. Leaders' contributions include synthesizing and extending the purposes of followers as well as constructing conditions under which followers can be transformed into leaders. Thus, in terms of a vision or common purpose, the relationship between leaders and followers need not and cannot be equal—but it *must be equitable*, that is, fair. To us this means that the contributions of leaders and of followers, which are inherently unequal in kind, must be equal in effort and in commitment to one another and to a shared vision.

We do not disagree with Rost's definition of leadership as "an influence relationship among leaders and followers who intend real changes that reflect their mutual purposes." We do, however, find this definition to be incomplete; what gets lost in Rost's argument, we think, is the leader as a source of vision or motive. Rost and some others seem to think that transformational leaders exist primarily to focus and help carry out the visions of followers. There is some truth to this and in this sense leaders are, as Robert Greenleaf has so beautifully said, servants. However, transformational leaders do not simply identify and build a clear vision from the visions of followers. They also identify what followers themselves might wish to envision but have not and perhaps cannot. And they provide followers with conditions that permit followers to achieve the goals and aims they share with leaders; leaders enable followers themselves to change, to realize more fully their potential. In sum, transformational leadership involves real, unique contributions from both followers and leaders, a point that Rost says he agrees with but which seems to us to be missing in meaningful detail from his approach.

Conclusion

We believe that a paradigm shift has indeed occurred over the past decades with respect to leadership research, theory, and practice. This shift has as its source Burns's pioneering ideas. That work led to a variety of new transformational approaches; we have reviewed the most important in this chapter. While different in many ways, these new approaches are nonetheless consistent. The new transformational leadership paradigm confirms the unity of the concepts of leadership and followership. It accomplishes this in ways that, on the surface, appear to be paradoxical. However, the paradoxes we have described are paradoxes only if one tries to look at them from the perspective of the old transactional, or management paradigm. When we apply the new transformational paradigm we see that what at first appeared to be paradoxical actually makes logical sense.

The most general paradox involves the apparent inconsistency between being a manager and being a leader. This apparent paradox is resolved by recognizing that effective transformational leaders use transactional, managerial roles not simply to define, assign, and accomplish tasks and achieve goals but also to educate, empower, and ultimately transform followers. By doing so, leaders wind up transforming their organizations. The transactional approach views the sort of skills and behaviors defined and described by Bass, Kouzes and Posner, and Sashkin as essential managerial activities, important for communicating clearly the terms of exchange between managers and their subordinates. But leaders don't just communicate directions, they communicate values. What the transactional paradigm cannot explain is that leaders use these interaction skills not to convince followers to do as the leaders want but to become more self-confident, to use power and influence in a positive way, and to develop more complex thinking skills. These outcomes are more than rewards accepted in exchange for compliance; they are true transformations in followers, transformations that lead to transformation in the organization.

Our outlook does not, however, deny the need for management. From the vantage point of the new paradigm, management is more important than ever; only by using the context of management activities can leaders transform followers and organizations. Through this new transformational leadership paradigm, the study and practice of leadership itself has been transformed.

Note

The authors gratefully acknowledge the helpful comments on earlier drafts of this chapter from Edwin P. Hollander, Barry Z. Posner, Joseph C. Rost, and Walter F. Ulmer, Jr. We accept full responsibility for our interpretation and presentation of their views.

Suggested Readings

Organizations and Management by Chester I. Barnard (Cambridge, MA: Harvard University Press, 1948). Chester Barnard was an executive at AT&T

TABLE 5.1   Transformational Leadership Measures

Multi-Factor Leadership Questionnaire (Bass and Avolio)	*Leadership Practices Inventory* (Kouzes and Posner)
Laissez-faire	Challenging the Process
Transactional Leadership	—Search for opportunities
—Contingent-reward	—Experiment and take risks
—Management by exception	Inspiring a Shared Vision
—active	—Envision the future
—passive	—Enlist others
Transformational Leadership	Enabling Others to Act
—Charisma	—Foster collaboration
—Individual consideration	—Strengthen others
—Intellectual stimulation	Modeling the Way
—Inspiration	—Set the example
	—Plan small wins
	Encouraging the Heart
	—Recognize contribution
	—Celebrate accomplishments

	The Leadership Profile (Sashin and Rosenbach)
	Transactional Leadership
	—Capable managment
	—Reward equity
	Transformational Leadership Behaviors
	—Communication leadership
	—Credible leadership
	—Caring leadership
	—Creative leadership
	Transformational Leadership Characteristics
	—Confident leadership
	—Follower-centered leadership
	—Visionary leadership
	—Principled leadership

for many years. He was also a serious management thinker and his work is still considered important by both scholars and thoughtful managers.

Bass & Stogdill's Handbook of Leadership (3rd edition) by Bernard M. Bass (New York: Free Press, 1990). This is a comprehensive reference resource that organizes just about everything ever written on the topic of leadership.

Leadership and Performance Beyond Expectations by Bernard M. Bass (New York: Free Press, 1985). This was the first formal attempt to apply Burns's idea of transformational leadership to leadership in organizations instead of nations.

Leaders: The Strategies for Taking Charge by Warren Bennis and Burt Nanus (New York: Harper & Row, 1985). This very readable book reports the authors' study of ninety exceptional chief executives and a model of organizational leadership based on what they learned.

Leadership by James McGregor Burns (New York: Harper & Row, 1978). Burns's work is the most important original source for the concept of transformational leadership. His book is also very readable.

"Legitimacy, Power, and Influence: A Perspective on Relational Features of Leadership" by Edwin P. Hollander, in *Leadership Theory and Research: Perspectives and Directions*, edited by Martin M. Chemers and R. Ayma (New York: Academic Press, 1993). This is the most clear and current statement of the "pure" transactional approach. The author tries to interpret and explain transformational leadership in terms of the older transactional paradigm (though misunderstanding the nature of transformational leadership by confusing it with charisma).

Executive Leadership by Elliott Jaques and Stephen D. Clement (Arlington, VA: Cason Hall, 1991). This very readable explication of Jaques's important theory of organization and leadership is based on his concept of "cognitive power" and the notion that individuals' levels of cognitive power must be matched to their positional levels in the organizational hierarchy.

The Leadership Challenge by James M. Kouzes and Barry Z. Posner (San Francisco: Jossey-Bass, 1987). These authors used much the same approach as Bass did to create a tool for measuring leadership, but they did not start from a theoretical base, and their focus was more behavioral. The five aspects of leadership they identified and measured, however, are very similar to and consistent with the five "strategies" originally defined by Bennis and the five behavior categories defined and measured by Sashkin.

"Power Is the Great Motivator," by David C. McClelland and David H. Burnham (*Harvard Business Review*, March–April 1976, pp. 100–110). This is a very readable report of McClelland's ground-breaking work on how the need for power comes into play in organizations and how it can be used for good or for ill.

Structure and Process in Modern Societies by Talcott Parsons (New York: Free Press, 1960). This is a very unreadable (but important) reference source. Parsons was one of the most important modern social scientists. He developed a very simple, perhaps even elegant, way of understanding what goes on in organizations and why.

Leadership for the Twenty-first Century by Joseph Rost (New York: Praeger, 1991). Rost provides an exceptional overview of the history of leadership study, as well as a leading-edge analysis of the new paradigm of transformational leadership.

"Understanding and Assessing Organizational Leadership" by Marshall Sashkin and W. Warner Burke, in *Measures of Leadership*, edited by Kenneth E. Clark and Miriam B. Clark (West Orange, NJ: Leadership Library of America/Center for Creative Leadership, 1990). This is the most accessible synopsis of Sashkin's Visionary Leadership Theory, including extensive data and research results up to 1990.

"Assessing Transformational Leadership and Its Impact" by Marshall Sashkin, William E. Rosenbach, Terrence E. Deal, and Kent D. Peterson, in *Impact of Leadership*, edited by Kenneth E. Clark, Miriam B. Clark, and David P. Campbell (Greensboro, NC: Center for Creative Leadership, 1992). This update of Sashkin's earlier report focuses on additional research evidence for his approach and explains how transformational leaders achieve their effects.

Organizational Culture and Leadership (2nd edition) by Edgar H. Schein (San Francisco: Jossey-Bass, 1992). Schein applies Parson's concepts in an understandable manner, clarifying the underlying nature of organizational culture and identifying many of the values and categories of values that are the most important ingredients of organizational culture.

PART 2

Climate, Culture, and Influence

And in the end, through the long ages of our quest for light, it will be found that truth is still mightier than the sword. For out of the welter of human carnage and human weal the indestructible thing that will always live is a sound idea.
—Gen. Douglas MacArthur

Climate

The climate of an organization can be sensed by talking with people, observation, and feeling the sense of spirit and energy that is expressed through word and deed. How people treat each other and what they say and do tell us a great deal about the leader. Often, we can then anticipate the responses of the followers to the leader. In a sense, this is the "personality" of the organization. Effective organizations reflect confidence and optimism. Organizations in trouble communicate fear and uncertainty. Leadership style sets the stage, and we believe it is the major influence on climate.

Leadership climate is reflected in the expectations followers have for the leader and the expectations the leader has for the followers. When we describe effective leadership, we mean there is a climate that supports the leader and the actions that result from shared decisions. Put simply, the leader's behavior sets the tone and creates the climate. If the leader is an effective communicator, there will be openness and candor in organizational information exchanges. When a leader has integrity and communicates her or his values, the organization will reflect strong values. A leader who works hard and sets high expectations will create a climate where people give their best; they know what it takes to be superior. When leaders stand by their people and allow them to make mistakes as learning experiences, the organization will be characterized as innovative and risk-taking.

73

Culture

There is a unique culture in the military as well as in each of the armed forces. Characterized by tradition, mores, norms, and socialization, a unique set of social patterns is, at once, a strength and a shortcoming. Organizational culture is a set of shared assumptions, beliefs, and values that form the basis for individual and collective behaviors. Perhaps the best articulation of the special culture of the military is represented by the famous phrase *duty, honor, and country*. Men and women entering the military know that it will be different from the lives they left. Those who are in the military know that they are set apart from the rest of society. This culture is communicated through stories, rituals, and symbols, and it is one that is implicit as well as explicit.

It is important to recognize that there are distinct groups within the military that represent subcultures with unique patterns of values and philosophy that are not inconsistent with the dominant values and philosophy of the military. In contrast, countercultures have a pattern of values and philosophy that outwardly rejects those of the larger military organization. For example, the first week of President Clinton's presidency (1993), the press was filled with arguments over whether homosexuals would be allowed to state their sexual preference and still serve in the military. Some argued it was time to be more inclusive; others were shocked and morally outraged. Each side claimed the other was a minority counterculture.

Whereas continued existence of countercultures is damaging to organizations, very large organizations, including the military, import potentially important subculture groups from our larger society. The leadership implication is in the relevance that the subgroups have to the organization as a whole. At one extreme, leaders can merely accept the subcultures and work within the confines of the larger culture. At the other extreme, leaders can value diversity but systematically work to block the transfer of societal-based subcultures into the fabric of the organization.

If one set of values is accepted to the exclusion of others, there may be high turnover and conflict. More important, it will be difficult to create a sense of ownership in shared goals and it will be impossible to build teams. We need to understand and appreciate a diversity of values, molding unit structures and processes in ways that permit individuals to work together— no matter the gender, age, or cultural background. Values that differ from our own are neither bad nor good; they are just different and should be recognized as such. Critics lament the "good old days" when a person's values were predictable. We believe that effectiveness can be achieved in a variety of ways, and allowing people to live their values will permit them to contribute in meaningful ways.

Influence

Influence is a form of power. It defines the relationship between leader and follower in a way that articulates the behavioral relationship. Primarily coming from the reality that personality matters, we believe that leadership is truly an influence process. Our ability to influence others depends upon our willingness to share ideas and our ability to communicate. The process is a reflection of our personal values.

Leaders must understand their values and the values of their followers. We find, for example, that generational differences create some interesting problems. Ranking officers and senior noncommissioned officers often hold to values such as giving one's best, accepting all assignments out of duty, welcoming competition, and constantly striving for the top command positions. Some junior officers and younger noncommissioned officers may, with equal fervor, seek the minimum acceptable standards of performance (while meeting those standards quite well), expect assignments that provide a desirable quality of life, question, prefer collaboration over competition, and be content to remain in a particular job throughout their careers.

Our self-knowledge is based upon values; self-confidence is the behavioral outcome of knowing and believing in one's values. Our values play a large part in determining the type of follower or leader we are. Leaders reveal their values in the way they make decisions, the way they work with people, the choices they make in routine and unusual situations, and the people and actions they reward. Thus, good leadership is marked by a congruency over time between actions and words. People know our values by observing the consistency of what we do with what we say. Thus, the values drive our actions and result in our ability to influence.

Implications for Leadership

In "Leaders, Managers, and Command Climate" (Chapter 6), Lt. Gen. Walter F. Ulmer defines "climate" in terms of the leader's example and the standards of performance expected in the group or organization. How well people adapt to the climate can be evaluated by peer and subordinate ratings as well as traditional performance evaluations. Ulmer believes that the command climate can be changed by altering the leadership and managerial habits of senior officers, for they are the ones who set the standards of performance. It is still the combination of leadership and management that moves from routine good intentions to routine best practice that will make a difference. He advocates credible standard methods for evaluating command climate to enhance leader development.

Lt. Col. Karen O. Dunivin addresses contemporary issues in "Military Culture: Change and Continuity" (Chapter 7). With a framework of U.S.

military culture, she compares the traditional model with an evolving model. Inclusion replaces exclusion, egalitarianism replaces separatism, and tolerance replaces hostility. Dunivin notes that conservatism, moralism, combat, and the masculine warrior elements remain the same in both models. With most social change in the military externally imposed, she notes that an evolving model continues to challenge the military with women in combat and homosexuals in the services. Dunivin advances that the military must challenge the male-only paradigm and the traditional combat-only identity. Her ultimate concern is that the military retain its culture within the social framework in which it exists rather than becoming a counterculture.

The complexity of American society is chronicled by Amy Waldman in "GIs—Not Your Average Joes" (Chapter 8). Even as society in general wrestles with cultural diversity, Waldman notes that the military continues to develop good citizens and is widening the gap between people in the military and civilians. The military continues to provide character-building responsibilities in young people in ways not thought possible by those outside the military. Working daily with diverse groups of people and demanding a sense of discipline, military leaders develop a confidence in their skills, which are unique. In today's all-volunteer environment, there is increasing evidence that an obligation to serve is no longer a widely held value among Americans. Thus, she notes that only in the military do we find the integration of people from a diversity of socioeconomic backgrounds. As fewer of those people considered as the "elites" participate in the military, there is an increasing gap between those enculturated by the military and the civilian populace.

In "Women in Combat, Homosexuals in Uniform: The Challenge of Military Leadership" (Chapter 9), Richard H. Kohn suggests that leaders who oppose social change need to think carefully. With regard to gender, history has demonstrated that women have fought successfully with men in other times. Fairness, practicality, and cohesion must be approached differently as military leaders cope with change. The services must redefine acceptable behavior, and Kohn is confident that military leaders will adjust, just as they have throughout history. The strength of the military depends ultimately upon the beliefs of the people—their values and ideals—because it is the people who are served by the military.

Finally, in "The Doctrine of Dissent" (Chapter 10), Lt. Col. Mark E. Cantrell notes that the history of every military organization includes leadership disasters. In most cases, someone saw the disaster coming. Either they did not speak out effectively or the commander did not listen. Cantrell suggests that we should develop doctrine for dealing with dissent and the mistakes that inspire it. Equally important is the need to reinforce the doctrine through training and rewarding those who practice the doctrine.

6

Leaders, Managers,
and Command Climate

Lt. Gen. Walter F. Ulmer, Jr.

The Setting

In spite of the enormous contemporary stresses upon the institution, America's military continues to be better than it has been in at least forty years. Whether or not this same laudatory evaluation will be accurate five years from now is unclear. Dwindling budgets, awesome advances in technology, structural reconfigurations associated with "downsizing," a widening array of missions, and critical scrutiny of roles and doctrines have created extraordinary pressures on our armed forces. The decade of the 90's has seen competence and tradition in action—from the spectacular 1991 excursion in the Gulf through the confusion of Mogadishu, the peculiarities of Haiti, and the "peacekeeping" in Bosnia, not to mention the hurricane and flood relief tasks close at home. However, in spite of many indicators of robustness and tactical excellence, we are far from capitalizing on the human potential in our armed forces. In order to sustain the reliable and efficient military machine our nation needs, we must attend immediately to the revitalization of the overall organizational climate.

No institution is more serious about inculcation of leadership and managerial techniques than our armed forces. Still, we have imprecise, unstudied, and randomly supervised concepts for building and sustaining a climate that fosters innovation, aggressiveness, calculated risk-taking, and the special unit tenacity necessary for battlefield superiority. Listening to students at War College seminars or reading the professional journals, one

Revised by the author from *Armed Forces Journal International* (July 1986), pp. 54–69. Reprinted by permission.

might conclude that different officers had come from different armies. Their stories of motivational techniques, leader priorities, organizational values, training distracters (i.e., any activity required of a commander or his troops that takes away from the critical training mission), and mentoring are extraordinarily diverse. The good stories reveal the enormous power of a proper command climate. The others describe frustration amid mindless bureaucracy . . . an invitation to avoidable and ultimately debilitating mediocrity.

The Role of Climate

These described variations in the quality of our organizations do not stem from differences in geography, new equipment, or availability of training devices. Nor do they derive exclusively from leadership style differences. Rather, they evolve from diverse combinations of leadership and management competencies that produce either a supportive or a dysfunctional organizational climate. And what is the essence of a "supportive" climate that promotes esprit and gives birth to "high performing units"? It may be easier to feel or sense than to describe. Most experienced people can quickly take its measure. There is a pervasive sense of mission. There is a common agreement on the top priorities. There are clear standards. Competence is prized and appreciated. There is a willingness to share information. There is a sense of fair play. There is joy in teamwork. There are quick and convenient ways to attack problems and fix aberrations in the system. There is a sure sense of rationality and trust. Such climates are the product of strong, insightful leadership embedded in enduring values.

Recent studies confirm that within the officer corps there remain widely varying opinions about the quality of leadership and favorability of command climates. Some sources contend that the bold, creative officer cannot succeed in today's military, where only spotless and politically correct actions will ensure "survival." Naturally, some complaints may represent merely the cries of unsatisfiable idealists or the whinings of non-selectees. My personal experience and recent observations support the disturbing contention that inappropriate constraints on boldness and candor do exist. Some young officers disenchanted by their local situation are voting with their feet. However, the fact that excellent units are seen to exist side by side with those of low or erratic effectiveness confirms that pathways to high performance can be found even in today's hectic, stressful environment.

Trust and Leadership

Leadership is of course not the exclusive factor determining climate and combat effectiveness. Other non-material factors include the mental and physical abilities of the followers, the managerial skills of the leaders, the level of commitment to institutional values, and the mode of processing information through the organization. One critical component of the morale and cohesiveness mosaic, and whose absence or dilution is particularly detrimental to effectiveness over time and under stress, is *trust*. Trust plays an enormous role in large and small organizations. Trust can generate magic. Nourishing it among soldiers coming from a skeptical, periodically traumatized free society is ever more often a challenge. The development of trust represents the consummation of a thousand small acts, while its undermining may be precipitated by a single isolated event. It works or fails upward, downward, and sideways. Our future performance is significantly affected by the trust (or lack of it) our boss places in us. A World War I story has Brig. Gen. Douglas MacArthur in the trenches with an Infantry unit just before dawn. He takes the Distinguished Service Cross ribbon from his own tunic and pins it to the chest of a young major about to lead the battalion in an attack, explaining that he knows the major will do heroic deeds that day. One general officer serving in a troop command in the 1990's observed the opposite end of the spectrum: "We . . . occasionally practice what we preach, but all in all we're gripped by our collective distrust of our people." Distrust inhibits soldiers from sharing responsibility and taking initiative and is, therefore, of more than clinical interest in a military unit.

American bureaucracies have a penchant for solving problems, whether caused by individual ethical flaws or systemic discontinuities, by grafting another set of regulations or another gang of overseers onto the existing superstructure. NASA's quest for safety guarantees via checklists, the Defense Department's use of oppressive regulations to ensure integrity in the procurement process, the Environmental Protection Agency's flood of minute environmental guidelines, and some bizarre revelations of Vice President Gore's examination of nonsense in the Federal bureaucracy highlight our tendency to rely on detailed proscriptions rather than on ethical common sense. Distrust is the lubricant for oversupervision and centralization.

A few years ago, the U.S. Army implemented a policy (that, I hope, is now forgotten) whereby a company commander could not be relieved of command without prior approval of a general officer (except in tactical or life-threatening emergencies). This directive sent two messages. The message policymakers intended to send was that relief was a serious move and that company commanders should be protected from arbitrary and capricious actions by battalion and brigade commanders; the second, unintended message was that the system did not trust the judgment of battalion and brigade commanders. The second message was stronger. The directive was severely misguided, and its author to this day probably remains unaware of his damage.

Some military scholars and defense establishment thinkers have developed recently the concept of a contemporary *Revolution in Military Affairs (RMA)*. The initials *RMA* are starting to appear in military journals and Department of Defense memoranda here and there. The basic postulate of the *RMA* is that the microprocessor and other technological innovations will enable a smaller force propelled by creative doctrine to substitute for the larger, slower formations of the Cold War. In the current discussion of structural and doctrinal change that happens to fit comfortably into the era of reduced defense spending, there are few references to the challenges to leadership and leader development that will attend any such an *RMA*. At the top levels of the Department of Defense in particular, fascination with technology, finances, and geopolitics continue to relegate human issues—except for a few pet social projects—to the back bench. In fact, any *RMA* will sooner than later come to depend more on the sustainment of fighting spirit than on the utilization of cyberspace.

The tools for building routinely supportive organizational climates are available. Development and implementation of a systematic approach to climate-building are the specific avenues to dramatically improved combat readiness. And the prescription is not expensive. The question is not one of leadership versus management, it is one of good leadership versus bad leadership, good management versus bad management, and integrating enlightened leadership and sensible management to create the proper climate. It is absurd to imply that skilled managers cannot be skilled leaders. On the contrary, leadership and management must be complimentary to create the climates from which high-performing units emerge.

Measuring and Developing Leaders

If we are serious about identifying and developing leaders, we must provide a model for measuring leadership. In this context we define "leadership" as essentially an influence process whereby one gains the trust and respect of subordinates and moves them toward goals *without reliance upon positional authority*. (Exercise of positional authority is of course legitimate and often necessary, but *reliance* on formal authority alone does not constitute "leadership" as we are using that term.) Given that our standard mode of performance appraisal is exclusively superiors assessing subordinates, it is remarkable that we do as well as we do in selection and development. We would do much better by having subordinates augment the system with periodic input about their superiors. When, as occasionally happens, a general makes a spectacle of himself through arrogant or capricious behavior, his boss is often surprised and disappointed. The troops might be disappointed also. But they are never surprised.

An Army War College study in the early 1970's examined leader behavior from three perspectives—self/peer, superior, and subordinate—and eventually incorporated input from more than thirty thousand questionnaires. The data confirmed what we intuitively knew: Self-delusion about leadership effectiveness is commonplace. Peers, superiors, and subordinates often see an officer quite differently from how the officer views himself. These data are similar to that collected in the corporate sector fifteen years later by researchers at the Center for Creative Leadership. Leadership, no matter which definition you use, does not speak of something that happens to, or occurs within, the leader; it speaks of something that happens to, or occurs within, a group of followers. Only followers reliably know how well the leader has led. This is particularly true in evaluating such leader behaviors as candor, commitment, and caring. In any formal organization, but within the long shadow of military tradition in particular, accepting the fact that our subordinates are the ultimate judges of even one facet of our performance is difficult. And such acceptance becomes even more threatening and counterintuitive as we become "successful" and more chronologically gifted!

Why does any leader ever promote somebody who everybody but the leader knows is the wrong person for the job? The answer is rarely cronyism or disregard for leader behaviors. The leader is simply ignorant of the leadership reputation of his candidate. Seniors' evaluations of colonels or brigadier generals are especially difficult to make because they are often based on infrequent or intermittent personal contact and tend to be skewed by single, highly visible incidents. Rarely do we provide useful developmental feedback to colonels and generals—or admirals either. The crucial model of successful adult learning with performance feedback as the essential ingredient is absent from our leadership texts and from our service school curricula. (As of this 1995 writing, there are embryonic efforts to confront these realities. The fact that such issues are being seriously discussed is encouraging; the history of sustained implementation of leader development at senior levels in either military or commercial organizations is not.)

Because superiors cannot alone measure leadership capability reliably, we must conclude that peer and subordinate input into the evaluation system are essential if the organization wants to identify, reward, and develop leadership. There is simply no alternative, particularly remembering that leadership strengths and weaknesses and ethical imperfections often reveal themselves last to even an experienced boss.

Peer and subordinate ratings raise emotional issues of competitiveness among peers and perceived challenges to authority, often creating theoretical confusion between popularity and competency. Such ratings have been used at our service academies, in other officer training programs, in Ranger school, and in special situations. However, although it is essential for decision makers to have access to the viewpoints of subordinates and peers when assessing leader effectiveness, any such input is not intended to substitute for the commander's decision. There may be justifiable occasions when the boss says, "I know he is not a great leader, but I need him in that job anyway." And finally, input from subordinates and peers can be packaged and administered in relatively unemotional and supportive formats and provided as constructive feedback even within the constraints of an hierarchical organization.

A second powerful, underutilized mechanism for providing insight regarding leader strengths and weaknesses is the behavioral assessment. Our senior service colleges have been using a limited battery of psychological tests to provide some awareness of individual tendencies of personality. A longer, more comprehensive session of assessment earlier in an officer's career is warranted. Assessment should be integrated into the normal sequence of promotion, schooling, and assignment and made a formal part of our programs. The results should be used for screening prior to commissioning and for self-development in the middle years, and should be made available to selection boards for key staff and command positions in grades of colonel.

Further, we should give serious consideration to an outrageous concept proposed by Army Col. Mike Malone. He suggests that an officer make application for the position of brigade commander or equivalent, and that the application process would include anonymous evaluations of the candidate's leadership from designated peers and subordinates in his prior command assignments.

To further complicate the process of evaluating leadership outcomes is the unseemly reality that we are not capable of assessing accurately the short-term changes in unit combat effectiveness. Not only are important attributes such as morale, pride, and mental toughness difficult to appraise, but also even the more tangible components of readiness, such as materiel status or tactical proficiency, defy precise peacetime evaluation. The inherent difficulty of evaluating unit effectiveness is exacerbated by the omission of that subject within the military education system.

Climate and Quality

Examinations of climate and culture are anything but new. Systematic but aborted organizational effectiveness initiatives in the military and similar efforts in industry have spotlighted the interaction between environment and productivity. Industrial giants such as Goodyear, Procter and Gamble, General Electric, and Ford continue to invest big money in reshaping the motivational context of work. "Self directing," or "self-managing," teams (SMT's) have moved past the conceptual stage. Total Quality Management

(TQM) has entered the lexicon. Both SMT's and TQM have erratic records of success in the corporate world. They will fare no better in the governmental sector. These attempts toward greater employee autonomy coupled with a dispersed sense of responsibility for quality output were not conceived from altruistic motives. These efforts stem from a bottom-line necessity to remain competitive in the international marketplace. However, we have found that such efforts ultimately succeed or fail within the context of a supportive organizational climate. When top leaders know how to lead and manage, SMT's and TQM can produce wonders. When leadership and knowledge of organizational climates and culture are lacking, SMT's and TQM become passing fads or chaos builders. Still, decentralization, trust, clarity of organizational vision, and empowerment appear to be the direct route to unlocking American initiative and producing better tires, paper towels, and switchboards. But it takes leadership of greater energy and confidence to decentralize and empower than to exercise rigid, centralized control! "Freedom to do one's work" (meaning latitude in getting the job done) within the realm of clear goals and priorities is *the* key stimulant to productivity. Environmental factors in the workplace are even more powerful than personal qualities of the workforce—including exceptional cognitive abilities—in producing innovative solutions. A stifling, overpressured climate with poorly articulated goals and priorities and a dearth of trust is also the primary stimulant for ethical misbehavior as employees or soldiers attempt to meet impossible goals with marginal resources. Arthur D. Little, Inc., concludes in its report, Management Perspectives on Innovation, that "creating a favorable climate is the most important single factor in encouraging innovations." And "innovation" translates quickly into the mind-set of intelligent risk taking and creative problem-solving needed by every fighting element in our armed forces, with or without the *RMA*. We must get serious about unleashing and focusing our enormous, uniquely American reservoir of human initiative. Too much of it remains pinned beneath the weight of a relentless bureaucracy.

Enhancing Organizational Climate

How can we change the organizational climate? Effective climate-building steps will mean altering the managerial and leadership habits of many of our colonels and generals. Therefore, it must be supported and over-watched by the top team. Crucial to leadership at the flag officer level is an understanding of the following: how to communicate a clear vision of an idealized future, how to build supportive, coordinated, internal operating systems, how to modernize methods for evaluating people and units, and how to reinforce traditional values through personal behavior.

As we move to create an environment that builds high-performing units, the criticality of competence in management must be recognized. While the MacNamara era did emphasize "management" to the detriment of "leadership," any diminution of managerial competence and practice is as threatening to organizational effectiveness as is incompetent leadership. Poor managerial practices soak up so much energy that leaders become too tired and frustrated to lead. Current systems for evaluating unit readiness, for tracking fund expenditure, and for ensuring rationality in local procurement of supplies, for example, create an administrative morass that can cripple any efforts to create a positive climate. Again, our service schools have not taught us about the essentiality of a supportive climate, or how to create, sustain, and measure it. Our systems for measuring progress in units—systems that often highlight short-term results, compromise morale, distort priorities, and worship statistics—represent another area of managerial challenge. They sit alongside the challenges of articulating a vision, decentralizing while maintaining high standards, developing loyal disagreement, generating trust, and scrubbing the nonsense out of the systems.

In relative terms, the American military as an institution may be as good as there is on earth. That special aura of selfless commitment and wonderful camaraderie unique to the brotherhood of arms still permeates most of our units. But we must be better if we are to survive the perilous times ahead. That can only be done by attracting, developing, and retaining individuals of strong character and quick intellect throughout the forces, and in the first instance by constructing organizational climates that will nurture and excite the enormous human potential at our disposal. Good people are increasingly intolerant of organizational stupidity and vacillating leadership. Poor organizational climates will slowly and quite silently demotivate the brightest and the best. We need to analyze and learn from specific successes and failures of senior officers as they energize or demoralize their commands. Supportive climates will sustain hope and build the emotional muscle necessary for battlefield success. Their teachable creation can be commonplace even in an era of budget austerity. They are in fact the most cost effective force multiplier imaginable. And the responsibility for moving from routine good intentions to routine best practice clearly falls on those of us who have been, are, or will be the senior leaders of our armed forces.

7

Military Culture:
Change and Continuity

Lt. Col. Karen O. Dunivin

Social scientists commonly use three interrelated concepts—ideal types, models, and paradigms—to study and explain social phenomena (e.g., poverty, crime, culture, and change). This article uses these theoretical concepts to examine both change and continuity in the American military culture.[1] At the risk of oversimplification, the article 1) briefly describes the three concepts; 2) applies each to the current American military culture; and 3) examines how the military's dominant "paradigm" conflicts with its evolving "model" of culture. First, it is important to establish the conceptual framework of analysis.

Theoretical Concepts

An "ideal type" is an abstract definition of some phenomenon in the real world, focusing on its typical characteristics.[2] As abstractions of reality, ideal types do not fit any single case in the real world exactly. Dictionary definitions are ideal types. For example, Webster's dictionary defines "family" as,

> A fundamental social group in society consisting esp. of a man and woman and their offspring; ... A group of people sharing common ancestry; ... All the members of a household living under one roof.[3]

Reprinted by permission of Transaction Publishers. "Military Culture: Change and Continuity" by Karen O. Dunivin, *Armed Forces and Society*, 20:4 (Summer 1994), pp. 532–547. Copyright © 1994 by Transaction Publishers; all rights reserved.

This definition, or ideal type, describes a family's typical characteristics to some degree, but it does not necessarily fit the experience of any single family perfectly. In sum, ideal types define social phenomena and thus instill some sense of order in our complex and dynamic social world.

When we conjure up mental pictures of these ideal types, and speculate how well they fit reality, we build "models." Models organize complex ideal types so we can simplify and understand social phenomena.[4] For example, what is the "correct" model of family in America? Is it the traditional model of a married man and woman with their biological offspring? Or a single parent with his/her child(ren)? Or a childless heterosexual or homosexual couple? Each form represents alternative models of the American family. From our construction of family models, we can speculate what shape (i.e., new model) the family may take under certain conditions such as war, divorce, unwed pregnancies, or homosexual couples.

Finally, a "paradigm" is the underlying collection of broad, often unstated, assumptions, beliefs, and attitudes that shape our ideal types and models.[5] A paradigm is a particular perspective or view of the world. As the foundation for our values, attitudes, and notions, paradigms are important because they influence the kinds of ideal types and models we create to explain social phenomena. For example, the American family model is influenced by society's dominant Judeo-Christian religious paradigm. We tend to create and evaluate family models based on common notions and beliefs about monogamous marriage. If we lived in another society, we might use a polygamous marriage paradigm to construct family models.

Unfortunately, analysts use paradigms and models interchangeably, failing to distinguish between the two. For instance, recent defense models propose new U.S. military missions and roles as the world order shifts from a bipolar Cold War to unpredictable regional conflicts throughout the world.[6] While analysts create defense models (often calling them paradigms), they tend to ignore the underlying paradigm (i.e., beliefs and attitudes) that shape the development of their new defense models. It is important to understand that a paradigm and model may not be complementary, the focus of this study.

In summary, these theoretical constructs—ideal types, models, and paradigms—are a useful, analytical way to study and think about complex social phenomena, including culture. With this brief description of the analytical framework, we can apply each concept to military culture.

U.S. Military Culture

Typically, scholars create models to simplify and explain military organization, culture, and social change.[7] However, models are only one-third of the explanatory equation, as noted. Using the three conceptual tools, this article examines the American military culture and explains the emerging conflict between its dominant paradigm and evolving model as it undergoes major social change.

Ideal Type

For this study, "culture" (an ideal type) is defined as, "a way of life that is learned and shared by human beings and is taught by one generation to the next."[8] While cultures differ in form, all cultures possess certain qualities. Specifically, culture is 1) learned from previous generations; 2) broadly shared by members; 3) adaptive to the conditions in which people live; and 4) symbolic in nature—agreed-on symbols help people create order and make sense of their world.[9]

Although military culture is a unique way of life, it fits the definition of "culture" and possesses these four qualities. Military culture is learned (via socialization training such as boot camp); broadly shared by its members (e.g., saluting); adaptive to changing conditions (e.g., integration of blacks); and symbolic in nature (e.g., rank insignia and language jargon make sense only within a military context). To fully comprehend and appreciate military culture one must understand its underlying paradigm.

Paradigm

Military culture is characterized by its combat, masculine-warrior (or CMW) paradigm. First, the military's core activity, which defines its very existence and meaning, is *combat*.[10] Military structures and forces are built around combat activities—ground combat divisions, fighter air wings, and naval aircraft carrier battle groups. The Services organize and train themselves around their combat roles, distinguishing between combat arms and support activities. Since the primary role of the military is preparation for and conduct of war, the image of the military is synonymous with the image of combat.[11]

The second element of the military's cultural paradigm is the *masculine-warrior* image. As an institution comprised primarily of men, its culture is shaped by men. Soldiering is viewed as a masculine role—the profession of war, defense, and combat is defined by society as men's work.[12] Thus, a deeply entrenched "cult of masculinity" (with accompanying masculine norms, values, and lifestyles) pervades military culture.[13] In *Bring Me Men and Women*, Stiehm wrote,

> ...how can one distinguish between male culture and military culture, and how can one make female culture legitimate in a military setting?[14]

In summary, the combat masculine-warrior paradigm is the essence of military culture. This paradigm persists today even with the presence of "others" (e.g., women and gays) who do not fit the stereotypical image of combatant or masculine warrior.[15] Given this entrenched CMW world view, we can examine two concurrent models of military culture.

Model

Table 7.1 depicts a continuum of military culture. The traditional model is characterized by conservatism: a homogeneous male force, masculine values and norms, and exclusionary laws and policies. At the other end of the spectrum is an evolving model that is characterized by egalitarianism: a socially heterogeneous force, diverse values and norms, and inclusionary laws and policies. Of course, military culture does not fit either model perfectly. However, the evolving model alerts us to emergent trends within military culture.

As theoretical constructs, these models are open to debate. Some may argue that the military is tolerant (or too tolerant) of force diversity and inclusionary policies.[16] Others may contend that the military remains a socially conservative culture that opposes most social change.[17] While there are different opinions of where military culture is along the continuum, the models illustrate change in military culture. First to consider is the traditional model.

TABLE 7.1   U.S. Military Culture

Cultural Variable	Traditional Model	Evolving Model
Ethics/customs	Conservatism, moralism	Conservatism, moralism
Enculturation	Combat	Combat
Laws/politics	Masculine warrior	Masculine warrior
Force structure	Exclusion	Inclusion
Attitudes	Homogeneity	Heterogeneity
Majority/minority	Separatism	Egalitarianism
Interactions	Hostility	Tolerance

Traditional Model of Military Culture

As a reflection of its traditional CMW paradigm, the military has adopted a complementary traditional model of culture (Table 7.1). The military espouses conservative, moralistic ideology as reflected in its ethics and customs. For example, each service academy's honor code ("We will not lie, cheat or steal [nor tolerate those among us who do]") guides the ethical development of cadets and midshipmen in preparation for their service as "officers and gentlemen." It is assumed that officers are honest, trustworthy, and male. Typically, military culture assumes a moralistic tone as well. For instance, service members who oppose gays in the military often argue that homosexuality is a sin, quoting the Bible.

These ethics and customs are supported by conservative laws and policies. Under the Uniform Code of Military Justice (UCMJ), service members may be punished and/or discharged from service for conduct including sodomy, "behavior unbecoming an officer" (e.g., adultery or financial irresponsibility), and fraternization (e.g., friendship between officers and enlisted members).

In addition, the laws and policies tend to be exclusionary, reinforcing its CMW paradigm. For example, previous laws segregated blacks in units commanded by white officers, limited the number of servicewomen in uniform, and prohibited women from performing duties aboard combat ships or aircraft. As an extension of such laws, military policies have excluded women from combat-related roles including flying, infantry, armor, and sea duty.

The military often justifies exclusionary laws and policies on the grounds of preserving combat effectiveness. Proponents argue that combat effectiveness and unit cohesion are best achieved in homogeneous combat units. As a former Marine Corps Commandant noted, "If you want to make a combat unit ineffective, assign women to it."[18]

The exclusionary, universal masculine model of warrior (with its hidden assumption of male normalcy and female deficiency) has evaluative overtones.[19] For example, DoD's Under Secretary of Defense for Personnel and Readiness, Edwin Dorn, in testimony before Congress, noted that combat exclusion laws and policies that restrict women's assignments lead some members to perceive women as inferiors:

> The combat exclusion reflects and reinforces widespread attitudes about the place of women in the military . . . Put bluntly, women may not be regarded as 'real' soldiers until they are able to do what 'real' soldiers do, which is to kill and die in combat.[20]

Finally, the conservative culture promotes enculturation, attitudes, and interactions that complement its CMW paradigm. As a socializing institution, the military reinforces masculine norms and values.[21] In particular, combat arms provide men the opportunity to demonstrate their masculinity, and the warrior role is one way to prove one's manhood. As Arkin and Dobrofsky observed,

The military operationalizes the equation of masculinity-warrior, not through the process of anticipating maturity but with a more efficient aggressive conditional model of creating the masculine male. Recruits end up internalizing much of the ethos of masculinity.[22]

This "masculine mystique" is evident during basic training when traditional images of independent, competitive, aggressive, and virile males are promoted and rewarded.[23]

In a "cult of masculinity" with a core principle of exclusion, women and homosexuals are viewed as outsiders and deviants in a man's world. Their presence and participation (especially in war) challenge the ancient paradigm of the combat, masculine warrior.[24] As noted in a recent editorial,

Logically, there is no argument against allowing women to pilot combat aircraft. The real problem lies not with the abilities of women, but in the minds of men such as Gen. Merrill McPeak, Air Force chief of staff. Two years ago, in testimony before Congress, General McPeak admitted that if ordered to choose between an inferior male pilot and a much better female pilot, he would choose the male. 'I admit it doesn't make much sense, but that's the way I feel about it,' he said. In other words, for General McPeak the issue is not job performance or ability, or even military effectiveness. The existence of female combat pilots would simply offend his sense of proper gender roles.[25]

Separatist attitudes (i.e., "they"ism) along with hostile interactions (e.g., sexual harassment or gay bashing) often emerge. Perhaps the most notable manifestations of the "cult of masculinity" are illustrated by two recent incidents: 1) Tailhook '91; and 2) the debate over gays in the military. In both incidents, the attitudes of and interactions among some service members reflect virtual intolerance of "others" who contradict the military's fundamental CMW world view.

In summary, the traditional model of military culture is characterized by an underlying combat, masculine-warrior paradigm, with complementary ethics/customs, laws/policies, force structures, enculturation, attitudes, and interactions. Traditionally, the military has recruited, trained, and rewarded soldiers that embody its CMW ideology—a homogeneous force comprised primarily of white, single, young men who view themselves as masculine warriors. However, times are changing.

Evolving Model

First and foremost, the military still embraces its CMW paradigm. Even with dramatic social change in America and the expansion of military missions and roles beyond traditional combat activities (e.g., disaster and humanitarian relief operations), the military still views itself as the primary instrument of national power whose combat mission, performed by masculine warriors, characterizes its very existence and meaning. Consequently, military ethics and customs still tend to be conservative and moralistic, as described earlier.

The military continues to promote its combat, masculine-warrior image, as evidenced by the Marine slogan, "Every man a rifleman." Similarly, airplanes on display at the Air Force Academy are combat aircraft (e.g., F-15s, B-52s, F-111s, A-10s). You will not find cargo or air refueling airframes at this "proving ground." In addition, the sculpted inscription above the archway leading to the Air Force Academy reads "BRING ME MEN." Although female cadets have been present nearly two decades, the bold pronouncement continues to send a message to cadets and visitors alike. It also serves as a symbolic reminder of a masculine tradition of days past, and perhaps days present. Finally, it demonstrates an institution's reluctance to shift from a cult of masculinity to cultural diversity.

While we see continuity in the military's CMW paradigm, other dimensions of military culture are changing to some extent, as portrayed by the evolving model (Table 7.1). Laws and policies are more inclusionary, reflecting greater acceptance of "others." For instance, in his Executive Order in 1948, President Truman ordered the "equality of treatment and opportunity for all persons in the armed forces without regard to race, color, religion, or national origin."[26] In addition, laws barring women from duties aboard combat aircraft and ships were repealed by Congress in 1991.[27] And the services have begun to assign women to combat aircraft and ships.

Proponents of inclusionary laws and policies cite social equality and military effectiveness as reasons for change. Dorn observed, "There appears to be a consensus in the United States that the armed forces should be a reflection of the society."[28] In other words, the military should mirror society's social demographic makeup (regional, economic, racial, ethnic, and gender diversity) as well as its core values (e.g., equality and civil rights). Furthermore, these proponents of inclusion advocate full utilization of ability. To them, excluding whole groups of "others" (e.g., women) from combat diminishes the pool of talent available for our nation's defense.

In response to social pressures, the services began revising their exclusionary policies. In 1948, the military began integrating its racially segregated units. In 1971, the military rescinded its policy that involuntarily separated pregnant women; in 1976, the service academies admitted women; in 1993, the Navy proposed opening all jobs, including combat roles, to women. Finally, in April 1993, former Secretary of Defense Les Aspin rescinded exclusionary military policy by directing the services to open assignments in combat aircraft and aboard combat ships to women.[29] As a result, the military's force structure is more heterogeneous in terms of race, ethnicity, and sex. Today, the military is a socially diverse force whose women and minorities perform many nontraditional jobs heretofore performed primarily by white men.

While the transformation to a pluralistic culture is painful at times (e.g., Tailhook '91), some recent signs suggest an improved social climate, at least in the work place. For example, the services conduct training to sensitize soldiers about racial, ethnic, and women's issues. In addition, the services have a zero-tolerance policy which punishes racist and sexist offenders (one could argue how well the services enforce these policies).

Recent survey data suggest changing attitudes as well. A 1992 Roper poll of over 4,400 service members showed that,

> nearly three out of four service people believe combat assignments should go to 'the best-qualified person, regardless of gender.'[30]

Anecdotal evidence also indicates that service members are acutely aware of prejudice in the work place. For the most part, soldiers conscientiously ensure that their words or actions are not construed as racist or sexist. Thus the Services and their members are taking steps to minimize polarization.

Consequently, both institutions and individuals seem more tolerant of "others" as partners in national defense. For example, the recent policy allowing women in combat reflects changing ideas about "combat" as a gender-exclusive role performed only by men. Some egalitarian attitudes also are emerging. As Major C. R. Myers, a male Marine Harrier jet pilot, noted:

> The military has a natural resistance to change; it's a male-dominated kingdom afraid to admit a few . . . that don't necessarily fit the mold. African Americans of past decades probably remember their entry into the military as a less than joyful event, yet they succeeded. . . . To think that women and gays in combat can't do the same is to deny the principle that all men (and women) are created equal. . . . If a woman or gay person is the most qualified candidate, let her or him in.[31]

Is this observed change permanent or temporary? Most social change within the military has been externally imposed. For example, the integration of blacks resulted from Truman's executive order. Women's inclusion at the service academies resulted from strong feminist pressure and legislative mandate.[32] Finally, the increased presence of minorities and women in the military since the early 1970s evolved from external forces: civil rights laws, the women's rights movement, more women entering the labor force, and the creation of the All-Volunteer Force. The military's pattern of incrementalism (e.g., slowly loosening restrictions that exclude "others") demonstrates its equivocation toward social change.[33]

In summary, although military culture still embraces its CMW paradigm with complementary ethics, customs, and socialization processes, other dimensions of military culture—inclusionary laws/policies, diverse force structures, and improved attitudes and interactions—reflect some social change. However, the evolving model of military culture contradicts the fundamental CMW paradigm.

Conflict Between Paradigm and Model

In a recent interview, former Secretary of Defense Aspin remarked that he asks three questions when facing a tough issue: 1) what is the fight really about; 2) who will win and who will lose; and 3) what are the true implications?[34] We apply each question to assess military culture as it undergoes major social change.

What's the fight really about?   The present "battle" is between the military's evolving model of culture, which is out of sync with its underlying combat, masculine-warrior paradigm. Current social change challenges the very heart of the military because it undermines the military's core CMW paradigm. As previously noted, paradigms are important because they shape the kinds of models we create. In the case of military culture, the CMW paradigm influences how the military views soldiering and how it organizes, equips, and trains its soldiers. However, in order to survive and thrive, cultures and institutions must adapt to changing conditions—the evolving model of military culture reflects this evolutionary adaptation to ongoing social change.

The recent debates over women in combat and homosexuals in the military epitomize this "battle." While the evolving military culture (as expressed by inclusionary laws and policies) has accepted women to some degree, there remains strong opposition to declared homosexuals in uniform. This attitude is not surprising in the context of its paradigm. The military defines itself as a combat, masculine-warrior organization—a characterization that, by the military's definition, excludes women and homosexuals. As long as the military retains its CMW world view, it will resist integrating women and especially gays (whom the military perceives as stereotypical effeminate homosexual men) into its combat arms because both groups are viewed by many as anomalies who do not fit the military's image (or paradigm) as masculine combatants. This "battle" will continue—major social change will evolve, and problems (e.g., sexism and gay bashing) will persist because the evolving model contradicts the underlying paradigm.

Although the current "battle" is between the military's CMW paradigm and an evolving cultural model, the long-term "war" is over the military's paradigm. Will the military retain its conservative CMW paradigm as it wants? Or will the military succumb to external pressures and adopt an equality view of soldiering? Only time will tell. Until the military and society embrace a mutually shared cultural paradigm—whether CMW, equality, or some combination—clashes will persist. External forces will pressure the military to adopt social change; liberals will push for equality for all service members. In response, the military will resist social change that challenges its core CMW paradigm, the raison d'etre for its existence. In summary, the military will accept some social change (as evidenced by the recent inclusion of women in combat), but it will draw a line in the sand on certain issues (e.g., declared homosexuals in its ranks) and resist that which threatens its CMW paradigm.

Who will win and who will lose?   That depends on one's perspective. From the military's point of view, its entrenched CMW paradigm, enculturated over generations, has served the military and nation well, producing superb soldiers who win wars. Drawing from a combat, masculine-warrior paradigm, traditionalists stress that the military's core activity remains combat, and the military should not be a laboratory for social experimentation.[35] Two marines recently emphasized this point:

> The institutional values that once defined a proud force are rapidly being eroded by inroads into its culture by feminist and homosexual-interest groups who view the military as a platform for their politically correct agendas.[36]

Such traditionalists cite combat readiness and unit cohesion as essential to success and thus resist social change (e.g., integration of women or homosexuals) that may destroy combat effectiveness, degrade cohesion and morale, or create an ill-trained, unprepared "hollow" force. These traditionalists conclude that both the military and nation will lose if sweeping social change subsequently destroys the military's cohesion and readiness to fight and win.

Conversely, liberals advocate an ideology of equality and denounce the military's practice of exclusion. They believe that social change is both mandatory and manageable. For example, in testimony before the Senate Armed Services Committee, Lawrence Korb (a former Assistant Secretary of Defense) noted that the inclusion of gays is not that disruptive,

> I find no convincing evidence that changing the current policy would undermine unit cohesion any more than the other social changes that society has asked the armed forces to make over the past 50 years.[37]

According to Korb, training and strong leadership can minimize any disruption. Interestingly, the RAND report on the military's homosexual policy made similar observations.[38]

Drawing from a paradigm of equality, liberals note that the military, as a servant of society, must reflect societal core values and culture or be labeled an anachronism. Without paradigm evolution, the military runs that risk—divorcing itself from society. In turn, the military may lose public confidence, respect, and support (e.g., funding, resources, recruits).

Like conservatives, liberals also are concerned with military effectiveness. However, these activists cite military effectiveness as justification for social change. They contend that when the military excludes whole groups of "others" (e.g., women and gays), the pool of talent is reduced, which undermines combat readiness and effectiveness. In their view, the military and nation lose because military forces do not include the most talented soldiers for crucial but difficult jobs, including combat.

What are the true implications? While the focus has been upon the evolving model of military culture (Table 7.1) and its incongruence with the dominant CMW paradigm, the real issue is the underlying paradigm—is the military undergoing a cultural paradigm shift?[39] As it moves toward the twenty-first century, will the military be a proactive agent of inevitable social change or a reactive guardian of conservatism and the status quo? Its cultural paradigm is the key.

In order to accommodate current social change (e.g., women in combat arms), the military must adopt an ideology of inclusion and reduce its practice of exclusion. In short, it must alter its CMW paradigm. First, the military must rethink its traditional combat identity.[40] As demonstrated by recent military operations, including disaster relief (Hurricane Andrew) and humanitarian support (Somalia), the military is not merely an instrument of war. Thus, the military must adopt an identity that encompasses warfighting, peacekeeping, and disaster relief roles.

Second, the military must alter its prevailing view of warrior as a male-only vocation. In the emerging pluralistic, egalitarian military, combat includes soldiers (e.g., gays and women) who do not fit the traditional mold of "masculine warrior." Their very existence and success challenge the military's traditional notion of warrior. Therefore, the military must begin to view the warrior as a soldier whose job extends beyond combat and whose ability transcends gender or sexual orientation.[41]

Dramatic alteration of the military's paradigm is very difficult—it is tough to change an institution's fundamental beliefs and attitudes, which are enculturated by generations of soldiers. If President Clinton is to successfully institute the social change he proposes, he may have to implant "new thinkers" in the military who embrace broader visions and paradigms.

Conversely, the military may successfully retain its CMW paradigm (and resist current social change), *if* society supports this paradigm. For example, does mainstream America believe that: 1) homosexuality is morally wrong; and 2) the military is a unique institution that may discriminate against individuals in order to field an effective fighting force? Recent survey data seem to support these beliefs. In a 1991 national survey, 71 percent of the respondents said that homosexual relations between adults are "always wrong."[42] Moreover, a 1993 Gallup national poll showed 53 percent of respondents agreed with the statement, "President Clinton should not change military policy to allow gays to serve."[43] These studies suggest some societal support for the retention of the military's CMW paradigm.

However, if the military retains its CMW paradigm and moves in a cultural direction contrary to that of its egalitarian society, it could become an isolated counterculture—an alienated warrior class divorced from the society it defends. Some military leaders do not support such divergence, including the Air Force's General McPeak, who commented, "We simply must not permit today's debates about . . . social issues to divide us from the society we serve."[44]

Conclusion

While cultural change is inevitable, its outcome is uncertain. Futuristic novelist Michael Crichton noted in *Jurassic Park*, "All major changes are like death . . . you can't see to the other side until you are there."[45] As a result of this uncertainty, military culture entails both change and continuity. There is change, as evidenced by the military's evolving model of culture, but there remains continuity in its traditional combat, masculine-warrior paradigm.

As the military undergoes social evolution, we will not know the final outcome until later. But that does not mean we must wait idly. Theoretical constructs such as ideal types, models, and paradigms provide an objective, analytical framework that we can use to study culture and change in institutions such as the military.

These analytical constructs also provide a means of assessment for military leaders. As shown by recent charges of racism, sexism, and hazing, military culture is not immune to dysfunction. Using this analytical framework, leaders can conduct internal reviews of military culture (e.g., identify potential cultural conflicts, examine effects of exclusion upon individuals and military effectiveness, and develop potential courses of action for change as the military moves toward greater cultural diversity). Such objective self-analysis allows the military to be proactive (versus reactive) in its management of social change.

Notes

Author's Note: Views, opinions, and findings contained in this paper are mine and should not be construed as an official position, policy, or opinion of the Department of Defense. I thank colleagues Steve Sellman, Jane Arabian, and Tom Ulrich for their constructive comments on an earlier draft of this manuscript.

1. This analysis of "culture" is at the macro, institutional level, examining core values, norms, beliefs, attitudes, and behaviors common to all of the military services. Although the Army, Navy, Marine Corps, and Air Force are culturally unique, they are subcultures of the military institution. Thus, this analysis is applicable to each service because elements of military culture described in this paper are found in each service, division, wing, squadron, company, and platoon.

2. See William C. Levin, *Sociological Ideas* (Belmont, CA: Wadsworth Publishing Company, 1991), 23. Max Weber (*The Theory of Social and Economic Organization*, ed. and trans. A. M. Henderson and Talcott Parsons [New York: Macmillan, 1946]) "invented" the concept of "ideal type" to explain bureaucracies.

3. Webster's II, *New Riverside University Dictionary* (Boston: Houghton Mifflin Company, 1988), 463.

4. Levin, *Sociological Ideas*, 25–26.

5. Ibid., 26–27; Thomas Kuhn, *The Structure of Scientific Revolutions* (Chicago: University of Chicago Press, 1962); Thomas Kuhn, "Second Thoughts on Paradigms," in Frederick Suppe, ed., *The Structure of Scientific Theories* (Urbana: University of Illinois Press, 1974).

6. Recently, each service revised its roles and missions to mirror the priorities of a changed world. For instance, Air Force missions reflect less emphasis on nuclear arms with the reduced nuclear threat from Russia. The Army unveiled a new doctrine that emphasizes contingency operations in regional "hot spots" around the world. (See Vince Crawley, "Johnny-on-the-Spot Army," *European Stars & Stripes*, 7 June 1993, 1; Barton Gellman, "Army's New Doctrine Manual Sees High-Tech, Distant Battles," *Washington Post*, 15 June 1993, 19.)

7. See, for example, Morris Janowitz, *The Professional Soldier* (New York: Free Press, 1960); Charles C. Moskos, "From Institution to Occupation: Trends in Military Organization," *Armed Forces and Society*, 4 (1977): 41–50; Karen O. Dunivin, "Gender and Perceptions of the Job Environment in the U.S. Air Force," *Armed Forces and Society*, 15 (1988): 71–92.

8. Levin, *Sociological Ideas*, 399.

9. Ibid., 117–119.

10. See Frank R. Wood, "U.S. Air Force Junior Officers: Changing Professional Identity and Commitment" (Ph.D. diss., Northwestern University, 1982), 10. See also David R. Unruh, "Characteristics and Types of Participation in Social Worlds," *Symbolic Interaction*, 2 (1979): 115–130. Although a military may not be engaged in war, its core activity remains combat. For example, combat readiness through training is an important peacetime activity.

11. See Melissa S. Herbert, "From Crinoline to Camouflage: Initial Entry Training and the Marginalization of Women in the Military," *Minerva*, 11 (1993): 41–57.

12. See, for example, Martin Binkin and Shirley S. Bach, *Women and the Military* (Washington, DC: The Brookings Institution, 1977); Cynthia Enloe, *Does Khaki Become You?* (London: South End Press, 1983), 7–15.

13. Charles C. Moskos, Jr., *The American Enlisted Man* (New York: Sage, 1970); Michael L. Rustad, *Women in Khaki* (New York: Praeger, 1982); Enloe, *Does Khaki Become You?*

14. Judith H. Stiehm, *Bring Me Men and Women* (Berkeley: University of California Press, 1981), 65–66.

15. Although masculinity and homosexuality are not mutually exclusive, the military paradigm narrowly views combat, masculine warriors as heterosexual, masculine men.

16. Brian Mitchell, *Weak Link: The Feminization of the American Military* (Washington, DC: Regnery Gateway, 1989).

17. Judith H. Stiehm, *Arms and the Enlisted Woman* (Philadelphia: Temple University Press, 1989).

18. General Robert Barrow, quoted in William L. Stearman, "With Women Aboard, the USS *Stark* Might Have Sunk," *Washington Times,* 16 June 1993, G-3.

19. Carol Tavris, *The Mismeasure of Women* (New York: Simon & Schuster, 1992), 309.

20. Edwin Dorn, quoted in Grant Willis, "Advocates of Gays, Women, Blacks Nominated for Personnel Post," *Air Force Times,* 12 April 1993, 3.

21. See, for example, Lois B. DeFleur and Rebecca L. Warner, "The Impact of Military Service on Women's Status: A Neglected Area of Inquiry," in Nancy H. Loring, ed., *Women in the United Stales Armed Forces* (Chicago: Inter-University Seminar on Armed Forces and Society, 1984), 1–16; Karen O. Dunivin, "Adapting to a Man's World: U.S. Air Force Female Officers" (Ph.D. diss., Northwestern University, 1988), 34.

22. William Arkin and Lynne R. Dobrofsky, "Military Socialization and Masculinity," *Journal of Social Issues,* 34 (1978): 155.

23. See, for example, Joseph H. Pleck, "The Male Sex Roles: Definitions, Problems, and Sources of Change," *Journal of Social Issues,* 32 (1976): 155–164; Martha A. Marsden, "Sex-Role Attributes, Mental Health, and Job Satisfaction Among Enlisted Army Women in Traditional and Nontraditional Military Units," in Loring, *Women in the United States Armed Forces,* 173–180.

24. See, for example, Stiehm, *Bring Me Men and Women;* Rustad, *Women in Khaki;* Enloe, *Does Khaki Become You?*

25. "Let Women into Combat," *Atlanta Journal and Constitution,* 9 April 1993, 12.

26. Harry S. Truman, quoted in Bernard C. Nalty and Morris J. MacGregor, eds., *Blacks in the Military* (Wilmington, DE: Scholarly Resources, 1981), 239.

27. Defense Authorization Act, Public Law 102–190, 5 December 1991.

28. Edwin Dorn, "Race and the American Military: Past and Present," in N. F. Dreisziger, ed., *Ethnic Armies* (Waterloo, Ontario: Wilfrid Laurier University Press, 1990), 115.

29. Les Aspin, Memorandum on "Policy on the Assignment of Women in the Armed Forces," 28 April 1993.

30. Survey cited by Don Ward, "Women Not Welcome—Yet," *Navy Times,* 4 January 1993, 30.

31. C. R. Myers, "Breaking the Military Mold," *Washington Post,* 25 May 1993, 18.

32. Jeanne Holm, *Women in the Military* (Novato, CA: Presidio Press, 1982); Stiehm, *Bring Me Men and Women.*

33. "Equality—Not Equivocation," *Los Angeles Times,* 15 April 1993, 10.

34. Bob Woodward, "The Secretary of Analysis," *Washington Post Magazine,* 21 February 1993, 9–11, 20, 22–30.

35. Jim Wooten, "Don't Make Military a Laboratory," *Atlanta Journal and Constitution,* 11 April 1993, G-5.

36. David S. Jones and Hagen W. Frank, quoted in Suzanne Fields, "When the Uniform Is Not Cut to Fit," *Washington Times,* 8 April 1993, G–1.

37. Lawrence Korb, quoted in Eric Schmitt, "Calm Analysis Dominates Panel Hearing on Gay Ban," *New York Times,* 1 April 1993, 1.

38. RAND Corp., *Sexual Orientation and U.S. Military Personnel Policy: Options and Assessment* (Santa Monica, CA: RAND, 1993), xxiii, 27.

39. Paradigm shifts are major changes in world views, and occur whenever a major change causes us to view the world differently. For example, Darwinian evolution forced a paradigm shift in how we view human evolution. Likewise, major cultural change can force a paradigm shift, as shown by the American civil rights movement during the 1960s.

40. There seems to be some paradigm shift from the military's traditional combat identity. In his "Bottom-up Review" (presented to the House Armed Services Committee on 30 March 1993), former Secretary Aspin noted that the fiscal year 1994 budget includes $398 million for anticipated peacekeeping, humanitarian, and disaster relief operations. In addition, Aspin cited "economic danger" as one of four post–Cold War dangers that the military must plan for in the future. The Army recently adopted new doctrinal thinking (Field Manual 100-5, "Operations") which includes peacekeeping, humanitarian assistance, and disaster relief among its military missions. All of these actions suggest a paradigm shift from the traditional combat identity to a broader view of the military that encompasses both combat and noncombat roles.

41. There appears to be some paradigm shift from the military's traditional masculine warrior identity. For example, in the wake of Tailhook '91, Admiral Frank Kelso (former chief of Naval operations) acknowledged that "Tailhook brought to light the fact that we had an institutional problem in how we treated women. . . . In that regard, it was a watershed event that has brought about cultural changes." (See John Lancaster, "Tailhook Probe Implicates 140 Officers," *Washington Post,* 24 April 1993, 1.) Shortly after his statement, Admiral Kelso offered to open Navy combat roles to women. Such statements and actions indicate a paradigm shift in the Navy (or at least Admiral Kelso), shifting from a masculine-warrior paradigm to a more inclusionary, egalitarian paradigm.

42. National Opinion Research Center, annual survey (February-April 1991), cited in the American Enterprise, *Public Opinion and Demographic Report* (March-April 1993), 82.

43. Gallup Poll for Newsweek (January 1993), cited in the American Enterprise, *Public Opinion and Demographic Report* (March-April 1993), 83.

44. General Merrill A. McPeak, quoted in John Lancaster, "Accused of Ridiculing Clinton, General Faces Air Force Probe," *Washington Post,* 8 June 1993, 1.

45. Michael Crichton, *Jurassic Park* (New York: Ballantine Books, 1990), 314.

8

GIs—Not Your Average Joes: What the Military Can Teach Us About Race, Class, and Citizenship

Amy Waldman

Like much of southeast Washington, D.C., 8th Street has seen better days. But at the corner of I Street sits one local landmark unscarred by age, crime, poverty, or neglect—a symbol, you might say, of tradition untouched by progress: the U.S. Marine Corps barracks.

Amid urban chaos, it is an oasis of order. A guard mans the gate; inside, crisply uniformed men and women move with purpose. The lush, manicured parade, maintained by a horticulturist and a staff of 20, spreads to the foot of the commandant's residence. From the band room drift sounds of the United States Marine Band—"The President's Own"—rehearsing a haunting classical refrain.

But not only the physical contrast to the surrounding streets is stark: Those who live within this haven's walls are a breed apart as well. The young enlisted Marines I meet, none older than 24, have poise and self-possession well beyond their years. They carry themselves with pride and speak in modulated tones, their words laced heavily with "ma'ams." Their answers are thoughtful. They have come, by and large, from the South, and from the working class, the children of seamstresses and social workers, farmers and factory workers. But from the first day of boot camp they abandon their inherited identities to be reborn into the military class.

Reprinted by permission from *The Washington Monthly*, 28:11, pp. 26–33. Copyright by The Washington Monthly Company, 1611 Connecticut Ave., N.W., Washington, D.C. 20009 (202) 462-0128.

They signed up for many reasons—patriotism, opportunity, challenge, to find their mettle. Corporal Gabriel Ford, 21, enlisted three years ago after growing up on a West Virginia farm and deciding college wasn't for him. His parents divorced early, and he wanted to make something of himself before making a commitment like marriage. The Marines promised to make the most of him. "They break you down to ground zero," he says, "and then build you up. You realize you can be a leader, that you have all these qualities that you never knew you had."

For others, the lure is practical. Corporal Adrian Santiago, 21, was born in Mexico and raised in Chicago, where a persuasive Marine recruiter snagged him on the cusp of high school and adulthood. The recruiter convinced him that the Corps offered what he wanted from life: the chance to travel; to grow up; to afford more education. Such blandishments may seem to have cultish echoes, but they all happen to be true. Indeed they are time-honored reasons for military service. Chief Warrant Officer Joe Boyer says he signed up 20 years ago because everyone from his Illinois small town high school was "going to the farm or going to work at Caterpillar to make bulldozers." Neither option appealed to him; slaying dragons and seeing the world did.

Yet Boyer says civilians have told him he must have gone into the military because he was too stupid to do anything else. This white male Midwesterner looks at me and says, "I am a stereotyped minority." He's right. Among the well-educated and well-off, the perception persists that the military is the blue collar option of last resort.

Twenty-five years ago, that notion had some merit. Once the educated began to evade the draft, and then were let off the hook entirely by the draft's end, the military became a place for people with few options. Drunkenness, drug use, desertion, illiteracy, and racial tension were rife. Forty percent of Army recruits were high school dropouts.

But beginning in the early 1980s, the armed forces began raising standards and requiring, if not a high school diploma, at least a GED (and only a tiny percentage of recruits have a GED instead of a diploma). Today, the caliber of recruits is the highest in history—more than 90 percent of enlisted men are high school graduates—and the services regularly turn away those who don't meet their standards. And because they have volunteered, recruits are truly committed.

If the raw material is impressive, so is the finished product. The military remains one of the few institutions in American life concerned with turning out good citizens who seek leadership, practice discipline, and believe in public service; and it has successfully tackled problems—most notably race and affirmative action—that continue to bedevil society at large. The military certainly isn't flawless, but it does have a lot to teach us. It's hard to learn at a distance, though, and the distance between the military and civilian populations has arguably never been greater.

All They Can Be

In 1989, Tenn Chowfren immigrated here from Jamaica. He had 19 years of life experience, a high school degree, and "no skills." So his parents did what desperate parents have done for generations: They encouraged him to enlist. In no time, he found himself in Army basic training. Soon, he not only had plenty of skills, but also what he calls "mental toughness," girded by a five-month deployment in Persian Gulf heat. He quickly ascended the ranks, then decided to go to college and become an officer. Today, he is an electrical engineering student at Howard University, as well as its Reserve Officers' Training Corps (ROTC) battalion commander. If he stays in the military, he will rise far. If he does not, he now has the skills and leadership experience "corporate America is looking for."

The military has always been an important force in assimilating and equipping immigrants like Chowfren for success. More remarkable, perhaps, is what it has done for a group of native-born citizens: African Americans. No group has benefited more from the upward mobility the military offers, because no institution in America has offered blacks more opportunity.

That's the thesis of *All That We Can Be: Black Leadership and Racial Integration the Army Way*, a new book by sociologists Charles Moskos and John Sibley Butler. Moskos and Butler trace the military's, and in particular the Army's, success not just in recruiting blacks, but in promoting them to positions of authority. Colin Powell is the most notable, but far from the only, symbol of that success. Seven percent of army generals are black; 11 percent of all officers; and 30 percent of enlisted men. The Army has made affirmative action work without quotas, without lowering standards, and without a white backlash.

Moskos and Butler identify several principles the Army has relied on and civilian society could learn from. The first is to promote on merit—but only after enlarging the pool of qualified blacks from which to select. The Army takes proactive steps to ensure that pool is big enough: recruiting heavily on historically black campuses, for example, and establishing education programs to bring the skills of potential recruits and officers up to par. Standards stay inflexibly high, which means everyone promoted has earned it—and everyone working under them knows it.

Moskos and Butler also stress that the Army worries more about creating black opportunity than eliminating white racism. In truth, though, the nature of the military means that anything that gets in the way of mission accomplishment is unacceptable. Racism gets in the way. "From day one of boot camp," Marine Corporal Ford, who is white, tells me, "everyone is green." The military forces integration; in doing so, it illuminates why that ideal is still worth fighting for. Lance Corporal Tashawna Craig, a 19-year-old African American from Houston who followed her five uncles into the

Marines, says growing up in the South made her wary when she saw the races freely mixing at boot camp. "I never thought I could work with [whites]," she says. She learned she could. "When I go home to the South I can feel the tension," she says. "I've never felt racial tension here."

Military race relations aren't perfect, of course. And if the peacetime benefits are high for blacks, so are the wartime costs: Blacks will be deployed in disproportionate numbers to their presence in the population (although a disproportionate number of blacks deployed are not sent into combat). That's why some black civil rights leaders look askance at military service: Upward mobility shouldn't require the willingness to strap on a uniform. That it too often does, however, tells us more about society than it does about the military.

The armed services also happen to be the only place, Moskos loves to point out, where blacks routinely boss around whites, who quickly learn that it's just like being bossed around by . . . whites. The military isn't just providing lessons for civilian society, in other words: It is also shaping its charges.

In many ways. The military builds character—in the sense of resilience, courage, and leadership—by giving young people responsibility unimaginable to most civilians. At age 23, John Brown, a Marine second lieutenant now training at Fort Sill, Oklahoma, will have under his command a group of enlisted men ranging from privates fresh out of recruit training to a staff sergeant with 10 years of service under his belt. "Some of the junior enlisted men will have personal problems," Brown says, "their wives still in high school, pregnant, with bills to pay. I will have to think things out to such a greater degree than I ever have before. I have to look out for them, help them take care of problems so the unit can function effectively." And military service will inspire an empathy—are his men cold? homesick? scared?—that he will carry into civilian life.

Brown will also acquire a deeply bred sense of ethics. The military operates under a code of honor most of us would find unsustainable. Write a bad check in the civilian world, and your bank subtracts $25 from your account. Do the same in the military, and your career may be over. The West Point creed reads, "A cadet will not lie, cheat, or steal, nor tolerate those who do," but even shading the truth or resorting to technicalities is frowned upon. This isn't always lived up to in dealings with civilians— think of military spokespeople misleading the press in Saigon or Riyadh, or Col. Oliver North's star turn before Congress—but in intramilitary interactions, it is an everpresent ideal.

More profoundly, those in the military grapple with moral dilemmas most of us skirt: When should you put your life on the line for your fellow man? Is it ethical to put completing a mission before saving a life? Is it honorable to put saving your own life before completing your mission? "If you go to war," one former Army artillery officer says, "you are morally compromised. Your hands have stains you'll never wash off if you've killed someone or ordered someone killed." Anyone who might go to war must contemplate what justifies crossing a line civilian society considers unbreachable.

Then there's the discipline, which to most civilians seems both archaic (who cares if your pants are creased properly?) and arbitrary (why should you do what someone tells you just because of his or her rank?). In fact, the discipline is anything but arbitrary: In combat, you must react instantly, as a unit, and you must react correctly; discipline hones those reflexes. As Brig. Gen. Richard Stillwell lectures a class of cadets in Rick Atkinson's *The Long Gray Line*, "West Point is tough! It is tough in the same way war is tough."

The discipline is bearable because those giving the orders have survived the same trials, and thrived; and—the occasional sadistic sergeant aside—they generally have their underlings' best interests at heart. The trust is earned. And while complete deference to authority isn't something we want to replicate in civilian life, there is a virtue in learning to do things you might not want to, and learning that you can survive that, too. Those with military experience say it endowed them with unshakable confidence in their ability to overcome any stress that civilian life has to offer.

Perhaps the greatest gap between the military and the civilian world is the relative weight each gives to rights and to responsibilities. American society is centered increasingly on individual rights, which in the American military are always subservient to individual obligations. People in the military learn self-discipline, but they also learn selflessness. That's what drew Major Ralph Peters into the Army 20 years ago. After growing up in a military family, he rebelled and became a musician. Then, in 1975, he was volunteer teaching at a refugee camp housed on a military base. He saw soldiers staying up until 2 a.m. to prepare for classes they were teaching the refugees; it was a sharp contrast to the "lazy, loudmouthed" civilians he knew. At age 23, he joined the Army.

Beyond the many things the military does daily in the service of society is the fact that its members have literally signed their lives over to protect that society. As our tolerance for military casualties diminishes, in the foreseeable future it is unlikely that thousands of men and women will have to give up their lives for us. But they are prepared to. As a result, they have thought deeply about what it is they are protecting: They are patriots, who will tell you emotionally that of the 20 countries they have visited, America, flaws and all, is the best; or about how they have seen people dying abroad for rights we take for granted. "People don't see the direct connection between their ability to walk around, have protests, vote how they want—and the military," says George Flowers, a Marine second lieutenant

based at Fort Sill, Oklahoma. People don't, in fact, see the connection between the presence of a strong military and their right to disparage it.

A Corps Apart

Given that people in the military seem to have both bigger muscles and
stronger moral fiber than many of us, it's no wonder that increasingly they
exude disdain for nonservers and the mores they live by. Thomas Ricks of
The Wall Street Journal provided a classic case study when he followed a
group of Marines home from boot camp in 1995: They described their old
friends as "losers." The Marines I met concur. When she first came back
from boot camp, Tashawna Craig says, civilians suddenly seemed "so stupid, so silly," and most of all, "so undisciplined."

The Marines may be hard-core, but they are not unique. At Howard University, Army ROTC cadets with prior service as enlisted men express dis-
taste and sometimes dismay at the behavior of their college peers, who talk
in class, goof off, and party too much. Todd Mielke, a 23-year-old freshman who enlisted at 17, wants his degree so that he can become an officer,
but he is palpably uncomfortable with civilian life. Among his pet peeves:
the litter. In the army, you damn well pick up after yourself. "We've got really high personal standards," Mielke explains. But on campus, he says,
people just throw their trash down.

The truth is that spending time around a group of Marines makes you
very aware of your imperfections—from messy hair and tardiness to flabby
thighs and white lies—which I suspect is one reason a lot of civilians keep a
distance. (One Army officer I interviewed launched into a tirade on the terrible eating habits of civilians: They can't handle a knife and fork, they
chew with their mouth open, and so on. I was thankful we were on the
phone, and not at lunch). Such standards of behavior are simply foreign to
most civilians.

Which is why, more and more, those drawn to the military lifestyle are
themselves the products of military families. Consider Lance Corporal
Christina L. Wright, one of the young Marines at the Washington, D.C.
barracks. Her stepfather was in the Marines; from the time she was five, he
conducted room inspections while she stood at attention. From then on,
she says, she knew that she too would be a Marine—as is her older brother,
as, she expects, her two younger brothers will be. She doesn't like the city,
doesn't trust most of the civilians around her, and will always be far more
comfortable with the Corps. The 18-year-old's goal is to become the Marine Corps' first female sergeant major (the highest ranking noncommissioned officer).

Indeed, more of those joining the armed forces are also making a career
of it, and the combination of these trends is troubling. We have inadver-

tently developed a professional military caste. "I'm concerned we're losing touch with the society we're supposed to serve," Joe Boyer says. Thomas Ricks wrote earlier this year that "It now appears not only possible but likely that the U.S. military over the next 20 years will revert to a kind of garrison status, largely self-contained and increasingly distinct as a separate society and subculture."

Reversing this trend requires understanding how the last 30 years brought us to this point: As society was shifting radically away from military values such as patriotism, and towards individualism and anti-authoritarianism, the proportion of that society serving in the military dwindled to a tiny minority. And most conspicuous in the nonserving majority, of course, were society's decision makers and opinion shapers.

High Class Dodgers

In his autobiography *A Good Life*, Ben Bradlee recalls chomping at the bit to escape Harvard to go fight in World War II. Three decades later, another Harvard student and future journalist, James Fallows, was starving himself to avoid the draft, an experience he recounted in a 1975 *Monthly* story. Bradlee's enthusiasm was widespread among his classmates; so was Fallows's recalcitrance.

What happened? Well, Vietnam most cataclysmically. Until approximately 1963, military service was a rite of passage for many young men, including those either born to the upper classes (Kennedys) or destined for the upper ranks of the meritocracy (Elvis Presley). It was fairly rare to find a government leader—or sports star, or movie star, or journalist, or businessman—who had not experienced military service. It was the moral thing to do, and a generational bond. Two-thirds of Charles Moskos's Princeton class of 1956 went into the military after graduation. Among the Princeton graduates drafted or enlisting around then: Neil Rudenstine, now Harvard's president; *The New York Times's* R. W. Apple; sociologist William Julius Wilson.

But as the Vietnam war machine geared up, leaders began opening loopholes, notably educational deferments, that told the rich and educated they were exempt from the obligation to serve. As the war's ignoble character became apparent, the well-educated and well-off rationalized evasion as moral, and service as stupid or wrong. Meanwhile, those without the education or know-how for escape, or those who believed it was their duty, went to Vietnam. The result was the politicization of military service, and indeed of patriotism: You were "with" America, or against it, in the military or opposed to it—and most young elites were opposed.

By 1973, when we officially instituted an all-volunteer force, the notion that not serving was the moral thing to do had been cemented. The system now reflected that: Instead of selecting soldiers from the population as a whole, we would purchase a proportion of our youth on the labor market. That, naturally, changed even more who served—and who didn't. No longer would the children—or youthful versions—of Fortune 500 executives, Ivy League professors, senators and congressmen, and journalists have to evade service; they could simply ignore it, and they did. The military became middle- or working-class, or just plain poor. And so only a minority of the generation now assuming power in government, media, academia, and business has served—a circumstance that will become more dramatic as World War II and Korean War veterans retire or expire.

One sign that the privileged feel no obligation to serve is in the numbers signing up from Ivy League schools and similar institutions. In the Princeton class of 1995, for example, 13 graduates went into the military. It's not entirely surprising: The military doesn't bother recruiting at many elite universities, and campus culture militates toward Wall Street, law school and consulting, where the milieu is familiar and the pay bountiful. The few who are interested in public service opt for programs like Teach for America or the Peace Corps. Nor do campuses offer many role models of military service, because few professors are veterans. Moskos, for example, is the only one in his department.

Indeed, it is professors who have often led the charge against one of the few conduits for elites into the military: ROTC programs, which once drew significant numbers into the armed services. During and after Vietnam, many prestigious private colleges phased ROTC out in the face of student opposition. In the 1970s and 1980s, ROTC made something of a comeback. But then came the fight over gays in the military, and once again, ROTC programs became political sacrificial lambs. (Some campuses also barred military recruiters.) In 1991, 62 ROTC programs were closed. That certainly wasn't all due to the controversy over gays in the military (as tuition has risen, the number of scholarships the military can pay for has fallen) but some of it was. And this time, the opposition was led by professors—the same generation who had been students voicing similar opposition during Vietnam. Where ROTC survived, as at Princeton and Dartmouth, it was largely because students resisted professors' opposition to the program.

Expelling ROTC programs from elite campuses may send a message, but it also has costs. For many students, the loss of ROTC is a lost opportunity—a ROTC scholarship at a "Tier-1 Alpha" (i.e., expensive) school like Princeton can pay up to $20,000 annually. Ivy League campuses also have been a wellspring for more liberal-minded officers over the past few decades. The military is an inherently conservative institution, made more so by the end of conscription, which essentially meant the end of white liberals in the army. By bringing in students from diverse campuses, ROTC helped mitigate that homogeneity. "A lot of people in the military don't want Harvard grads," says Air Force Colonel Charles J. Dunlap. "They want people from conservative schools in the Bible belt. They don't want an insider with a different outlook—and that's very bad for a military in a democracy."

If elite service benefits the military, military service also benefits the elite, or at least broadens their horizons, by doing what public schools once did: integrate people of different socioeconomic backgrounds. "You learn arrogance in the Ivy League," says a former Army lieutenant who graduated from Princeton and is now a Harvard graduate student. "You learn humility in the army, because some guy from a college you have never heard of knows a lot more than you do." He describes working with young enlisted men from backwater high schools in Louisiana and being profoundly impressed by their motivation and intelligence. When he told them so, many said he was the first person who had ever told them they were smart.

That few similarly privileged youth share that experience is troubling, because they often grow up to be powerful adult leaders. Georgetown University's School of Foreign Service trains the elite of the foreign policy establishment, and it would seem logical that students have some interest in the military as a key foreign policy tool. Not so, as Richard G. Miles, a U.S. Army Reserve captain, found when he enrolled at the school. "The sum total of [my classmates'] knowledge about military matters—ranging from tactics to tanks—came from movies and magazine articles," he wrote in *Newsweek*. The Princeton-educated former Army lieutenant says he joined the military partly because he was interested in a career in politics or diplomacy. "I thought it would be inappropriate to strive for a position where I would be directing the military without having been directed myself." That is an uncommon perspective among aspiring political leaders these days.

Close to 60 percent of men in the Senate are veterans, but only 36 percent of the House (and a fifth of the freshman class). Only 20 percent of Senate-confirmed Clinton appointees are veterans, and only 4 percent of the White House staff (a fact that understandably has aroused the ire of vets who wonder why the administration looks like America in every category except military service). And consider the roster of possible presidential candidates who avoided active military service: Clinton, Gramm, Quayle, Cheney, Forbes, Kemp, Gingrich. Says one Army officer: "If Clinton tells an 18-year-old to go fight, he expects him to go whether or not he thinks it's a good idea. Yet he didn't think Vietnam was a good idea, he didn't want to serve, and he didn't. I'm not saying he didn't make a morally responsible choice. But given what he does [command the armed forces] ... it's a problematic choice." The same applies to all those with similar pasts who want his job. And it explains why Dole keeps running on his war record: He knows it resonates with the generation for whom service was a moral obligation.

Civilian leaders not serving isn't just morally, but also pragmatically, problematic. For a civilian to command the military, he must have the military's respect. To earn the military's respect, he must understand military culture. Fewer and fewer civilian leaders do. Thus, the Clinton administration has been marked by a litany of real and perceived slights and faux pas. Officers mutter about how Clinton salutes sloppily, with a shame-faced demeanor. They have not forgotten the White House staffer who allegedly told Gen. Barry McCaffrey, "I don't talk to people in the military." They have not forgiven the administration for making gays in the military its number-one priority. They ridicule Clinton's attempt (under the Soldiers and Sailors Relief Act of 1940) to use the president's role as commander-in-chief to delay Paula Jones's suit. Clinton managed to reopen old wounds when he said he felt "vindicated" in his avoidance of military service by Robert McNamara's concession that Vietnam was a mistake. And the perception that Clinton is morally challenged doesn't help his credibility in the socially conservative armed forces.

It is obviously important to have some leaders in government who haven't served, who have a skeptical attitude toward, not a vested interest in, the military. But it is crucial as well to have people in the White House and Congress who understand the institution, who know what questions to ask, as Dwight Eisenhower did, and who have the credibility to get answers. That's all the more true because at least some of the leaders who avoided service sometimes seem less skeptical about the military than guilt-ridden about their own past. "Thirty years later, now elected to positions of prominence, those who evaded service now truckle and fawn to demonstrate the depth of their regard for men in uniform," writes Andrew J. Bacevich, a professor at Johns Hopkins's School of Advanced International Studies.

Thus we have Bill Clinton, who somehow manages simultaneously to piss off and kiss up to the military. Eager to curry the military's approval, or fearful of incurring its wrath, Clinton has shied away from responsibly downsizing the military-industrial complex. Instead, there's hairy-chest beating, as the administration boasts about the size of its defense budget (which, of course, has less to do with military readiness than making smart decisions about how to spend the money). And, as *The Wall Street Journal* recently noted, Clinton just can't say no to Veterans Affairs Secretary (and war hero) Jesse Brown, whose budget keeps increasing even as his department's hospital system is vastly underutilized.

What matters even more is whether leaders have children or relatives who are serving, or know people who do. There is no authoritative count of how many of the children of congressmen or administration officials have served, but by all accounts it's a tiny percentage. "Ask any group of male community leaders over age fifty how many served in the military," former Navy secretary John Lehman has written, "and eight of ten hands will rise; ask how many have children who have served and it will rarely be one or more."

Yet many of these leaders are deciding to send the military into risky situations, particularly in the post–Cold War era, when "military operations other than war" have become commonplace. Where our national interest is not at stake, but our "values"—a much broader rubric—are, will we sacrifice American lives? That's never easy, but it is slightly easier if you are sending abstract "brave men and women in uniform" rather than Bobby Jones from your hometown. Easier, too, when the bodies come back. Consider that of 220 Marines killed in the 1983 Beirut bombing, 78 were Catholic and 64 were Baptist, the denominations most common to the working class. There were two Episcopalians, two Presbyterians, and no Jews. Of the 19 Americans recently killed in the Saudi Arabian bombing, 10 were Roman Catholics, and five Baptists.

The same standard, of course, ought to apply to journalists who are exhorting the president to send troops for a peacekeeping or humanitarian operation. Yet many journalists expressing such opinions also have nothing—or no one—at stake. Many of those covering the operations also have no military experience. That doesn't make good coverage prohibitive, but it makes it harder. During the Gulf War, for example, reporters stuck to what they knew: They based themselves in five star hotels in Dhahran, and reported—literally—from poolside (although they didn't tell their viewers that). They allowed themselves to be herded around by a Pentagon whose assertions went unchallenged. It took a week, for example, for the press corps to wake up to the fact that the Pentagon's boast about an 80 percent success rate in air missions in the Gulf was based on "arriving at the target and delivering the ordnance," not whether the ordnance actually hit the target.

Off-base notions about the military don't just surface in nonfiction. The intellectuals who shape popular culture and public perceptions no longer do military service either. Herman Wouk, James Jones, Irwin Shaw, Norman Mailer wrote, and imagined, great novels about war and the army from experience. Most of today's novelists aren't serving—and neither are producers, screenwriters, or directors, which is why so many of today's military characters are caricatures. (Two recent movies, *The Rock* and *Broken Arrow*, both feature mad vets holding cities hostage.)

No wonder so many of us are so ignorant about today's military—and so many elites so dismissive of it. "Working-class folks respect the military because they constitute most of it," says Ralph Peters, who now works in the Office of Drug Policy. "But when I meet academics, or people in government or the private sector, they're absolutely astonished that I'm in the military and can also speak in complete sentences."

Peters not only can speak in complete sentences; he's actually quite brilliant. He is a Russia specialist—fluent in the language, conversant in the literature, authoritative on policy and culture. He has an M.A. and four years of education beyond that. He is writing his seventh novel. Believe it or not, "military intellectual" is not an oxymoron.

The irony is that even as we fail to recognize the brains in the military, we imbue it with all sorts of other superhuman qualities, romanticizing what we don't really understand. The national hysteria over Colin Powell was akin to the second coming of Christ; somehow, we projected his ability to lick Saddam Hussein onto bad schools, drugs, the economy. Clinton boasted during the first presidential debate that he had "appointed a four-star general as drug czar . . . the most heavily decorated soldier in uniform when he retired," as if the correlation between a successful military career and the ability to deter drug use is perfectly clear.

This rosy, hazy view of the competent modem military encourages civilians to expand the military's purview into peacekeeping, drug interdiction, humanitarian intervention, riot control, disaster relief, even chauffeuring Olympic athletes, an inclination compounded by the fact that we now have a 1.5 million person military with no Cold War and no clear mission. A belief in the omnipotent military sends more soldiers into harm's way; it also gives a potentially dangerous level of political power to the military.

The combination of a powerful and self-righteous military and a naive and guilt-ridden civilian leadership isn't a good one. A military is crucial to a democracy but is not itself democratic, and we don't want a society in its image. What we want are civilians who understand and respect what the military is and what it does, and who share the burden of public service it increasingly shoulders alone.

Universal Service

John Keegan's masterpiece of military history, *The Face of Battle*, contains a striking scene from the battle of Waterloo. The British are defending a chateau against a fierce French onslaught when a British officer, Captain Wyndham, spots a French Grenadier clambering over the gate. Wyndham has a weapon in his hand, but rather than shooting the interloper himself, according to an eyewitness report, he "instantly desired Sergeant Graham, whose musket he was holding while the latter was bringing forward another piece of timber, to drop the wood, take his firelock and shoot the intruder." The blood would be on the sergeant's hands, which was exactly Keegan's point: The officer class had begun to find killing in battle distasteful and therefore were delegating the dirty work.

Waterloo is now battlefield lore, but this story has its modern permutations. Who gives the order to kill, and who executes it, isn't just a wartime dilemma. Any democratic society that wants to ensure its preservation grapples with the same decision—or ought to—on a daily basis, especially when the military is under civilian command. I'm certainly not in a position to condemn those who haven't served in the military; I didn't rush off to a recruiting office after college. But I think if we are going to ask others to do what we ourselves are unwilling to, we should consider the implications of an all-volunteer military. It's harder to do that when the military is an isolated abstraction.

The obvious solution, one this magazine has long advocated, is to resurrect the draft. That remains a noble ideal, but an increasingly impractical one. The military today is much too small to sustain the numbers universal conscription would churn up. Much of its operation also requires a technological sophistication that draftees would have difficulty acquiring in a year or two; there is less of a place for conscripts in an increasingly professionalized military. A draft, remember, might not just draw in the elite; it could also pressure the military to accept those it now prides itself on weeding out.

So how do we stem the growing alienation between civilians, especially elite civilians, and soldiers, and recover the class mixing, character building, and community sustenance that democratically distributed military service once provided? Various educational measures could improve civil-military relations: Require military officers to go to civilian graduate schools and civilian decision makers to spend time at military academies; preserve or restore ROTC on campuses, both to provide access to the military and because its mere presence can educate students about military affairs; and have undergraduates study military history and culture.

But we need to take more dramatic steps, especially as military service becomes less a calling than a ticket. Recruiters now rely more on appeals to bread-and-butter needs and aspirations than to patriotism and public service. "Are you in the market for skill training, a guaranteed salary, and money for college?" the phone message at one Army recruiting office asks. These are certainly valid reasons for joining the military, and pay and benefits need to be generous enough to lure good people and recognize the service they perform. But the danger is that gradually the civilian ethos of serving yourself will overwhelm the military ethos of serving the country, that young people anxious to compete with their peers and surpass their parents will shun the less lucrative returns military service provides.

Reversing this trend ultimately may have nothing to do with getting more people to serve in the military—and everything to do with getting more people to serve, period. The fact is, a tiny proportion of college graduates go into the Peace Corps or Teach for America. Most go to work for themselves—a fact those in the military, or considering the military, can't help but notice. People are simply out of the habit of serving.

As a remedy, Moskos and Butler propose national community service for young people. But since we can't afford a national service program for all young Americans, the best compromise may be a national service lottery: If your number comes up, you can do military service (if you meet the military's standards); or, as in Germany, you can opt for civilian service. Those going into the military will, of course, be putting more on the line; their compensation should reflect that.

Such a program could draw a wider pool of people into the armed services, including at least a few more children of the powerful and privileged. A lottery would also provide the military with more short-termers and fewer lifers, which would mean a healthy injection of skepticism and self-criticism by those whose careers wouldn't be on the line. For those serving, it could renew a national sense of obligation, an understanding that rights require sacrifice. It would impose discipline on its participants and demand responsibility. And it would throw together young Americans of every stripe.

National service is, of course, popular among neoliberals, but what surprised me was how many military people I talked to proposed it—indeed were passionate about it. This is, in part, because it would make those who volunteer for military service feel less alone in shouldering the burdens of citizenship. But it is also because they believe in duty, honor, and country—and understand that paying tribute to those words has little to do with wearing a uniform.

9

Women in Combat, Homosexuals in Uniform: The Challenge of Military Leadership

Richard H. Kohn

Bill Clinton's promise to end the ban on homosexuals serving openly in the military, and the continuing furor over women in combat, threaten an ongoing civil-military battle that could damage military professionalism, alienate an otherwise friendly incoming Administration, and, ultimately, ruin the military effectiveness of the American armed forces for the foreseeable future. Military leaders who oppose these changes ought to consider some facts and principles that might change their minds.

First, history. Women have fought successfully, sometimes integrated with men, as in the World War II Allied underground, where they proved just as adept at slitting throats, leading men in battle, suffering torture, and dying, as men; sometimes segregated, as in Soviet air force units, which produced many female aces fighting the Germans. Homosexuals have for centuries served honorably and effectively, in the United States and abroad. Arguments against open service assume that proper policies and effective leadership will fail, even though the services succeeded in integrating African-Americans and women, switching to a draft military in 1940 and then back to an all-volunteer force after 1973, and adjusting to other very divisive social changes over the last half century.

Second, there is fairness. In times of emergency, service is a fundamental obligation no citizen should escape unless disqualified physically or excused

Reprinted from *Parameters: Journal of the U.S. Army War College* (Washington, D.C.: Government Printing Office), 23:2 (Spring 1993), pp. 2–4. Copyright© 1993 by Richard H. Kohn. Reprinted by permission of the author.

on religious or moral grounds, or because their skills need to be used in some other capacity. But also, participation in combat—dying for one's country—has historically enabled minorities to claim the full privileges of equal participation in society, something basic to our form of government. That is why African-Americans for generations "fought for the right to fight" and why combat and military service are so important to women and homosexuals. Combat and service promote equal protection of the laws and undermine prejudice and discrimination.

Third, the very real practical problems can be overcome. Without question, change will be complicated and costly and take time, and military efficiency will suffer in the short term. Unless carefully explained to the American people, these changes could harm recruiting, precisely in those areas and among those groups which have been traditionally supportive of military service. To accommodate women on combat ships and in flying units (few advocate women in ground combat units), facilities and perhaps weapon systems will need modification. There will be ticklish, perhaps intractable, problems of privacy and personal discomfort (there already *are* in the military). The services will be distracted from their primary peacetime duties of readiness, preparation, and modernization. Leadership at all levels will be challenged to maintain morale and effectiveness in circumstances where, historically, macho behavior and explicit sexual banter helped forge the personal bonds that enabled units to train and fight effectively.

Cohesion, the key to military success, will be more difficult without traditional methods of male bonding. The strict authority, harsh discipline, and instant obedience required for victory in battle have always been subject to abuse, and adding more women and ending discrimination against gay men and lesbians will increase the problem. To deal with it, military leaders will have to redouble their efforts to define appropriate conduct and to punish or expel those in the ranks who cannot or will not control their language and their behavior. The problem, as Tailhook so clearly reveals, already exists; the fundamental issue in the short run will not be attitude, but behavior, and the military can be extremely effective in controlling behavior. The services will have to review policies on acceptable conduct, on and off duty. Research on maintaining cohesion without scapegoating homosexuals and treating women as sex objects will have to be undertaken. The challenge to our military leadership, at all levels, will be enormous, and it will last as long as sexism and homophobia afflict significant portions of our population.

And yet, our military can adjust—once again. It is natural to resist because change poses a diversion from the primary purposes of preparing for and deterring war, and engaging in combat. That is why as outstanding a public servant as General George C. Marshall during World War II opposed racial integration, believing it divisive and concerned that the Army could not afford to act as a "social laboratory" during a national emergency. But civilian control means that our military will be organized and will operate according to the nation's needs and desires. Historically our national security and our social, legal, and constitutional practices have had to be balanced. The services know that military efficiency and combat effectiveness do not always determine our military policies, and less so in times of peace and lessened threat.

If President Clinton follows through on the promise to let gay men and lesbians serve openly, and if, for reasons of fairness and justice, he permits women to fight in combat units at sea and in the air, then the American military must comply, and without resistance. To resist would only make the adjustment more time-consuming and disruptive, and would itself undermine military effectiveness.

In the long run, the services should find that their effectiveness, as in the experience of racial and gender integration, will be enhanced rather than diminished. The strength of our military depends ultimately upon its bonds to the people; the armed forces will be stronger the more they reflect the values and ideals of the society they serve.

10

The Doctrine
of Dissent

Lt. Col. Mark E. Cantrell

A yes man on a staff is a menace to a commander. One with the courage to
express his convictions is an asset.
—MacKenzie Hill (pseud., Maj. Gen. Orlando Ward, USA) c. 1934.

Every school, from Officer Candidates School through the Marine Corps
War College, increases an officer's knowledge and confidence. Similarly,
every promotion and every billet from platoon commander through division commander increases an occupant's professional competence and
awareness of that competence. Ultimately, if an officer is one of the few selected for a major command, he will be treated with a high degree of respect and courtesy. Such a process would give any mortal considerable faith
in his own judgment.

But no officer commands alone, so our hypothetical commander sur-
rounds himself with staff officers who think as he does, and who can best
implement his policies, because they are most sympathetic with those policies. He is far from the corporals and lieutenants, but he has a staff to feed
him the information he wants. His subordinates expect him to dictate policy and be brilliant, so he dictates policy and usually is brilliant. Yet sometimes, like even the best humans, he will act emotionally or without a few
key facts. The staff, duly informed of their commander's wishes, will hur-
riedly produce estimates and numerous briefing charts in support of those
wishes. Some subordinates, perhaps with the benefit of fewer preconceived
notions or perhaps having facts unknown to the commander, might see

Reprinted by permission from *Marine Corps Gazette*, 82:11, pp. 56–57.

folly in his plan. However, the commander may be too senior and intimidating or they may be too junior or too cautious to approach him. They, might look to *FMFM 3-1, Command and Staff Action,* but they would find no clear advice on how to respond to a commander's misguidance. Nor would they be likely to remember anyone at The Basic School talking about how to react to legal but flawed orders. If the commander is lucky, these concerned subordinates might speak to their immediate superiors, but the chief of staff (or executive officer) might disagree. Someone might wish to protect the commander from being upset by officers too junior to see the "big picture." The commander might find it difficult to admit, even to himself, that he is wrong. For whatever reason, the mistake might go uncorrected. Although the commander would be solely responsible, in such a case he would not have fouled up alone. Really big blunders often take teamwork. In this case, the commander's misstep went uncorrected because of staff groupthink, subordinates too timid to speak up, a chief or executive officer unwilling to trouble the boss with dissent, and an institution that failed to prepare them all.

Since we can never completely eliminate misjudgments, we should create an environment where subordinates are more likely to identify and invite attention to those misjudgments. This will require effort by all three parties to the problem—subordinates, seniors, and the institution that trains them.

Subordinates

We will all occasionally find ourselves doubting the wisdom of an order. Your first reflex should be to make very sure that the boss really is wrong. After all, he is the boss because he has more experience and quite possibly more wisdom. He may also be privy to information unknown to his juniors. If your analysis supports the commander's decision, you will have learned from the exercise and you will be better able to implement the order. If your analysis indicates that the commander is wrong, the information you gather will enable you to better argue your position. Make sure your analysis includes a suggested alternative. If you cannot offer a better idea, there is little to gain by poking holes in the plans of your superiors.

Your next task is to decide what, if anything, to do about your disagreement. If the issue is trivial or it is too late to intervene, you may reasonably decide to do nothing. For example, you normally wouldn't want a showdown with the boss over his choice of color for the conference room tablecloth. Nor would it be wise to question his scheme of maneuver after crossing the line of departure. On the other hand, you have a duty to do something if the issue is significant and there is time for debate.

Once you decide to speak up, you must choose the manner for your presentation. If time is short, you may have no choice but to argue your case verbally. If there is time and the issues are complex, you may find a staff paper more effective. In either case, you will want to get your ducks in line and get it right the first time. It will be much harder to bring the matter up again if you have already been shot down once.

Timing and surroundings are at least as important as your method of presentation. It is difficult for anyone to admit a mistake, especially in front of an audience. Therefore, a staff meeting is a lousy place to suggest to a commander that he is wrong. Ideally, you should head off a bad order before its announcement at a staff meeting. Failing in that, you should tactfully mention your reservations at the meeting, rather than letting the order gather inertia by its announcement to the command as a whole. In either case, you may simply want to mention that you have reservations and ask for a little time to gather facts. The delay will allow you to build your case and usually arrange for a more private hearing. It will also spare the commander from having to unexpectedly defend his order and deliberate alternatives in front of the staff.

When the time comes for your presentation, use a calm and tactful, but forceful approach. Although important issues will often be emotional, you'll want to keep those emotions in the background if you wish to be persuasive. Even rational arguments sound suspect if delivered with too much feeling. By the same token, you want to keep your superior in a calm, unemotional frame of mind. You can do that by avoiding approaches that would predictably put him on the defensive or make him angry.

If your best efforts are unsuccessful, you face an even more difficult decision. In most cases, you should say "aye, aye" and cheerfully execute the order to the best of your ability. History may prove you right, in which case there will be no need for an "I told you so" and you'd be ill-advised to try to squeeze one in. If history proves you wrong, you will have learned from the experience.

But what do you do if the issue is too important and you are too sure of yourself to let it go? You can gather more evidence and ask for another audience. Failing in that, as a last resort—and if the issue is critically important—you can go over your commander's head. Have the courage and courtesy to inform him, tactfully, that you are doing so. It is better to be thought of as a stubborn fool than a disloyal coward. Also, stick to your chain of command. Right or wrong, you'll make few friends by going to the press or Congress to resolve a problem that could have been corrected by Marines. If you are right, there is a Marine somewhere in that chain who will see it.

Seniors

Just as the subordinate is duty bound to voice dissent, the senior should consider himself obligated to listen if time allows. In fact, the wise commander will actually encourage his subordinates to voice disagreements. One of the best ways to do this is to conceal your own views until you've heard the recommendations of your subordinates. Even if you've already decided on a course of action, ask your staff for recommendations. They may come up with something you like even better. If not, and they cannot successfully defend their ideas over your own, at least you can be confident that alternatives have been considered. In any case, the staff will have learned from the experience. I don't advocate denying your staff planning guidance. It is very frustrating to develop a recommendation only to have it rejected due to assumptions or criteria that were deliberately hidden. If you have preconceived acceptability criteria, by all means announce them, but you should avoid announcing any bias towards a particular course of action. To do so would inevitably limit the staff's consideration of alternatives.

Like the dissenter, the commander must be concerned about an appropriate time and place for hearing a subordinate's views. Again, a crowded conference room is not ideal. An audience puts you on the spot and clutters your mind with concerns other than the issue at hand. When possible, invite the subordinate to your office for a private discussion. However, don't make it sound like a trip to the woodshed, or you'll have a tough time wringing candid opinions out of that audience in the future. Also, don't be so quick to argue that time does not allow reconsideration. Few situations are too rushed for at least some discussion.

Once you have set the appropriate time and place for the dissident to present his views, keep an open mind and hear him out. If you need time to deliberate or seek other opinions, take it. Remember that there is no shame in changing your mind, but it is shameful to press on with a bad idea out of pride of authorship. You will find fewer people to speak up if it becomes obvious that you never change your mind.

Regardless of the outcome, seniors must reward those with the courage to voice dissent. Even if you believe him wrong, the dissenter deserves a thanks and a pat on the back for speaking up. If his methods are clumsy or inappropriate, gently correct them, but his ideas still deserve a fair hearing, and he still deserves congratulations for his backbone.

Finally, any commander would be wise to include a few bright, outspoken, and disagreeable officers on his staff. It may be more pleasant to work with officers who think as you do. However, an occasional disagreement will discourage groupthink and maybe even help you avoid some serious mistakes.

The Institution

It isn't easy for seniors or subordinates to transform dissent from a threat into a constructive force. Both must, to some extent, act against human nature. So the Marine Corps, as an institution, must do more to train officers for both roles. This training must start in our formal schools. It isn't enough to hold leadership discussions on My Lai. While that is needed too, few of us will ever be faced with blatantly unlawful orders. Yet every officer will be faced with orders that are ill-advised. We should stop pretending that commanders never make mistakes and develop a doctrine for dealing with those mistakes. Lieutenants should not be left to develop their own methods through trial and error and seniors shouldn't be encouraged, by the absence of such a doctrine, to pretend that they are infallible.

Once we develop a doctrine, it should be acknowledged in our publications. Such an important and ticklish subject should not be passed on in whispers like some dirty little secret. There seem to be a few unwritten rules already. Let's write them down in our leadership texts, in *FMFM 3-1*, and in the *Marine Corps Manual* for starters.

Conclusion

The history of every military organization includes leadership disasters. In most cases, someone saw that disaster coming. Either they did not speak out effectively or a commander didn't listen hard enough. We can do much to attack both problems. Specifically, we should develop doctrine for dealing with dissent and the mistakes that inspire it. Then, we must teach that doctrine and reward those who practice it well.

PART 3

The Personal Challenge

The rare quality of being an effective leader cannot be attributed to any single trait, practice, characteristic, or "golden rule." Effective leadership is a delicate combination of integrity, perseverance, technical knowledge, mission, awareness, a sense of fairness, and genuine concern for one's soldiers.
—Sergeant Major Sweeny
(source unknown)

In the modern military, the leader can no longer afford to be the most skilled individual; technical skills of followers must exceed those of the leaders if the unit is to be successful. Leaders are evaluated in terms of having people in their units who are brighter and more capable than they are. It is just not possible to keep up with changing technology while coping with the incessant demands of command.

A leader's success depends upon self-knowledge, self-confidence, and commitment to lifelong education and training. There are no surefire methods of developing leadership. No seminar, workshop, training school, or short course can turn individuals into leaders. We believe that accurate self-knowledge is the only way a person can prepare for the challenge. The discovery of one's own strengths and weaknesses enhances self-confidence. Taking risks and learning from failures are critical to leadership development. The more we learn about ourselves, the more effective we can be in the roles of leader and follower.

Followership

Leaders come from the ranks of followers. Few leaders can be successful without first learning the skills of followership. Aristotle's *Politics*, Plato's *Republic*, Homer's *Odyssey*, and Hagel's *Phenomenology of Mind* affirm the mastery of followership as the sine qua non of leadership. Hence, the contemporary study of leadership must examine followership and leader development as they affect organizational success. Good followership is, in effect, a prerequisite for effective leadership.

Most of us are followers more often than we are leaders. Even when we have subordinates, we still have those above us. Followership dominates our lives and our organizations, but a preoccupation with leadership often constrains us from truly appreciating the nature of the follower.

Qualities that make effective followers are paradoxically the same qualities found in effective leaders. What distinguishes effective followers from effective leaders is the role they play. Effective followers and leaders easily move from one role to the other. In many organizations, the leadership role is the path to success, the one that is most focused upon for development and reward. That is unfortunate, because most organizations need good followers more than they need emerging leaders. A few organizations, such as the military, recognize the importance of the role of follower.

In a quest to create harmony, many organizations have replaced the use of terms like "subordinate" or "follower" with "associates," "partners," "team members," or "colleagues." What we call "people" matters less than how we treat them. We have observed associates and team members being treated poorly by those in charge; nomenclature is not what is important. What we all want is for our leaders to help define the direction and create a path to the future. By following, we do not want to be perceived as inferior. We are in it together. If every leader is also a follower, then it stands to reason that developing effective leadership is understanding and experiencing effective followership.

The Human Dimension

Leadership is a person-based phenomenon. Dynamic qualities of personality linked with situation and opportunity are expressed in terms of vision, decisiveness, risk-taking, self-confidence, morale, and trust. Leadership is thus an influence process. Personal interactions between leader and follower are a necessary component of leadership. One thing is certain: Leadership comes from the *person*.

It is the interaction between our personality and the personalities of the follower that allows leadership to occur. And though we should be able to adapt to changing situations, the reality is that we have preferred ways of acting. Moreover, our values drive our decisions, and so adapting may work in the short-run, but over time our behavior is a result of our personality. The result is that we may find ourselves successful in one context and ineffective in another. The situation may be unique or the personality of the followers may be different. How we relate to the followers will change accordingly.

Yet effective leadership is more than personality. The environment in which we are asked to lead is important. The military moves leaders among units with regularity. But there is a leadership culture and a sense of loyalty involved. It is different from politics and business. In those environments, culture is not necessarily one of leadership expectations; new leaders must prove themselves capable within the environmental constraints. There is a difference, then, between leadership in the military and leadership in other organizations.

Some people would argue that the stakes are highest in the military. The lives of followers and entire societies are dependent upon effective military leadership during times of crisis. Success and failure do not appear as significant in the normal course of politics and business. Thus, the environment places different strains on the leader, and the relationship between leader and follower seems to be more clearly defined. And even though personality is important in all arenas, we believe that the military provides a more challenging and, ultimately, clearer demand for leadership related to the time and place of events.

The Leadership Dimension

Earl H. Potter III, William F. Rosenbach, and Thane S. Pittman present their conceptual model of followership in "Followers as Partners: The Best Evidence of Good Leadership" (Chapter 11), which was revised for this edition. They describe effective followers as partners in an enterprise who are committed to high performance and healthy relationships with their leaders. The authors agree that leaders who encourage partnerships as well as followers who seek to be partners characterize organizations that keep pace with the rapidly changing global environment.

James M. Kouzes, in "When Leadership Collides with Loyalty" (Chapter 12), describes the results of a study he conducted with Barry Z. Posner, which indicates that leaders are expected to be forward-looking and inspiring. Leaders and followers each want the other to be capable and effective; they need to be able to depend on trust and one another and set aside their own agendas for that of the organization. Yet being forward-looking and inspiring is often incompatible with being cooperative and dependable, which presents another dilemma. The leader who usually is both must make an either-or choice between leading and following.

James L. Stokesbury, unlike many writers, uniquely differentiates leadership from headship in "Leadership as an Art" (Chapter 13). He focuses on the leader as a person and does not address those who merely serve (as "heads") in positions of leadership. In an attempt to define leadership, he says that we are trapped by the inadequacies of the language and often wind up with a tautological definition. Stokesbury deals with this dilemma by defining leadership as an art and by suggesting that the best method for learning about leadership is to study the examples provided by history. He chose four historic leaders: the Marquis of Montrose, Alexander Suvorov,

Robert E. Lee, and Philippe Pétain, all of whom had little in common other than sharing attributes that Stokesbury believes constitute the art of leadership. He concludes by observing that the higher elements of leadership remain an art, whereas the lesser elements can be learned scientifically and can be treated by artifice. He ironically observes that the better times are, the less artifice works, and the more that art is needed.

In "A Charismatic Dimension of Military Leadership?" (Chapter 14), David M. Keithly and James J. Tritten review the common theme of charisma as related to leadership. The term "charisma" is often employed to describe effective leaders with little definition as to the characteristics and behaviors involved. The authors examine the meanings of charisma in the literature with a special emphasis on applications for military leadership. They explore the psychological, situational, cultural, and other factors associated with charisma. Charismatic leaders are often change agents, but they can also be at odds with the tenets of traditional authority. Leaders who rely upon charisma find success in new organizational environments, but they rarely succeed beyond their own personality.

An interesting and often-made comparison between business and the military is explored by Micha Popper in "Leadership in Military Combat Units and Business Organizations: A Comparative Organizational Analysis" (Chapter 15). In peacetime, we find many comparisons between military leaders and business managers. Popper suggests that the organizational context is quite different and, as a result, that the leadership patterns vary between the two environments. Military leadership is based upon a response of commitment coming from emotion. Business leadership elicits a transactional leadership response based upon social, material, and professional rewards. He concludes by noting that the actors (leaders) may not be as different as the stage or context as well as the rules by which the leaders operate.

In "Leadership: Between a Rock and a Hard Place" (Chapter 16), Maj. Lee E. DeRemer notes that military leaders may be faced with dilemmas for which no comfortable solution exists. Competing or conflicting interests often accompany high military rank. Since we cannot compromise integrity, DeRemer suggests, we must change the constraints. If even that is not possible, leaders must sacrifice themselves professionally to change those constraints in a way that preserves the mission and the safety of their people. Citing the specific example of Gen. John D. Lavelle during the Vietnam War, DeRemer recalls the problems, the solution, and the ramifications of the choice. The conclusion is that personal integrity is essential to effective leadership.

Finally, in "Once a Leader, Always a Leader?" (Chapter 17), David Stauffer discusses the importance of organizational context. With the high turnover in the military and the opportunity for second careers, he cites the difficulties with successful senior military leaders moving to the private and public sectors as well as politics. Great leadership comes at critical junctures of organizations and where there is a sense of urgency. It is not clear that in transitioning from the military (or even within the military) that there is a transference of leadership skills. Stauffer makes a good case for self-knowledge and self-confidence remaining as the key attributes for leaders of the future.

11

Followers as Partners: The Best Evidence of Good Leadership

Earl H. Potter III, William E. Rosenbach, and Thane S. Pittman

This chapter is written for those who want to be more effective leaders. If you are one of these people, it is also likely that you want to achieve personal success as well to lead effectively. However, it is also likely that you are not completely sure about what it means to be an effective leader. It is not uncommon for emerging leaders to be confused about leadership effectiveness today. What their seniors say and what they do may not be the same. Moreover, the ways that organizations measure performance do not always include all aspects of leadership effectiveness. Thus it is possible for "successful" officers or NCOs to be less than fully effective leaders. Surely this cannot be good for a service. The mission suffers and those who are learning to lead are confused. What is right and what works? Is the answer to these two questions the same?

These days the senior leaders of every U.S. military organization espouse a commitment to the people in their organizations. This commitment should mean that the military services can attract and hold the best talent. Yet there are signs that not all is well in the military services of the United States. Every U.S. military service except the Marine Corps is failing to meet recruitment quotas, and low retention of midgrade talent is driving services to make costly emergency interventions. Some attribute these conditions to a booming economy; others blame them on the hardships associated with meeting demanding mission requirements with downsized forces. We believe that the behavior of leaders is key to understanding this situation.

Fifteen years ago Dr. Nicholas Allen asked the leadership teams of Coast Guard commands to identify and rank the importance of the indicators they used to evaluate the effectiveness of ships under their command. The admirals and their staff officers ranked material condition number one and crew morale number eighteen. Allen then asked these leaders to rank order the ships under their command in terms of overall performance. The factor that was most strongly related to overall performance was crew morale.

When Allen looked more closely he found surprising contradictions at the root of this relationship. The commanding officers of every ship said pretty much the same things about their mission and priorities. Furthermore, they believed that their crews understood both their mission and the captain's priorities. On the ships judged to be the highest performing, this was true. However, on the ships ranked at the lower end of the performance scale, there was a striking difference. While the captain's "espoused" priorities included the welfare of the crew, the crew felt that the captain's most important priority was his own career.

The "bottom line" seems to be that the judgment of followers concerning the effectiveness of leaders is the same as the judgment of their seniors. This is true even if the seniors do not weigh the judgments of "the crew" as an important factor in their own evaluations of effectiveness. Crew members like being part of a successful enterprise, and they appreciate being treated as a valued part of that enterprise. These factors are what drive the kind of morale that enables crews to endure hardships and teams to achieve outstanding results. This understanding corresponds with the beliefs of expert civilian and military leaders like William Marriott, CEO of Marriott Hotels, and CDR Michael Abrashoff (see Chapter 20), former commanding officer of the USS *Benfold*.

Both of these leaders believe that frontline employees or crew members have a wealth of knowledge that leaders, if they are to be effective, must respect and tap. In fact, CDR Abrashoff goes so far as to say that "the most important thing a captain can do is to see the ship from the eyes of the crew." This belief should not be confused with "softness." Whenever Bill Marriott visits one of his properties, he makes time to listen to employees, but he also inspects every detail of the hotel's operations. The USS *Benfold* under CDR Abrashoff's leadership had the best combat readiness in the Pacific Fleet. These leaders match their belief in people with a high commitment to performance. In CDR Abrashoff's words, "Innovative practices combined with true empowerment produce phenomenal results."

These results include followers who share the same commitment to performance and behave as if the leader's priorities were their own. Followers like these behave like partners in every sense of the word.

Therefore, we believe that leaders should have the goal of turning their followers into partners. Moreover, the best signal of an effective leader in command is that his or her leaders behave like partners.

The astute reader may well object at this point that this is a fine thing to say to Bill Marriott or CDR Abrashoff, but what about the young leader who must work under another's command? Even more to the point, what if the young leader's boss hasn't read this article and has different ideas about how leaders should relate to followers? We do not take these questions lightly. Every leader is, in fact, both a leader and a follower. For the leader as a follower, everything we have said thus far applies with the following qualification: Unless the boss is truly intent on doing something illegal, the follower's best course of action is to work to make his or her boss successful. If young leaders do this while at the same time seeking to engage their own followers as partners, the chances of success are greatly increased.

The model that follows offers a tool that should help leaders assess their own strategy for developing effective followers and offers followers a tool for planning their approach to followership.

A Model for Evaluating
Followers as Partners

Partners and Other Followers

Our basic assumption is that no one gets up in the morning and goes to work with the intent to fail. All who can survive in the workplace give what they believe will be at least enough effort to keep their job. Likewise, leaders do not intend to purposefully alienate the people on whom they depend. Yet experience and prevailing wisdom have seldom taught followers that those who take the personal initiative to strengthen the relationship with their leaders will be more effective. In fact, efforts to build an effective relationship with the boss are more often understood by both parties as ingratiation and advantage seeking rather than a sincere effort to build an effective partnership. This view may be accurate when the follower pursues a better relationship with the boss without a commitment to high performance. However, the most effective followers are intent on high performance and recognize that they share the responsibility for the quality of the relationship they have with their leaders. More than that, however, they know that they cannot be fully effective unless they work in a partnership that requires both a commitment to high performance and a commitment to developing effective relationships with partners (including their boss) whose collaboration is essential to success in their own work.

Taken together these two dimensions, *performance initiative* and *relationship initiative,* define four types of followers who are familiar to military leaders: the *subordinate,* the *contributor,* the *politician,* and the *partner.*

Types of Followers

Subordinate. The subordinate is the "traditional" follower who does what he or she is told—competent at a satisfactory level but not one to whom the organization looks for leadership or to whom challenging assignments are given. The subordinate keeps a job and may rise in a seniority-driven organization but demonstrates neither a sensitivity to relationships nor a commitment to high performance. The subordinate is the only kind of valued follower in hierarchical organizations that operate only with orders from the top and obedience from the bottom. In organizational settings where this is desired behavior, "good" followers will exhibit these characteristics even when they are fully capable of and even desirous of behaving like the other types of followers we describe.

This is also the likely style of a somewhat or completely disaffected follower who is not interested in giving anything extra, or whose job is not one of his or her primary concerns.

Contributor. This type of follower behaves in an exemplary way—one who works hard and is known for the quality of his or her work. This person rarely seeks to understand the perspective of the boss, however, and generally waits for direction before turning to new challenges. Although this person is thorough and creative in obtaining resources, information, and skills that are needed to do the job, the interpersonal dynamics of the workplace are not a primary concern. These individuals can develop into full partners by gaining skills and perspectives on the relationship initiative dimension. Alternatively, their valued inclinations can be accommodated and their work value maximized by allowing them to focus on tasks in which they excel and feel comfortable, removing or minimizing aspects of the job that call for interpersonal relationships with the boss.

Politician. The politician gives more attention to managing relationships than to maximizing performance. This person "possesses" valuable interpersonal qualities that are often misdirected or misunderstood. Followers such as these are unusually sensitive to interpersonal dynamics and are valuable for their ability to contribute when interpersonal difficulties have arisen or might arise. They can provide valuable assistance to the leader because they are willing and able to give insights into group relationships. However, often these followers neglect the defined aspects of their jobs in favor of the more relationship-oriented or political aspects of their relationship with the boss. This is a particular problem when others rely on them for job performance. Politicians can become full partners by focusing on job performance and learning how to balance these two concerns, or they can be accepted as they are and given responsibilities that call primarily for the skills and inclinations they possess.

Partner.   The partner is committed to high performance and effective relationships. In fact, the energy given to the development of relationships serves the purpose of gaining the kind of understanding that leads to plans and actions that anticipate new directions and contributions that serve unmet needs. Organizations that anticipate and keep pace with change in the global environment are characterized by leaders who encourage partnership and followers who seek to be partners.

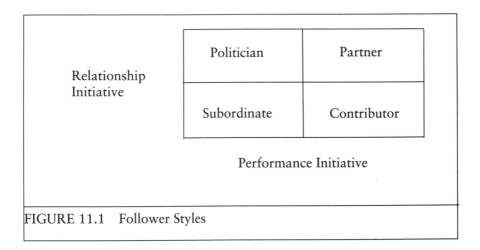

FIGURE 11.1   Follower Styles

Follower Behaviors

These four types of followers can be identified by describing their behavior on the performance initiative dimension and the relationship initiative dimension.

Performance Initiative

Performance initiative refers to the follower's active efforts to do a good job. Those who demonstrate a great deal of performance initiative find ways to improve their own performance in the organization that might include improving skills, sharing resources with team members, and trying new strategies. Those at the high end of this scale understand that their future depends on the future of the organization and are not content simply to do what they were asked to do yesterday. At the low end of this scale one stills finds satisfactory performers, and at the high end one finds experts who lead in their fields and whose contributions strengthen the performance of the organization.

To assess this dimension of follower initiative, we need to consider the extent to which the follower thinks of ways to get his or her assigned job done, the extent to which the follower treats him- or herself as a valuable resource, how well the follower works with coworkers, and what view the follower takes toward organizational and environmental change. Followers differ in the extent to which they take positive initiatives in each of the following four domains.

Doing the job. Followers vary in the extent to which they strive to be as good as they can be at what they do. At one end of this continuum are the followers who go through the motions, performing the tasks that are assigned to them up to the minimum standards required to keep their jobs, and doing little or no more. At the other end of this continuum, some followers care deeply about the quality of their performance. They set their own standards, which are higher than the minimum prescribed by the organization and which are focused on effective performance rather than on merely meeting defined standards. For these followers, work is an important and integral part of their lives. They take pride in what they do, and apply high personal standards for performance from which they can derive personal satisfaction.

Working with others. Another important dimension of follower performance is working with others in the organization. At one extreme is the follower who cannot work well with others, and therefore is continually involved in arguments and disputes, irritating everyone in the process. These followers actually interfere with the performance of others in the organization. In contrast, some followers work alone. They do not have difficulties with others, but they do not really work with them either. Their performance is dependent solely on what they themselves do (or so they think). But many followers do take advantage of working with others, to varying degrees. When followers work effectively with others, they are able to balance their own personal interests with the interests of others, discovering common purpose and working to achieve common goals. That means emphasizing cooperation over competition, finding success in the success of the whole group instead of in self-achievement only.

Self as a resource. Another important aspect of follower performance initiative lies in the extent to which the person treats him- or herself as a valuable but limited resource. Some followers pay little attention to their own well-being, neglecting physical, mental, and emotional health. Although this may yield some short-term benefits for the organization if the follower is effective in important ways, in the long run such neglect is likely to lead to burnout or stagnation, depending on the other aspects of follower performance initiative. Followers who will be effective over the long haul recognize that they are their own most valuable resource and take care to maintain their own physical, mental, and emotional health by balancing work and other interests (e.g., family and friends, community activities and relations, physical and nutritional fitness).

Embracing change. The other important dimension of follower initiative is the follower's orientation to change. In many cases, a follower's reaction to change is to ignore it or hide from it. Change is threatening and confusing, altering the time-honored and familiar. Some followers actively take the initiative to resist change, finding ways to prevent things from being done differently. At the positive end of this dimension are the followers who look for new and better ways to do things because they are committed to continuous quality improvement. These followers see change as an opportunity for improvement for themselves and their organizations. Such followers anticipate or look for change. They can be extremely effective as agents for change, by explaining to their coworkers the advantages of doing things differently, showing by example how different does not have to mean worse.

Relationship Initiative

Relationship initiative refers to the follower's active attempts to improve his or her working relationship with the leader. A person who demonstrates a high degree of relationship initiative finds ways to help the leader succeed because he or she knows that "you can't succeed if your boss fails." On the relationship initiative dimension there are several questions to be explored. To what extent does the follower understand and identify with the leader's vision for the organization? Does the follower actively try to engender mutual trust with the leader?

To what extent is the follower willing to communicate in a courageous fashion with the leader? How actively does the follower work to negotiate differences with the leader? At the low end of this dimension people take the relationship that they are given. At the high end they work to increase openness and understanding in order to gain a perspective that can inform their choices as a partner. The following subscales describe relationship initiative.

Identifying with the leader.   Followers vary considerably in the extent to which they understand and sympathize with the leader's perspective. Many followers simply do not. Viewing the leader as something strange and very different from themselves, they do not try to think about how things look from the leader's perspective or what the leader's goals or problems might be. In organizations with clear hierarchical structures and relatively strict chains of command, it is probably quite natural to see this element missing in the typical follower's approach to the leader. Followers may even be encouraged to think of their leaders as sufficiently different (i.e., superior) as to defy understanding by mere mortals. In contrast, some followers have thought more dispassionately about their leaders, understand their aspirations and styles, and have developed sufficient respect for the leader to adopt those aspirations as their own. These followers understand the leader's perspective, do what they can to help the leader succeed, and take pride and satisfaction in the leader's accomplishments.

Building trust. Followers can also take the initiative to act in ways that will build their leader's confidence and trust in them. This means that the follower will look for and take advantage of opportunities to demonstrate to the leader that she or he is reliable, discreet, and loyal. Followers who demonstrate these qualities to their leaders will in turn be asked for their opinions and reactions to new ideas. Followers who do not seek out such opportunities for building trust, who do not understand or see as important this aspect of their relationship with their leaders, will be treated accordingly and will not be in a position to help their leaders as much as they might.

Courageous communication. Part of building trust includes being honest, even when that is not the easiest thing to do. This aspect of relationship initiative is important enough to consider in its own right. Some followers fear (often with good reason) being the bearer of bad news, and are likely to refrain from speaking unpleasant truths. This can range from the classic notion of the "yes man" to simply refraining from speaking one's mind when that might be uncomfortable for the speaker and listeners. But followers who take the initiative in their relationships with their leaders are willing to speak the truth in order to serve the goals of the organization even when others may not enjoy hearing the truth. A follower who exhibits courageous communication takes risks in order to be honest.

Negotiating differences. Another aspect of relationship initiative concerns the follower's approach to differences that arise between leaders and followers. A follower who is oriented toward improving her or his relationship with the leader is in a position to negotiate or mediate these differences. In the case of a difference of opinion between a leader and follower, the follower may engage in open or hidden opposition to the leader's decisions, hiding his or her disagreement and quickly agreeing with the leader regardless of true personal opinion. Alternatively, the follower who is concerned about the leader-follower relationship will air these differences in order to have a real discussion that may persuade either party or lead to a compromise that is satisfactory to everyone.

Growing Professionals

Creating the conditions that lead followers to partnership requires first that leaders know what they are looking for in their followers. The model we have described offers a framework for this. Creating the right conditions for effective followership next requires a clear understanding of practical steps that invite followers to partnership. The following example may help readers think about the steps they might take.

The personnel inspection is the archetypal military ritual—the symbol of high standards and discipline. For many service members it is an occasion when someone with a lot of power surveys a lot of people with less power for the purpose of discovering discrepancies that the less powerful must correct. The experience usually carries some anxiety and usually ends with relief. Good officers pride themselves on a reputation for tough inspections. In general, one would not describe the inspection as a partnership—but what if it were?

Those inspecting and those being inspected would understand that the assistance of an expert observer is essential to help all come up to the high standards to which they aspired. An inspection "gig" would be information that would help the follower improve. The overall results of the inspection would be seen as information for the commanding officer concerning how effective the leaders of the command were at teaching the standards. Failure to perform would lead to problem solving in order to discover the underlying reasons for nonperformance, and every member of the command would take pride when all members had achieved the highest standards.

If you find yourself objecting that this scenario is unrealistic, remember the elite units you have known. Then remember the other inspections you have experienced. When the responsibility for quality and high performance is vested in the hands of the few, it is heavy work. When every member of a command understands and seeks to perform to the same high standards, the load lightens considerably. This is a simple example, but the climate of a command is the result of many such "simple" interactions.

The experienced military professional might observe that "sharp" followers never experience anxiety during an inspection. They are good and they know it—and that is the point. Good followers take responsibility for their own performance and seek to learn the expectations they must meet in the simple and complex tasks they must perform. But good followers first have to learn the attitudes and skills that support their independent initiative. The challenge of leadership is to develop in the modern military professional the habit of effective followership, and the effective follower will be a partner.

References

Allen, Nicholas H., and Potter, Earl H. "U.S. Coast Guard Efforts to Support Unit Cohesiveness: Studied neglect in sympathy with excellence." Paper presented at the meeting of the American Psychological Association, San Francisco, April 1985.

Boccialetti, Gene. *It Takes Two: Managing yourself when working with bosses and other authority figures*. San Francisco: Jossey-Bass, 1995.

Branch, Shelly. "So Much Work, So Little Time." *Fortune*, June 3, 1997, pp. 115–117.

Case, John. "The Open-Book Revolution." *Inc.*, June 1995, pp. 26–43.

Chaleff, Ira. *The Courageous Follower*. San Francisco: Berrett-Koehler, 1995.

Cohen, Allan R., and Bradford, David L. *Influence Without Authority*. New York: Wiley and Sons, 1990.

Herman, Stanley M. *A Force of Ones: Reclaiming individual power in a time of teams, work groups, and other crowds*. San Francisco: Jossey-Bass, 1994.

Kelley, Robert E. *The Power of Followership: How to create leaders people want to follow and followers who lead themselves*. New York: Doubleday, 1991.

Kouzes, James M., and Posner, Barry Z. *Credibility: How leaders gain and lose it, why people demand it*. San Francisco: Jossey-Bass, 1993.

LaBarre, Polly. "Grassroots Leadership: . . . The USS *Benfold*." *Fast Company*, April 1999, pp. 115–126.

Nocr, David M. *Healing the Wounds: Overcoming the trauma of layoffs and revitalizing downsized organizations*. San Francisco: Jossey-Bass, 1993.

Organ, Dennis W. *Organizational Citizenship Behavior: The good soldier syndrome*. Lexington, MA: D. C. Heath, 1988.

Ryan, Kathleen D., and Oestreich, Daniel K. *Driving Fear Out of the Workplace: How to overcome the invisible barriers to quality, productivity, and innovation*. San Francisco: Jossey-Bass, 1991.

Sashkin, Marshall, Rosenbach, William E., and Sashkin, Molly G. "Development of the Power Need and Its Expression in Management and Leadership with a Focus on Leader-Follower Relations." Paper presented at the 12th scientific meeting of the A. K. Rice Institute, Washington, DC, May 12, 1995.

12

When Leadership
Collides with Loyalty

James M. Kouzes

Despite our cry for more effective leadership, I've become convinced that we are quite satisfied to do without it. We would much rather have loyalty than leadership. Recall the fight between former General Motors board member H. Ross Perot and G.M.'s chairman, Roger B. Smith, that erupted when someone other than the official leader of the corporation began to articulate a strategic vision for the company.

Or take the case of a friend of mine, a former senior vice president of a large packaged goods company. A few years ago he faced a critical leadership challenge. New technology made it possible to introduce a substitute for his company's food product. His market studies clearly indicated that the future of the industry lay in the new substitute product. He was convinced that his company had to revise its long-range plans and develop its own entry into the market or suffer disastrous consequences.

But the board did not share his point of view. It authorized its own independent studies by two prestigious management consulting firms, which to the board's surprise supported the senior vice president's sense of the market. Still unconvinced, the board asked two law firms to determine whether entry into the new market would pose any antitrust issues. Both sets of lawyers agreed there would be no problem.

Despite the overwhelming evidence, the board then sought the opinion of yet a third law firm. This one gave it the answer it was looking for and it abandoned the new product.

Copyright 1988 by The New York Times. Reprinted by permission.

The senior vice president would not be false to his beliefs and subsequently left the company. He has since successfully applied his leadership talents to dramatically improve the performance of a business he now owns in another industry. And he was right about the future of his former company. It experienced serious financial losses, went through a dramatic downsizing, and has yet to recover fully from its myopic strategy.

This critical incident illustrates an extraordinarily difficult choice executives must often make: Do I lead or do I follow? While one is frequently a leader and a follower in the same organization, there are times in executive careers when the choice is either-or. That is because there are distinct differences [in] what we expect of followers. These expectations are in dramatic conflict.

During the course of doing research for a book, my co-author, Barry Posner, and I asked top-level managers to complete a checklist of the characteristics they look for and admire most in a leader. According to our study, the majority of senior managers admire leaders who are: honest, competent, forward-looking and inspiring.

In a separate study, we asked a similar group of executives about what qualities they value in a follower. The majority of executives in our study said they admire honesty, competency, dependability and cooperation.

In every survey we conducted in the United States, honesty and competency ranked first and second in our expectations of what we want from our leaders and followers. If we are to follow someone willingly, we first want to know that the person is worthy of our trust. Similarly, when a leader inquires into the status of a project he wants to know that the information is completely accurate.

We also want leaders and followers alike to be capable and effective. When a leader delegates a task he naturally wants assurance that it will be carried out with skill and precision.

But we also expect our leaders to have a sense of direction and a concern for the future of the organization. Leaders must know where they are going. We expect them to be enthusiastic, energetic and positive about the future. It is not enough for a leader to have a dream—he must be able to communicate his vision in ways that uplift and encourage people to go along with it.

Leaders want to know they can count on people to be team players. They want to know they will work together willingly and will be able to compromise and subordinate individual needs to the common purpose.

These qualities are absolutely essential for even the most mundane tasks in organizations. We must be able to rely on each other, to trust each other, and to set aside our own agendas for that of the organization. Without dependability and cooperation, nothing would get done, and politics would be rampant.

Yet being forward-looking and inspiring—two essential leadership qualities—is often not harmonious with being cooperative and dependable. This is what happened in the case of the senior vice president of the packaged goods company. His integrity demanded that he stand up for his point of view. The result was that he was perceived not to be a team player.

If an individual's vision of the future is opposed to that of his superiors, he may be perceived as uncooperative and disloyal even if his point of view is correct. Persistently selling a point of view only reinforces this perception and may diminish support within the organization. It may even lead to being branded a renegade and result in being fired, transferred, or "voluntarily" dismissed.

As essential as cooperativeness and dependability are, they can be inhibitors of organizational change. If they are too rigidly adhered to, they can result in faithful allegiance to the status quo and unquestioning loyalty to the party line. They also can inhibit the development of the leadership skills we so need in business today.

There is another crucial difference between a pioneering leader and a dependable follower. While success in both is founded on personal credibility, leadership requires the realization of a unique and ideal vision of the future. Following requires cooperative and reliable adherence to that common vision. When an individual's vision is in conflict with the existing strategic vision of an organization, he may have to make a choice: Do I lead or do I follow?

There is no easy path. If organizations inhibit the honest articulation of fresh strategic visions of the future, they will never grow and improve. They will never create a climate that fosters leadership. On the other hand, if individuals cannot learn to subordinate themselves to a shared purpose, then anarchy will rule.

In these times of business transformation, it is wise for executives to encourage and tolerate more internal conflict than we have allowed in the past. If we expect people to show initiative in meeting today's serious business challenges, then we have to relax our expectations of abiding devotion. Instead, we must support the efforts of honest and competent people to find solutions to the problems that are confronting our companies. In short, we must develop the leader in everyone.

13

Leadership as an Art

James L. Stokesbury

There is a certain sense of paradox, almost of impudence, in choosing as the opening title for a social science annual the topic, "Leadership as an Art." If one is thrown off balance by this, it is because society's perceptions have changed so radically over the past century. A hundred years ago, no one would have suspected that leadership might be anything other than an art, and impudence would have lain in asserting that there were scientific aspects to it.

Indeed, as late as fifty years ago the social sciences had still not come of age, and the most popular British historian of his time, Philip Guedalla (1923: 149), could dismiss them quite offhandedly as "light-minded young things like Psychology, with too many data and no conclusions, and Sociology, with too many conclusions and no data." In the 1960s, a distinguished American military historian used to tell his classes that the social sciences and statistical method were capable of telling us "all those things that are not worth knowing," a remark which the disgruntled humanist, pushed ever farther back behind the shrinking perimeter of his defenses, teaching Latin in his office or lecturing on Napoleon to an audience that confuses the Weimar with the Roman Republic, is likely to cherish lovingly.

Now the development of computer technology has finally given the social scientist the tools he needs to amass data as never before, and to extract from it conclusions that are necessarily changing our ways of approaching problems. Social science has come of age, and the humanistic protest that "there is more to it than that" sounds increasingly plaintive. Students who used to read the classics now study executive management, and where they

James L. Stokesbury, "Leadership as an Art," pp. 23–40 in *Military Leadership*, edited by James H. Buck and Lawrence J. Korb, Sage Publications, Inc., 1981.

once learned how Caesar addressed his men, or Napoleon tweaked his grenadiers' earlobes when he was pleased with them, they now absorb graphs and mathematical formulae that are supposed to guarantee magic results. It is a sort of acupuncture of the mind: If you put the needle in here, the object will respond by doing whatever it is supposed to do.

There remains, however, a place for art. The essence of science is in mathematics and predictability. It has become more and more feasible to forecast how more and more of any given group will respond to certain stimuli. If the President looks forthright on television, public confidence will strengthen; if he looks tired, or if his makeup is the wrong shade, the stock market will drop so many points. Elections, we are confidently told, depend on that ever-smaller number of mavericks whose reactions simply cannot be predicted.

In a way, history is repeating itself, as it always does, with twists and quirks. In the eighteenth century, at the height of the Enlightenment, critics of society thought that if only they could be rid of the few remaining irrationalities, they would then achieve the perfect society. Old anomalous institutions like the monarchy, and especially the Church, founded on emotion and faith rather than on the dictates of pure reason, had to be swept away, and once they were, all would be for the best in the best of all possible worlds, as Voltaire wrote in his jibe at Leibnitz. Unhappily, when people destroyed the old institutions, they got the Terror and the Napoleonic Wars, and reason turned out to be little better a guide than tradition, or emotion, or history. One suspects a tendency now on the part of the computer analysts to feel much as the philosophers did in their day: If only we could reduce everything to quantifiable factors, then we should have perfection.

Happily, we cannot, and though a great many of the things that matter in life have been shown to be more amenable to quantitative analysis and scientific predictability than was previously thought to be the case, there still remains the province of art. We still respond to the leader, in fact we hear more and more desperate cries for the emergence of one, and the leader, to bridge that last gap between corporate management and true leadership, still depends upon unmeasurables, that is, on art rather than on science. The elements of his gift, or his skill and how he develops it, are qualitative rather than quantitative, and the problem for the humanist describing the leader is that he is trapped by the inadequacies of the language to describe qualities that defy precise definition. A leader, he may say, needs courage, resolution, self-reliance, and on and on. But he can only define any one of these terms by reference to others of them, and in the end he has produced a tautology: The leader is a leader because he can exercise leadership. One can hardly blame the social scientist for finding this less than adequate, and for preferring to work with something he can pin down, i.e., can measure.

One way out of this dilemma is that history does teach by example. If it is no more than vicarious experience, it is also no less than that. It is useful to look at men whose place in history, large or small, has been guaranteed by the passage of time, and to try to extract from their careers, or episodes in them, elements that epitomize the qualities of leadership that men have most prized. In a not-quite-random sampling, consider the careers of the Marquis of Montrose, Suvorov, Robert E. Lee, and Henri Philippe Petain. These four all achieved pinnacles of leadership, but they are useful examples in that the external details of their careers had little in common. Each was from a different country, in a different century. Two were losers—most of the time, two were winners—most of the time; two fought in civil wars and two in external wars; two fought more or less unconventional wars, and two conventional. Two were in the pre-, and two in the post-industrial period. Though all are admittedly in the European tradition, that is after all our own, and it is legitimate to suggest in the aftermath of *Shogun* that some of the elements of leadership in other traditions may be so significantly different from ours as to be safely disregarded here.

The Marquis of Montrose

If the Stuart dynasty had been worthy of the devotion it inspired, there would still be a Stuart on the throne of England, and Elizabeth II would be just Mrs. Battenburg. James Graham, Marquis of Montrose, was born in 1612 and educated in Scotland and abroad. As a leading member of the Scottish nobility, he took part in the risings against the introduction of the Anglican prayerbook in Scotland in the 1630s, and was one of the foremost signers of the Solemn League and Covenant. When the Scottish Presbyterians became ever more insistent on their own interpretations of salvation and politics, Montrose drifted openly into the Royalist cause, and in 1644 he came out for Charles I. For the next two years, he routed army after army of Scottish troops, relying on his own brilliance as a tactician and a leader of men. His ultimate inability to hold Scotland for King Charles lay more in Charles's failure, or unwillingness, to support him fully, and Montrose's own lack of resources to overcome the tremendous power of the Campbells, the strongest of the western clans and the most determinedly anti-Stuart, than in any personal failing of his own.

Montrose's tiny army was finally routed in 1646; he himself got away to the Continent, where he remained until after the execution of Charles I. In a last chivalrous gesture, the Marquis returned to Scotland with a forlorn hope; most of his little band was shipwrecked; he himself was betrayed and sold to the Covenanters, and he was hanged in chains in Edinburgh in 1650.

It was a short but glorious career, and ever since its end the story of Montrose has seemed to epitomize all that courage and daring might achieve in the face of great odds. It is the more remarkable in that Montrose had no formal military training, though of course every gentleman of the day, and especially every great lord, was expected to know something of war. Nor did he ever have much in the way of troops. For the most part his army was made up of Irish peasants, often brought over with their families and following their own chiefs, or Scots of the Highland clans who came out for the love of fighting and the hope of booty.

Yet Montrose knew how to get the most from such men; he never asked for more than they could perform, though he asked much indeed of them. He took them into the Great Glen in the midst of winter and harried the Campbell lands when others said it could not be done, and he held his little army together in spite of reverses and the general sinking of the Royalist cause. Nothing typifies the spirit of his leadership more than his performance in his first battle, at Tippermuir. Here, with but 3,000 men, no cavalry and his musketeers down to one round per man, he met a well equipped army of 5,000 horse and foot. The Covenanters spent several hours in prayers and exhortations, but Montrose's speech to his men was short and to the point, and set precisely the right tone:

> Gentlemen! It is true you have no arms; your enemy, however, to all appearance have plenty. My advice therefore is, that as there happens to be a great abundance of stones upon this moor, every man should provide himself in the first place with as stout a one as he can well manage, rush up to the first covenanter he meets, beat out his brains, take his sword, and then I believe, he will be at no loss how to proceed! (Williams, 1975: 155)

The Irish and the Highlanders did exactly that, and when the survivors of the Covenanters fled back to Perth they had lost over 3,000 men; one of Montrose's men was killed, and a second later died of his wounds.

Such disproportionate figures as that would tend to the conclusion that Montrose's lopsided victory was no more than a fluke and that any reasonably resolute force would have defeated the Covenanters. However, Montrose did it again, at Kilsyth, in August of 1645. Once more outnumbered, by three to two this time, he attacked the overconfident Covenanters as they marched across his front. He lost three men; his enemy something more than 6,000. The clansmen and Irish slaughtered their fleeing foes for eighteen miles before they finally stopped from exhaustion.

Yet Montrose himself was not a bloody-minded man. He did his best to avoid the excesses of seventeenth-century warfare, and gave quarter where he could manage to do so. He remained a high-minded gentleman, courteous to his adversaries when he was not actively engaged in killing them, and was the very archetype of all that later Romantics saw as the virtues of the Cavalier party. He was something of a minor poet, too, and spent the night before his execution composing some appropriate lines. Probably best known, though, are the lines from *I'll Never Love Thee More* which have been attributed to him, and which sum up his career and his character as a leader:

> He either fears his fate too much,
> Or his deserts are small,
> That puts it not unto the touch,
> To win or lose it all. (Williams, 1975: 395–396)

Montrose had the conventional upbringing and education of the nobility of his day. His knowledge of warfare was instinctive and intuitive rather than studied, and that indeed remained the norm in the British service until well into the nineteenth century. Except for the scientific arms, engineers, and artillery, the function of British officers was to lead their men and, if necessary, to die well; the bulldog spirit was more important than technical expertise.

This was true of most armies of the eighteenth century, and most soldiers who studied war at all did so because they were interested in it, rather than because such study was a prerequisite for advancement. Knowledge could be an actual impediment in some cases; it was practically that in the career of Alexander Suvorov.

Alexander Suvorov

Born in 1729, the weak and sickly son of a former military officer who transferred into the civil service side of the Russian bureaucracy, Suvorov never wanted to be anything but a soldier. He read voraciously, and pushed his frail body to and beyond its limits. His father, much against his will, enrolled him as a cadet in the Semenovsky Regiment when he was thirteen. That was late for a Russian noble to start his military career—officers were often put on a regiment's list at birth—and Suvorov's rise was extraordinarily slow. He spent years in staff and routine work, and the ordinary chores of garrison duty. Even through the early years of the Seven Years' War he saw no action, though he was present at Kunersdorf in 1759, where Austro-Russians slaughtered half of Frederick the Great's army.

Not until 1761 did Suvorov see independent action, and from that point on he never stopped. His many years of dull service had given him a great contempt for the scheming courtier-soldiers he saw constantly promoted ahead of him, but an even greater love for the Russian soldier, conscripted for life, punished by the knout and the gauntlet, and consistently abused by his superiors. Suvorov understood such men, and empathized with them. He started making his name as a leader of Cossack irregulars, and his commander noted he was "swift in reconnaissance, daring in battle and cold-blooded in danger" (Longworth, 1965: 26).

After the war, as commander of the Suzdal regiment, he rewrote the drill and tactical manuals, and spent his time working up a unit that in spirit and performance resembled Sir John Moore's light infantry more than it did other Russian formations. There was active service in Poland against the armies that tried to reverse the Polish slide toward oblivion and Suvorov enhanced his growing fame particularly by the siege and taking of the fortress of Cracow.

Real glory came to him over the next twenty years as he was almost incessantly campaigning against the Turks in Catherine the Great's wars to expand Russia southward. His success is the more amazing in view of his constant ill health, and before one of his greatest battles, Rymnik, he was too weak to carry his own sword—but not too weak to lead his men personally on an all-night march that set up the victory.

His brilliance lay not only in intensive study allied to native military genius, but in his leadership qualities. More than any Russian before or perhaps since, he had the touch that appealed to his soldiers. On campaign he ate and slept with them, and was more than content with a pile of straw for a bed. This was a period when many Russian officers could not even address their men, having been brought up speaking French, and often those who could would not deign to do so. Suvorov, by contrast, was the common Russian writ large. In a gathering of officers, he looked like a tough weed among a bed of lilies. Regrettably, his popularity with his soldiers cost him both advancement and patronage, for just as he despised most of his fellow generals, he was hated by them. While Catherine lived he was protected, for she had learned to value his deeds more than his manners, but when she died in 1796, he was dismissed abruptly, and not recalled until Russia joined the Second Coalition against France in 1799. After a brilliant campaign in northern Italy, in which he again showed all the qualities that had made him a great soldier, he was caught up in the general Allied defeat in Switzerland, and forced to lead his starving army over the Alps and back to the Danube. Tsar Paul fired him a second time, refused to see him, and he died in disgrace in 1800.

His spirit lived on in the Russian army, however, and the great Encyclopedia Britannica edition of 1911 (Vol. 26: 173) compared the Russian Army to him in its "spirit of self-sacrifice, resolution, and indifference to losses," adding a remark which we would do well to remember in our own time: "In an age when war had become an act of diplomacy, he restored its true significance as an act of force." In 1941 and 1942, when war was universally recognized as being an act of force, Russian patriotic posters showed the ghostly figure of Suvorov, still leading Holy Mother Russia's sons into battle.

Robert E. Lee

Probably no American soldier has ever epitomized the art of leadership more fully than Robert E. Lee. Washington was often aloof, Jackson erratic for all his brilliance, MacArthur and Patton were both perhaps a little too overtly propagandistic to win the unreserved loyalties of their men, but it is safe to say of Lee that he was truly loved. On the Federal side only George H. Thomas approached Lee in this. McClellan came close for awhile, until his men found out he was so solicitous of them that he refused to risk their lives in battle, an apparently ironic fault which soldiers are quicker to perceive as such than members of less dangerous professions.

Where Suvorov was a fierce old war-horse, and a looter and slaughterer of civilians as well, Lee was every inch a gentleman. Few soldiers have ever fought a civil war more chivalrously; Lee was in the peculiar position of having been offered the command of the army against which he was fighting, and he studiously referred to the Federals as "those people," never as "the enemy."

In spite of a brilliant record in the Mexican War and being offered the command of the Union forces, Lee did not do anything outstanding in the Confederate service until after his appointment to command the Army of Northern Virginia in June of 1862. But the new posting proved a happy mating of leader and material. Both still had much to learn, as the following campaigns showed, but they had less to learn than their opponents, and they learned it faster. The result was to produce as nearly perfect a fighting force as the world is ever likely to see again. Consider the battle of Chancellorsville, universally regarded as Lee's masterpiece. Outnumbered by better than two to one, and virtually surrounded at the outset of the battle, he ended it by nearly surrounding his foes and driving them off the field in full retreat. And that against an army that was itself one of the great ones of military history!

Lee's brilliance as a commander was matched and sustained by his leadership of his men, and the love they bore him. Even in, perhaps especially in, defeat this relationship shone forth. After Pickett's immortal failure at Gettysburg, there was little sense that Lee had been wrong in sending the Confederates against the steady Union center. The famous diorama at West Point which shows the Rebels straggling back from their charge, and their officers reporting to Lee, reflects both his anguish at having sent them on such a mission, and theirs at having failed to do what he asked of them— even if flesh and blood could not do it.

Perhaps the most revealing of all episodes of Lee's career, however, is that of the fight at the Bloody Angle at Spottsylvania Court House. That was nearly a year after Gettysburg, and the shadows were gathering around the Confederacy. U.S. Grant had come out of the West to command the Union armies, and he was, as Lincoln said of him, "a man who knew his arithmetic." It was just before Spottsylvania that he wired back to Washington, "Our losses have been heavy, but so have those of the enemy. I propose to fight it out on this line if it takes all summer." Here was no McClellan, husbanding and pampering his troops to no purpose; here was a man who knew that if you killed enough men in grey and butternut brown, eventually there would be no Confederacy, and that was precisely what he intended to do. While that terrible litany of battles went on through the summer, Lee too came to recognize what fate held in store. As Grant slid south toward Richmond, Lee stopped him in the Wilderness, and entrenched next around Spottsylvania Court House, with his line forming an acute angle.

On the morning of 12 May soldiers of Hancock's II Corps swept like a blue tidal wave over the point of that angle, and the life of the Confederacy hung on a single thread. That morning Robert Lee rode among his soldiers, his sword uplifted, and proposed personally to lead the counterattack. His men would not have it, and shouting "General Lee to the rear" they went forward weeping, screaming, and cursing, to die in his place. For the rest of the day Confederates and Union soldiers fought as bitterly as men have ever done over a rotten little abatis. Lee lost one-fifth of his army, and Grant more than a tenth of his, and students who think that war is a matter of computers, or that Americans do not "know their arithmetic," would do well to study the Civil War.

Later, one day when it was all winding down to its sad finish, Lee lamented what might become of his country, and one of his aides interrupted, "General, for the last two years, these men have had no country; you are their country, and what they have fought for."

In the twentieth century, the tasks of leadership at the highest levels of authority have become strangely complicated. On the one hand the simple growth of the population has made it increasingly difficult for a leader to touch all his potential followers; on the other, the development of modern communications methods has made it easier for a leader to project at least an image of himself to vast numbers of people. That, we may all agree, has been a mixed blessing. We have moved rapidly from the era of the newspaper image, early in the century, when the public followed with bated breath the reports of royalty and nobility visiting this fair or launching that battleship, to the era of the radio, when men as diverse as Franklin Roosevelt and Adolf Hitler discovered the uses of the ether for informing or misinforming their constituencies. And we have moved even more rapidly still to the era of the television set, the all-seeing, all-telling eye that dominates our contemporary scene. If, in the age of mass man, the leader has to reach more people than ever before, he has in the instrument of mass communication an unprecedented means of doing so.

Such problems were in their infancy, and but imperfectly perceived, at the time of the First World War. Until 1914 men were convinced that modern masses could meet and overcome any challenge by the application of modern technology. There was then what now looks like a charmingly naive confidence that anything might be achieved. Had not man recently learned to fly? A few years earlier, when the machine gun was developed, writers had praised the new tool as a means by which the savages and natives of backward territories might be civilized and Christianized the more rapidly. That was the era of Samuel Smiles and self-help, and if you believed you could do better, then by golly you could do better.

That complacent confidence had evaporated by 1917. It had been slaughtered on the "corpsefield of Loos," blown apart on the slopes of Vimy Ridge, and ground into the mud on the Somme and Verdun. In April, when General Robert Nivelle led the French armies once more to defeat in the Second Battle of the Aisne, they finally broke and mutinied. It was for France the greatest crisis of the war, and the government resolved it by the appointment of the one man who typified the army's ideal of leadership, General Philippe Petain.

Philippe Petain

Petain had already made his mark several times over the years, and until fairly recently that mark had always been a black one. As a junior officer he had thoroughly identified with his men in the Chasseurs alpins, much as Suvorov had done in an earlier time. Like his famous predecessor, he was as unpopular with his superiors as he was popular with his men, and one of his fitness reports contained the always-quoted remark, "If this officer rises above the rank of major it will be a disaster for France." His chief problem was not his personality, though; it was his studying of modern tactics which led him to fly in the face of accepted French military dogma. In the late nineteenth century the French, falling behind Germany in all the statistics of great power status, convinced themselves that such statistics meant nothing, and that French spirit was irresistible. They adopted the idea of the all-conquering offensive as an article of religious faith, and Ferdinand Foch became its high priest. Petain was the heretic in the congregation. He believed in the superior power of the defensive, and to all paeans on the attack at all costs he replied with a laconic "Fire kills." By 1914 he was a disgruntled colonel, on the verge of retirement.

The outbreak of the war changed all that, and Petain, twelve years a captain, went from colonel to lieutenant-general in three months. He did well at the Marne, got command of the second Army in mid-1915, and a year later his name was a household word, for when the Germans launched the great Verdun offensive, Petain was sent to stop it.

He did so, at enormous cost in men and material. He instituted a rotation system, and it is estimated that 60 percent of the French army passed through the fighting at Verdun at one phase or another of the battle. He organized the supply system, sending an endless chain of men and materials up the *voie sacree*. When the battle finally ended, the French had lost more than a quarter of a million men, but they had held Verdun, and Petain's name, whatever it might become in another war, was irrevocably linked with this greatest of the Third Republic's victories.

So it was that when the army at last refused duty after Nivelle's vainglorious Aisne offensive—a sort of Fredericksburg writ [at] large—Petain was appointed to the supreme command, and set about to restore order and morale. He did so by the simplest of measures: He showed the soldiers that someone in authority was interested in them. That does not seem like much, but it was far more than most French soldiers had received so far in the war.

British writers charge that after Petain the French army was relatively inactive, and took little offensive part in the war. That is certainly true, but the fact derived more from the enormous wastage of the army before Petain took it over; in terms of generalship he did little but recognize reality. That, indeed, had always been his specialty, and accounted for his prewar unpopularity. As a leader, however, as a restorer of morale, a man who empathized with his troops and won their loyalty and respect, he had few equals in the twentieth century. That accounts in large part for the way in which he was greeted as a savior when he assumed power in 1940. His ultimate tragedy was that he lived too long, and the sad later years of his career should not obscure the enormous impact of his leadership on the soldiers of France in 1916, 1917, and 1918.

A Common Thread

All four of these men, in their own time and since, have been acknowledged as masters of the art of leadership. Do these cursory examinations of their careers reveal any general characteristics, from which it is possible to extract some of the essence of leadership? The answer is both yes and no. No, because there tends to be relatively little in common between them except that they were all soldiers, and, of course, great leaders. But the conditions of war under which Petain labored were not very similar to those of Montrose's day, and the personality of a Robert Lee was not very much like that of Suvorov. There are, however, some elements that can be isolated.

Each of these leaders believed in his men, in their power to rise to the heights of endeavor to which he called them. It is often preached that loyalty is a two-way street; unhappily it is less often practiced. The potential leader cannot demand the unswerving loyalty of his followers unless he is willing to return it. If he sees his men only as instruments to further his own career, he is not going to be very successful. Napoleon once remarked to Metternich that he could use up a million men a month, "for what does a man like me care for such as these," but that was after the legend was established, indeed, that was when Napoleon was already on the way down, and events were to prove he could not use up a million men a month. The leader who says, "You must be loyal to me, but I need think only of my next fitness report" will not go far.

These men also believed in a cause which transcended themselves and their own desires or ambitions. Those causes may in our own day be difficult to discern, but that is more our problem than theirs. Montrose believed both in the right of the Stuarts to rule Britain, and in his own concept of freedom of religion. Suvorov served the dynastic state in the person of Catherine the Great. Robert E. Lee believed in the Confederacy, in fact epitomized what was best in it, and Petain was similarly the embodiment of France, the real France of small villages and infinitely tenacious peasantry—in spite of a reputation for frivolity, the French are among the most dour nations on earth—and he inspired the same attitudes in his men.

It is probable that their followers believed less in these causes than they did in the men who led them. Montrose's Irish and Highlanders followed their own lords to war, and were no doubt but dimly aware of the constitutional principles involved in the English Civil War. Suvorov's peasant soldiers were not asked if they cared to aggrandize Russia when they were dragged off to the army for life. It was the humane treatment, the fact that he was actually interested in them, that made them follow Suvorov, and that made him subsequently a Russian legend, for surely there has not been much of that sort of leadership in Russian history since then. For the most part, leadership as practiced in Russia has been of the remote and awe-inspiring—or indeed fear-inspiring—variety.

Charles de Gaulle (1960: 65), who had some considerable professional interest in the problem, commented on this facet of leadership. He wrote between the wars,

It is, indeed, an observable fact that all leaders of men, whether as political figures, prophets, or soldiers, all those who can get the best out of others, have always identified themselves with high ideals. Followed in their lifetime because they stand for greatness of mind rather than self-interest, they are later remembered less for the usefulness of what they have achieved than for the sweep of their endeavors.

It is safe to say that de Gaulle and Bernard Montgomery agreed on little, but they both agreed on that. Montgomery (1961:17) thought that one of the prime requisites for leadership was "selflessness, by which I mean absolute devotion to the cause he serves with no thought of personal reward or aggrandizement."

The student is apt to retort that neither de Gaulle nor Montgomery, both of whom were acknowledged as great leaders, particularly lived up to this requirement. Both of them would insist, in rebuttal, that indeed they had. Both saw themselves, however historians have seen them, as essentially selfless men. Here is de Gaulle (1960: 64) again: "Every man of action has a strong dose of egotism, pride, hardness, and cunning. But all those things will be forgiven him, indeed they will be regarded as high qualities, if he can make of them the means to achieve great ends." He would therefore argue that selflessness does not mean self-abnegation; one may be ruthlessly thrusting and ambitious, provided that ambition is directed in the service of something that is perceived as a greater good, and equally provided that the leader has the ability to convey to his followers the importance of that greater good, and not just his own ambition.

Military history is littered with the names of great and good men who were not quite hard enough, and whose disinclination to get their men killed caused only more suffering in the long run; consider again McClellan's solicitousness for his men, which may well have prolonged the Civil War by years, or Ian Hamilton's reluctance to interfere with his subordinate commanders at Gallipoli, which threw away a campaign that might well have been won on the first day. Some writers maintain that one of the few deficiencies of Sir Harold Alexander as a field commander was his preference for the soft word, and it may have cost him the capture of most of the German army south of Rome in May of 1944. Napoleon summed it up when he sent Brune down to clean up the Vendee in 1800; he told his general it was better to kill ten thousand now, than to be too soft and have to kill a hundred thousand later on.

The leader therefore not only has to believe in his men, and have that belief reciprocated; he has to be able to inspire them to risk their lives for some greater end which they may only very dimly perceive, and he has to have himself the courage to demand that they do so. It is of course in this particular that military leadership differs from other kinds.

As we are now nearly a decade away from an active war, there is a tendency, unfortunate but perhaps inevitable in such periods, to regard military leadership as little different from directing, for example, a large company or a political entity. If a man can run a railroad, he ought to be able to run the United States Army, so we say. This, as it happens, is not the case, though the example of Montrose, moving smoothly from civilian to military leadership in his society, might seem to suggest that it was. In such times as these, we try to repress the knowledge that the military obligation, the "profession of arms," in Sir John Hackett's phrase, demands a greater commitment: It demands, in the last analysis, that men agree to die if necessary in fulfilling their tasks. That is rather a different affair from the possibility of losing one's job if one does not do well. The man who raises his right hand and dons a uniform is saying, in so many words, "I shall perform a certain task, and if necessary I shall put my life on the line to succeed in it." Not many trade unions, and not many managerial staff, would be willing to make that sort of statement (though if they were required to do so, Chrysler might have started making small cars several years ago). If the military leader has the advantage of trained and disciplined followers, he also has the disadvantages of the much higher risks of their profession.

This is not, it appears, an unnecessary laboring of the obvious. In recent years, in spite of having the television bring war into our front rooms, there has been a very real sense of suppression of this basic fact. People are not "killed," they are "wasted," or "terminated" in common parlance, and statisticians succumb to the same impulse that makes undertakers describe people as having "passed away"; bodies at the funeral home are "resting" rather than "dead." It may well be that this is a most unfortunate attitude, and that if there were clearer recognition that someone who is "killed" is "dead," there would be fewer temptations to resort to war as "an extension of politics," a mistaken definition which Clausewitz only too belatedly recognized.

The Problem of War

The problem of war, and of leadership, is that if your soldiers are brought to acknowledge the necessity of achieving their objective or dying in the effort, so are the enemy's. It is that which calls forth the leader's ability to deal with the unforeseen, "the contingent element inseparable from the waging of war [which] gives to that activity both its difficulty and its grandeur" (de Gaulle, 1960: 16). "Whimsy, the irrational or unpredictable event or circumstance, *Fortuna*" (Record, 1980: 19), these are the things that are not susceptible to computer analysis, these are what makes war an art, and therefore leadership an art as well.

There are of course those parts of the trade, or art, that can be studied, and therefore learned. There have been few great leaders who were not knowledgeable about the mechanics of the business; you cannot be an inspiring leader if you neglect the logistics that feed your men. They will not give you their confidence if you forget to bring up the reserve ammunition, or if you leave them with no way out of an ambush, or even if you consistently schedule two columns to use the same crossroads at the same time. All of that level of operation is subject to scientific principles, and can be taught. Any reasonably intelligent person can learn the routine of siting a battery, or even of administering a battalion. One can go very far on basic managerial skills, and one cannot do much without them. One of the difficulties, in fact, of dealing with the question of leadership is the tendency not to distinguish between the aspects of it that relate to making sound military decisions, and the aspects that relate to leading men in battle. The last people to insist that science was nothing, art and spirit were all, were the French military advocates of *l'attaque a l'outrance*, the *furia francese*, before World War I, and all they managed to do was kill off the better part of their army in the first couple of weeks of the war, as Petain had all too accurately foreseen. It has been pointed out that if Waterloo was won on the playing fields of Eton, Gallipoli and Singapore were also lost there.

It would therefore again be a mistake to insist on too wide a cleavage between science and art, and to say that either one was all, the other nothing. Every aspect of life has elements of both in it. To repeat the example above, there is an art to siting a battery, but it must be done on scientific principles, as the British discovered when they tried to unlimber within range of the Boer rifle pits at Colenso; they lost 1,100 men, and ten out of twelve of their guns, for a Boer loss of less than fifty. The higher elements of leadership remain an art, though the lesser ones can be learned scientifically, can be treated, as it were, by artifice.

Ironically, the better times are, the less artifice works, and the more art is needed. We live in what is undeniably the most prosperous society that has ever existed, with better conditions for more people than has so far been possible in human history. Artifice does not work, because our servicemen are for the most part sufficiently intelligent and sophisticated to see through it. Our society has become so free that preoccupation with freedom as an end in itself has led us to neglect the responsibilities and the obligations that have always been thought to accompany it. No state in history has been able to say to its citizens that they need not, if they do not choose, take any part in defending the unit against the outside world. Most states resorted to conscription of a sort; even Britain, if for two centuries it had no obligatory service, had the press gang when necessary, which was a type of lottery conscription: If you happened to be in the wrong place at the wrong time, you got caught. The United States, however, has only rarely in its history had to resort to a form of conscription that was always far more selective than it was universal. In recent years we have based our security forces on the thesis that enough money will answer our needs, and that if we pay our servicemen sufficiently, they will continue to be servicemen in spite of the siren song of civilian life, a thesis which does not seem, by and large, to be proving correct. The nature of the obligation, once again, and the constraints of military life, are such that even our society does not produce sufficient to pay enough men enough money to fulfill our needs.

To this fact that prosperity breeds a disinclination for the military life must be added the further one that our recent experience has not been such as to enhance the prestige and morale of the military forces. Our position in this respect is summed up, oddly enough, by de Gaulle (1960: 71–72) writing about France after World War I:

> The aversion felt for war in general has crystallized around the army. This is an anthropomorphic phenomenon of the same kind as that which makes us dread the dentist even more than the toothache.... But the mystique of our times must not be allowed to discourage or to humiliate those who wield the sword of France. What better guarantee can be offered to a people gorged with good things, looked at from abroad with embittered resentment, and whose frontiers are so drawn that a single lost battle may put its very capital in jeopardy, than the efficiency of its armed forces.

It is perfectly normal that after a period of unhappy foreign adventuring Americans should prefer to remain at home, that after a long wasting war which was actively opposed by a substantial portion of the population the military services, the most visible target for both fiscal retrenchment and public resentment, should be unpopular. But such attitudes, now hopefully diminishing in the face of returning awareness that there still is a world out there, and that it is not a very friendly one, make the task of leadership, and the exercise of it, all the more difficult.

The more difficult such leadership becomes, the more it requires skill approaching art. One is still left with the problem of precisely what that is, or how to inculcate it into one's potential leaders. But this is by no means a new problem. Ever since society departed, somewhere in the last century, from a stratified system in which certain persons were thought by right of birth to be capable of exercising leadership, men have attempted to grapple with it. Lord Palmerston, when pressed to support the idea of examinations for the civil and military service, wrote to a friend. "Success at an examination is certainly not a decisive proof of Fitness for official employment, because after all, examination is chiefly a test of memory acting upon previous Study, and there are other qualities besides Memory and Studious Habits required to make a Good official Man" (Ridley, 1972: 683).

How to produce the Good official Man, or how to recognize him, has remained one of the besetting problems of our time. If we believe, as our whole history attests we do, in the career open to talent, then talent must be recognizable and rewarded as such. But how to recognize it, and how to cut through the "media hype" that tries to convince us today that a man can walk on water, and the day after he is elected or put in command that he cannot walk at all?

De Gaulle (1960: 127), again, groped for a solution. "Enlightened views and supreme wisdom," he said,

> . . . are all a matter of intuition and character which no decree can compel, no instruction can impart. Only flair, intelligence and above all, the latent eagerness to play a part which alone enables a man to develop ability and strength of character, can be of service. It all comes to this, that nothing great will ever be achieved without great men, and men are great only if they are determined to be so.

"Intuition," "character," "flair," "greatness through determination to be great," all these are unsatisfactory to the social scientist as explanations of why men do the things they do. They are, in other words, in the province of art. Leadership remains the most baffling of the arts, and in spite of all the tricks that supposedly make it manageable, it will remain that way. As long as we do not know exactly what makes men get up out of a hole in the ground and go forward in the face of death at a word from another man, then leadership will remain one of the highest and most elusive of qualities. It will remain an art.

References

De Gaulle, C., *The Edge of the Sword* (G. Hopkins, trans.), New York: Criterion, 1960.

Encyclopedia Britannica, "Suvarov" (vol. 26), Cambridge: Cambridge University Press, 1911, pp. 172–173.

Guedalla, P., *Men of War*, London: Hodder and Stoughton, 1923.

Longworth, P., *The Art of Victory*, New York: Holt, Rinehart & Winston, 1965.

Montgomery, B., *The Path to Leadership*, London: Collins, 1961.

Record, J., "The Fortunes of War," *Harper's* (April 1980), pp. 19–23.

Ridley, J., *Lord Palmerston*, London: Panther, 1972.

Williams. R., Montrose, *Cavalier in Mourning*, London: Barrie and Jenkins, 1975.

14

A Charismatic Dimension
of Military Leadership?

*David M. Keithly and
James J. Tritten*

> *Don't confuse charisma with a loud voice.*[1]
> —Harvey Mackay

Over the years the charisma motif has surfaced and resurfaced in discussions of leadership. The term "charisma" continues frequently to be used in an imprecise, even ambiguous manner, referring in a somewhat grab-bag fashion to anyone with flair, flamboyance, or popular appeal. Partly as a result, inquiries into the subject remain regrettably limited in scope. The aim of this article is to determine the various meanings of charisma in the literature, with an eye to ascertaining the distinctive implications for military leadership. Notwithstanding the substantial amounts of literature on charismatic leadership, this remains largely uncharted territory. We endeavor here to integrate psychological, situational, cultural, and other factors customarily identified as consequential in examinations of charisma.

The German Army harbored a keen interest in charisma. Early in this century, Baron Hugo von Freytag-Loringhoven observed: "A great general is able to substitute his own personality in the eyes of his soldiers for their home country . . . In the long years of war the soldier finds a second home in the camp; and as a substitute for patriotism he has his esprit de corps and

The views expressed are the authors' own.
Reprinted by permission from *Journal of Political and Military Psychology*, 25:1, pp. 131–146.

his enthusiastic loyalty for his great leader."[2] At the same time, von Freytag-Loringhoven noted that the tendency to extreme centralization under a charismatic leader has a detrimental effect on the development of subordinates. Recently, the U.S. Armed Forces have embraced W. Edwards Deming's concept of Total Quality Management/Leadership (TQM/TQL), which advocates, above all, participatory leadership vis-á-vis more traditional forms of transactional leadership. As the Services describe it, TQM/TQL requires the adoption of a "positive, progressive" leadership style that encourages subordinates to come forward with ideas and initiatives.[3]

Recent research has demonstrated that charismatic properties can be taught with the result that subordinates tend to perform better and maintain a greater degree of job satisfaction. One experiment indicated that leaders exhibiting charismatic behavior in the supervision of a control group were able to elicit greater productivity.[4] The leaders in this case were professional actors who received thirty hours of training in charismatic behavior traits and used the same words to define work tasks to both groups. Such use of hired actors in laboratory experiments has significantly demystified charisma. Devising a controlled environment to study charismatic personalities is feasible, of course, only under specialized conditions. This circumstance occasioned Robert J. House to observe that most theoretical notions of charisma in the sociological or political science literature have not been subjected to sufficient empirical testing.[5] In fact, little historical material on charismatic leaders exists, although one can partially compensate for this by studying biographical information and placing the leaders in a particular context.

It is somewhat ironic that charisma is frequently associated with an office, not an individual. A new organization, where institutional norms have yet to be formed, are among the most likely sites for charisma's surfacing.[6] Followers, asked to share dreams of what could be, are inclined to vest founders with charisma. Traditionally, religious and military organizations have done much to create a charismatic aura for senior leaders. The charisma associated with religious and military offices, or that fashioned in individuals, may be only a substitute for natural charisma. Impression overshadows substance: what followers perceive as charisma becomes genuine for them. Since what really matters in practice is the willingness on the part of followers to accept leadership demeanor as charismatic, a fresh set of rigorously defined characteristics of charismatic leadership is unwarranted. Charisma must be understood in terms of adherents' cognizance and responses, not by what leaders are, nor even by what they perceive themselves to be, but by how followers come to regard them. Effect defines charisma.

Should charismatic leadership be nurtured? The short answer is a qualified "no." The record of charismatic combat leaders is in fact dubious: their actual contributions have been prodigiously inflated with the passage of time. Often, charismatic combat leaders have caused difficulties for the governments they served. Many military officers who cannot reasonably be described as charismatic were simply good leaders who served their country well in time of war. From a careful review of the literature, one would be hard-pressed to make the case that charismatic military leadership is opportune, either in a combat or non-combat environment. If anything, the evidence indicates that charismatic leaders are more trouble than they are worth. Be that as it may, since charisma is a facet of leadership, it is nonetheless worth inquiring how certain aspects of it can be forged through selection, promotion, and training.

Charisma and Authority

The first methodical study of charisma was conducted by the German sociologist Max Weber early in this century and published in the 1920s.[7] Weber took the concept from the Greek, which was used in the literature of early Christianity to refer to "the gift of grace." Charismatic authority, Weber argued, has a mystical quality, clothing a leader with power to captivate people.[8] Charisma has functioned as a cornerstone of religious communities and military structures. In a more contemporary analysis, David Easton holds that, in organizations where the behavior and personalities of the occupants of the authority role are of dominating importance, the basis of legitimacy may be highly personal. He submits that leaders engendering legitimacy through their persons are sometimes able to transgress prescribed molds, to be inattentive to usual arrangements.[9]

While the term "authority" generally refers to the regime ruling a particular group or society, legitimacy involves the ability of those wielding power to establish their right to do so. Leaders sufficiently devoid of legitimacy are at an impasse to wield power effectively. Easton identifies three types of legitimacy: personal, ideological, and structural. In the first case, a strong, charismatic personality fosters legitimacy for a particular regime. In the second, a popular commitment to principles and/or to a *Weltanschauung* might provide legitimacy. The third, the most enduring source and the one most closely resembling Weber's "right rules of the game," entails prevalent public deference to political processes. Weber stated that societies usually pass through a sequence of three types of legitimate authority: (1) charismatic; (2) traditional; and (3) rational/legal.

Whereas bureaucracies and organizational structures operating within certain parameters generally underpin traditional and rational/legal authority, religious communities and military *camaraderie* based upon charisma differ. Charismatic authority involves a special two-way relationship between followers and the leader in accordance with different and nontraditional patterns that leaders impart. Charismatic authority thus derives not from the office or status of the leader, but instead from the capacity of individual leaders to inspire the confidence on the part of others that itself is a source of legitimacy. Leadership must exist to some extent in each of Weber's three different categories of authority. Traditional and rational/legal forms of authority are not precluded from having leaders with strong charismatic traits.

Charismatic leadership, in its purest form, involves hero worship, whereby followers respond to a leader's authority in ways very different from that of rational/legal and traditional leaders. This relationship is tantamount to being on stage, but inattentive to the audience: the stage dialogue is between the leader and himself. The follower assumes the role of spectator, one oblivious to the separation between leader and led. The follower's intellect and emotions are no longer distinct.[10]

Observers have identified four major differences between charismatic leaders and traditional or rational/legal leaders.[11] The first is that followers attribute to the charismatic leader qualities commonly associated within that culture to be spiritual or preternatural. Second, statements and ideas of the charismatic leader are accepted by followers, often unconditionally, by virtue of the leader's having proffered these. Ideas are not first scrutinized for truth. Third, followers comply because they have been given a command by the leader—no other reason is necessary and the task need not be evaluated first. Fourth, followers respond emotionally to the leaders and, by extension, to his vision or doctrine, in a manner close to religious worship—devotion, awe, reverence, and blind faith.[12] Therefore, charisma is a special subtype of leadership involving personal qualities and interpersonal relationships between the leader and the follower that are not found in the general population of leaders.

Pure charismatic leaders in history are fairly rare. Those who have successfully mastered charisma in combination with ideological guidance constitute another group. According to Easton, ideologies are to be regarded as "categories of thought to corral the energies of men"; from an expressive viewpoint, one should consider them as "ideals capable of rousing and inspiring men to action thought to be related to their achievement." To its champions, Marxism-Leninism represented a systematic declaration of values and ideals. Hence, the symbiosis of ideology and charisma.

The lack of definitional criteria for determining who is charismatic, coupled with a desire on the part of many political leaders to claim charismatic status, complicates analysis. Because of the penchant of political leaders to portray themselves as charismatic, academic literature seldom addresses the question whether charisma can be created. Sociologists emphasize that charismatic leadership is situation-dependent, whereby a crisis often serves as the vehicle of the leader's ascent. That said, most observers agree that leadership style is substantially situation-dependent. Political scientists who want to review crises during which charismatic leaders have emerged usually fail to find a logical causal nexus and hence seldom concern themselves with such queries. Psychologists tend to look at the critical inter-personal relationships between leader and follower, or attempt to correlate personality traits with biographical experiences. Psychological studies of charisma usually have as a point of departure the notion that needy followers attempt to resolve inner conflicts between who they are and who they wish to become. Thus do followers substitute the charismatic leader for their own ideal. Social psychology and organizational theory approaches are predisposed to emphasize the attraction that followers have for the person and abilities of the charismatic leader. Organizational theorists often explore the role that the charismatic leader plays within an organization. The follower is depicted as being in awe of the leader's vision, communications skills, and ability to motivate and empower subordinates. Historians are perhaps most disposed to use the term unclearly, making reference to anyone with a flair for leadership or exhibiting unusual leadership qualities.

For the most part, studies of charisma have focused on political and religious leaders who have emerged from societies in crisis, when trust waned and the legitimacy of institutions abraded. Accordingly, charismatic leaders have generally, but not always, been agents of change. When challengers succeed in altering the existing order, they often claim popular support to effect that change, and in doing so, submit that their authority is charismatic.

Leadership treatises for business schools and aspiring managers continue to appear in large numbers.[13] Those dealing with charismatic leadership, like many previous studies, are frequently based on speeches and autobiographical writings. Moreover, these seldom accept the standard academic notions of charisma, using the term rather loosely by ascribing this trait to anyone who masters change and is perceived as "revolutionary" within an organization. Indeed, the studies usually question whether the "evolutionary" leader can be charismatic.

One of the more consequential findings in recent management literature is that charismatic leaders are not cost-free. Analyses of combat leaders such as Horatio Nelson have drawn similar conclusions.[14] The dark side of charismatic managers can cause their businesses major problems. For example, the dark side may skew the manager's vision of the future, or the person may be blinded by sheer ambition. Vision, though, is a function of insight; charisma is not. The charismatic leader is inclined to lose contact with followers corrupted by selfish ends and to eschew the feedback necessary to adjust goals in rapidly changing circumstances.

Equally disconcerting, business leaders exhibiting forceful charismatic traits have a strong propensity to foist personal demands and beliefs on constituents. They can quickly lose touch with the marketplace. They tend to be overly critical of others, but loath to recognize their own flaws. Charismatic leaders are known to misuse their considerable communications abilities to manipulate groups and organizations, the personal power to control others being a strong draw. They are often impulsive, autocratic, inattentive to details. Their management styles can foster alienation and rivalries and, as discussed below, charismatic leadership is usually unstable, at odds with its own foundation.

Yet, assisted by capable supporting staffs, business leaders with charismatic traits display a keen sense of strategic opportunity, similar to what Napoleon referred to as *coup d'oeil*, the inner eye's ability to assess a situation rapidly and to master it.[15] They are the ones most likely to take the risks necessary to achieve objectives. Studies show how organizations can deal with these flaws. Strong staffs sustained by proper management training and socialization can mitigate negative consequences. In some cases, businesses are simply willing to bear the burdens associated with charismatic leaders.

Strategic vision in the business sense is largely the product of an incremental process that in turn derives from past experiences, creative insights, opportunity, and not least, serendipity. As a rule, leaders with vision become adept in their respective businesses relatively early in their careers and consequently develop an intuitive sense about the enterprise's needs. Many are able to avail themselves of innovative ideas on offer and have had sufficient occasion to experiment. The result is often greater receptiveness to creativity.

Many business people face markets and technology that are largely beyond their control, notwithstanding their accurate assessments and their determination to shape events. When competent leaders sense an opportunity and are able to seize upon it, they may then be credited with having not only intuition, but charisma. Business literature describes intuition as the ability to synthesize diverse information, weed out the irrelevant, and visualize what remains. This is *coup d'oeil*. In an innovative and creative environment, the positive side of the charismatic leader often presents itself. The charismatic leader accepts uncertainty and is usually enamored of unconventional approaches. As a consequence, charismatic leaders are potential catalysts of change; frequently instrumental to the creation of new organizations.

With an eye to gleaning lessons for the private sector, the business world has demonstrated its recent interest here in military leadership. Business schools continue to borrow examples from the military and devote considerable attention to assorted types and styles of leadership. Analytical focus upon leaders within the context of their following is clearly a forte of the business school approach to leadership study. Much current management literature indicates that military organizations have been doing basically the same job for centuries. But should one study competitive, ambitious, or charismatic business leaders in order to assess the value of charisma in military combat leadership? Although combat leadership, certainly combat command, is usually more demanding than non-combat leadership, the same traits are critical in both situations. This is not to say that the successful non-combat leader will automatically make a good combat leader, or vice versa. Leading in combat can differ hugely from leading in peacetime. Any non-combat environment changes radically once the combat threshold has been crossed.

Training and education programs of the U.S. Armed Forces often fail to differentiate combat from non-combat leadership, though. This is regrettable, but the military seldom has the luxury of time to switch from non-combat to combat leadership. In the politically volatile world of the 21st century, in which the military will be involved in an increasing array of operations, with very different mission profiles, failure to distinguish between types of leadership could become a more salient problem. U. S. Army Field Manual 22-100 (FM 22-100), entitled *Military Leadership*, states: "Because of the increasing complexity of the world environment, we must prepare to respond across the entire spectrum of conflict." Yet, the military neglects to consider the ensuing ramifications for leadership. Largely by deliberate decision, it remains predisposed to avoid drawing crucial leadership distinctions, or dovetailing leadership skills to various military operations. Again, FM 22-100: "The purpose of leader development is to develop leaders capable of maintaining a trained and ready Army in peacetime to deter war, to fight and control wars that do start, and to terminate wars on terms favorable to US and allied interests." This fails even to address the problem, much less to resolve any leadership dilemmas.

TQL, characterized chiefly by empowerment of subordinates, involves leadership methods more appropriate in non-combat and low-stress environments, not in combat situations.[16] True, military doctrine underscores the importance of "decentralized execution," that is, the empowerment of subordinates. The command method known generally as *Auftragstaktik* has an undisputed place in Western military thinking. *Auftragstaktik* hinges on decentralized leadership, emboldening commanders to make their own decisions in fast-moving *combat* environments. That is just the point: this command method is one suited to high-stress, conflict circumstances.

Business schools have demonstrated a far greater ability to recognize crucial leadership distinctions. Above all, they are more apt than the Armed Forces to discuss and analyze the enduring quandaries of leadership. Studies of leadership under stressful conditions counsel that groups faced with crisis tend to shift their loyalties from a participatory-style leader to one more forceful and decisive.[17] Should the Armed Forces come to accept the critical differences between combat and non-combat leadership, then presumably they would alter professional training and education curricula where appropriate. They would also embrace mentoring programs, for instance, and introduce special notations on evaluations of combat leaders.

Follower perception, the fundamental determinant of the charismatic leader, on occasion leaves the field open to manipulation. So long as the leader can establish and maintain this special relationship, charisma can be said to exist. In seeking evidence of a charismatic presence, one should not closely scrutinize the leader's attributes, nor, as mentioned above, the leader's perception of himself, but instead focus on the responses of followers. Insofar as the path of charismatic leadership is this special two-way relationship, it is evident why leaders have engaged, for example, in image-building through the media. They are endeavoring to create charisma. Since charismatic leadership ensues primarily from the perceptions of followers, charisma is not only situation- but also culture-dependent.[18] Thus, although Peter the Great might have been charismatic in Russia at a particular time, he would have been less successful in another context. Hitler's rule of Germany is one of the most situationally dependent examples of charismatic leadership of all time: given different circumstances he would not have attained the powers he did. Hitler or Stalin exercising charismatic authority in another cultural context staggers belief. Furthermore, social-cultural contexts have profound impact upon the very concept of the charismatic leader. Japan, for example, has a strong tradition of downplaying individual leaders. Although the victory of Admiral Tôgô Heihachiro at Tsushima in 1905 led to his elevation to the status of national hero, officers of the Imperial Japanese Navy (IJN) did not accord much special recognition. Situation- and culture-dependency underscores the absence of a single charismatic personality type.

The Charismatic Personality

Any serious examination of the charismatic personality must continue to direct attention to the relationship of the follower with the leader. This relationship encompasses an emotional, spiritual, or non-rational feeling the follower harbors for the leader. It, not the leaders themselves, must be the focal point of the study. Charismatic leaders have been described as having exceptionally high levels of self-confidence, a need to influence, with an attendant ability to dominate, and a strong conviction in the moral righteousness of their beliefs. Some researchers have attempted to trace the roots of charismatic personalities either to very close childhood bonds with parents, which bestowed on them the self-confidence to be creative and self-reliant, or to the untimely death of parents, resulting in a drive to compensate for the loss.[19] They usually exhibit the following attributes: goal articulation, role modeling, personal image building, extraordinary self-motivation, compassion, as well as dynamic, resourceful, and responsive competence that rebels against authority and tradition, sometimes in the name of a group the leader values. Such individuals have exceptional skills of self-expression and are adept at nonverbal cues. They tend to possess considerable insight and are often untroubled by internal conflict.[20] Most are able to articulate a vision and to communicate aspirations that heighten the self-esteem of followers. In light of the lingering ambiguities and the attendant lack of criteria of acceptability, some scholars urge the use of a new expression, one suggestive of charisma but with a wider sweep. This is transformational leadership.

Transformational Leadership

Bernard M. Bass offers several contributions.[21] He argues that most studies involve styles of leadership in which leaders reward subordinates for services rendered, that is, "transactional" leadership. He suggests a new type of leader should be examined and that a model for educating leaders, to include military leaders, accordingly be developed. This new model is that of the transformational leader, first expounded by James MacGregor Burns in his pioneering book *Leadership*.[22] The transformational leader is one who articulates a reasonable vision of the future that can be shared and understood by subordinates, but at the same time empowers the group to act. Inspired by the charismatic-like transformational leader, followers accomplish more because they have a clearer vision of what needs to be done and consequently exert extra effort.

A 1986 management treatise *The Transformational Leaders*[23] further developed Burns's ideas. Noel M. Tichy and Mary Anne Devanna employ business case studies to produce their own transformational leadership concepts. Instrumental to these is right brain visioning. A list of transformational leadership characteristics includes: (1) self-identity as agents of change; (2) courage; (3) belief in people; (4) avowal to be value-driven; (5) commitment to life-long learning; (6) skill in dealing with complexity, ambiguity, and uncertainty; and (7) vision with an ability to translate this so others can share in the change process.

Bass argues that attaining charisma in the eyes of one's subordinates is central to the transformational leadership process. Charisma provides followers with a vision, a sense of mission they can appreciate. Followers then have faith in the leader and abet his focus of effort. Bass's research supports the conclusion that organizations receive higher payoffs when leaders articulate a shared vision of the future in a manner that arouses confidence and commitment. In like manner, Peter Senge underscores the linkage between charisma and shared vision, noting that the latter is one of the five cornerstones of what he terms the "learning organization."[24] Transformational leaders tend to thrive in an atmosphere of innovation and creativity and are more likely to emerge in times of stress and disorganization.

Bass synthesized surveys in which hundreds of business people, academicians, government leaders, and senior U.S. Army officers were evaluated by subordinates. He also conducted a study of U.S. Navy officers that likewise used assessments by peers and subordinates.[25] The results of other researchers employing the transformational leadership paradigm to evaluate U.S. Navy officers correspond closely to those of Bass.[26] Inherent to the TQM/TQL process is the empowerment of subordinates, a component of transformational leadership Bass endorses. Transformational leadership in turn includes a charismatic element. But the Services do not clarify what role transformational leadership assumes in TQM/L.

Transformational leaders tend to display concern for individuals within the organization and to spur subordinates intellectually by enabling them look at problems a new way. Empowerment as a means to attain goals is instrumental to transformational leadership. In sharp contrast to the charismatic leader, the transformational leader stresses innovative problem-solving. Recent studies have investigated why so many business leaders believe they are empowering subordinates, yet fail to understand enough about themselves and their respective organizations to know that they are not.[27] One scholar postulated that, in some cases, the pure charismatic leader does not empower his followers at all.[28]

Command Leadership

Few studies of military leaders have aspired to apply theoretical work on charisma to a specific military situation. One recent work that does is Garry Wills's examination of King David of Israel.[29] Wills utilizes one of the historical examples of charismatic leaders that Weber identified, one who is also perchance a military commander.[30] In King David a sympathetic model of a charismatic leader suggests itself.

King David stood outside the regular forms of authority. The ultimate test of this leader's charismatic authority was, of course, the followers' response. Was he a basically sympathetic figure in contrast to recent, less savory examples, such as Stalin, Hitler, or Castro? Clearly so. Was he a successful military leader? This he was as well. What drawbacks are most apparent? First, his authority, as with all authority, is subject to what Weber described as *Veralltäglichung* ("everydaying" or "routinization"). When charismatic authority reaches this point—King David's leadership was no exception—it must resort to other, more banal means to exercise power. Because the leader did not attain power by traditional accord or legal compact, authority necessarily wanes through routinization. As Wills puts it, the tired charismatic leader must resort to procedures that are anything but charismatic; in extreme cases, to secret police, spies, and executions. Should the reigns of terror that have periodically taken place in history, often in association with charismatic leaders, come as any great surprise?

In King David's case, despite a long and enlightened rule, he was unable to bequeath a united kingdom to an heir. In this botch, Wills argues is to be found the grimmest lesson of charismatic leadership. Specifically, it tends to be short-lived, not in accord with its own fundaments. Since charismatic leadership has an essential transcendental or spiritual element, any failure invariably and substantially undermines authority.[31]

Charismatic leaders evince heartfelt messages, or proffer visions of the future. It stands to reason that new doctrines or paradigms developed by a charismatic leader flow from the top down and are generally devoid of follower participation. Charismatic leaders are assumed to be able to ascertain the needs of followers and to deliver the message the latter want to hear. The message and vision of a charismatic leader have frequently, but not always, sprung from a climate of crisis and originated from leaders willing to challenge the existing order with new ideas. Such processes do not describe military doctrinal development in the U.S., although these may point to the role played by visionary military leaders attempting to introduce new technologies or ideas into the bureaucracy from a position within the organization. Doctrine has often changed with the introduction of new technologies, and doctrinal development can play a role in facilitating revolutionary change within the military.

Charismatic leadership theory portrayed the leader as an outsider, until historical evidence indicated that revolutionary forces can exist within organizations.[32] Although Hyman Rickover, the founder of the U.S. Navy's nuclear submarine force, repudiated the need for charismatic leaders, adding parenthetically that he himself had the charisma of a chipmunk, he did nonetheless have a special relationship with his followers. His uncommon facility to motivate others and his faith in his own authority as the sole source of legitimacy were attributes indicative of charismatic leadership. Since Rickover was not a combat leader, his case suggests the occurrence of both combat and non-combat instances of charisma in the military.

Studies of effective naval combat leaders during World War II disclose an evident lack of charisma. Raymond A. Spruance, for example, was one of the best known and most successful combat leaders of the Pacific War. Spruance's biography, entitled *The Quiet Warrior*, depicts Spruance as a dogged warrior but also as an intensely private individual, unconcerned with image, oblivious to his portrayal in history. Spruance was no charismatic leader.

Another case is that of Willis A. "Ching" Lee. Lee also was an effective combat leader in the Pacific theater of World War II. Commanding the fast battleships during most major engagements, he was an innovative thinker, determining, for instance, how to employ radar most productively in combat. Lee was scarcely a charismatic or pugnacious warrior: he usually is described as a scientist in uniform. His area of expertise before war was anti-aircraft gunnery. In 1944, he returned to the U.S. to direct work on defenses against *kamikaze* attacks. His organization eventually grew into the Operational Test and Evaluation Force (OPTEVFOR).

Here one might offer a few common-sense observations. Vision and insight, indispensable aspects of charisma, are facets of effective leadership. Vision and insight are indicators of the ability to conceptualize. Meeting the challenges of operational combat requires both insight and the mastery of execution. Insight derives from a willful receptiveness to a variety of stimuli from intellectual curiosity (although intellect itself does not guarantee insight), from observation and reflection, from continuous evaluation and testing, from conversations and discussions, from a review of assumptions, from listening to the views of outsiders, from a study of history, and from the indispensable ingredient of humility. Obstacles to insight are many: one's own propaganda, acceptance of the conventional wisdom, superficial thinking, blindness to reality, self-satisfaction, complacency, and arrogance.

It is notable that the U.S. Army conducted a study of the tactical proficiency of combat leadership during World War II, comparing the effectiveness of twenty-four representative divisions in the European theater—twelve German, five British, and seven American.[33] These divisions were rated in order of battlefield effectiveness; the top ten divisions were further analyzed. Nine of the top ten divisions were German, the only non-German division being the 88th Infantry Division of the U.S. Army. The 88th was commanded by a nondescript, non-charismatic group of leaders, the unit itself having been formed "from scratch" when mobilization began. The 88th's success was attributed to good training, but above all, to leaders with a vision of what would constitute a good military organization prior to combat.

The overall superior quality of the 88th's leadership was the essential component the U.S. Army found in each of these top-rated divisions in the European theater. These leaders showed:[34] (1) considerable capacity for independent action; (2) the determination to adhere to the mission,—i.e., a moral obligation to operate in the spirit of the assigned mission; (3) avoidance of a fixed pattern of action; (4) the facility to make clear and unambiguous decisions; (5) the ability to establish a definite point of main effort; (6) a constant concern for the welfare of their troops; (7) the preservation of combat efficiency. In sum, these are tenets of good leadership. Little evidence of charisma presents itself in the study. One might allow, however, that few German general officers were perceived as charismatic by their troops.

Conclusion

Charismatic combat leadership warrants future study. If analysts are in the main correct about the types of wars that will become prevalent in the future, then U.S. Armed Forces will increasingly face non-traditional forces, including militias, guerrillas and terrorists. New enemies require new thinking and non-traditional operations require fresh leadership techniques. Hence, the importance of understanding such things as charismatic and transformational leadership.

A common premise of most theories of charisma is that followers, not leaders, are the chief determinants of charisma's existence. Here we have stipulated that charismatic leadership entails an interpersonal relationship defined by the follower in which the leader is thought to have an extraordinary, even a preternatural status. Ideas and orders of the leader are accepted without question merely because they were issued by the leader, not his office, and an emotional bond, approaching the irrational, is extant between follower and leader. We have not sought to ascertain how charismatic leaders might view the world (a study has yet to do this), but have addressed the paramount question: should military organizations endeavor to recruit, cultivate, promote, or retain such individuals?

The appearance of charismatic leaders during crises suggests they are frequently change agents.

Charisma may coexist, however uneasily, with traditional and rational/legal authority. Purely charismatic leaders seem to score initial successes, most often in new organizational settings. But, as Weber observed, charismatic authority is ephemeral, prone either to become routine or be transfigured into another form of authority. Largely because of their inability to think or act beyond the constraints of their charismatic qualities, such leaders are, in effect, ultimately trapped by their own charisma.

Notes

1. Jonathan Lazear, *Meditations for Men Who Do Too Much* (New York: Fireside/Parkside Meditation Book, Simon and Schuster, 1992), p. 25.

2. Major General Baron Hugo von Freytag-Loringhoven, "The Power of Personality in War," in *Roots of Strategy*, Book 3 (Harrisburg, PA: Stackpole Books, 1991).

3. See John L. Byron, "Welcome to the Revolution," *U.S. Naval Institute Proceedings*, 117, no. 10 (October 1991), pp. 32–33.

4. Jane M. Howell and Peter J. Frost, "A Laboratory Study of Charismatic Leadership," in *Organizational Behavior and Human Decision Processes*, 43 (1989), pp. 243–269.

5. Robert J. House, "A 1976 Theory of Charismatic Leadership," in James G. Hunt and Lars L. Larson, eds., *Leadership: The Cutting Edge* (Carbondale: Southern Illinois University Press, 1977), p. 190.

6. Ronald A. Heifetz, *Leadership Without Easy Answers* (Cambridge, MA: Harvard University Press, 1994), pp. 64–66.

7. Max Weber, *The Theory of Social and Economic Organization*, A. M. Henderson, trans., Talcott Parsons, ed. (London: The Free Press of Glencoe, 1947) (originally published in Germany in 1924), esp. pp. 106, 265, 328, 364–366.

8. Quoted in Garry Wills, *Certain Trumpets: The Call of Leaders* (New York: Simon and Schuster, 1994), p. 290.

9. David Easton, *A System Analysis of Political Life* (Chicago: University of Chicago Press, 1979), pp. 302–303.

10. Abraham Zaleznik and Manfred F. R. Kets de Vries, *Power and the Corporate Mind* (Boston: Houghton Mifflin, 1975), pp. 246–247.

11. Ann Ruth Willner, *The Spellbinders: Charismatic Political Leadership* (New Haven, CT: Yale University Press, 1984), pp. 5–8.

12. David Apter, *The Politics of Modernization* (Chicago: University of Chicago Press, 1965), pp. 266–267.

13. Jay A. Conger, Rabindra N. Kanungo, and Associates, *Charismatic Leadership: The Elusive Factor in Organizational Effectiveness* (San Francisco: Jossey-Bass Publishers, 1989); and Jay A. Conger, *The Charismatic Leader: Behind the Mystique of Exceptional Leadership* (San Francisco: Jossey-Bass Publishers, 1989).

14. For example: Charles Benedict Davenport, *Naval Officers: Their Heredity and Development* (Washington, DC: The Carnegie Institution, 1919); and Alfred Thayer Mahan, *Types of Naval Officers: Drawn from the History of the British Navy* (Boston: Little, Brown and Co., 1918).

15. Karl von Clausewitz, *On War*, O. J. Matthijis Jolles, trans. (New York: The Modern Library, 1943), pp. 33–35.

16. John E. Hassen, Carol F. Denton, Fred Reis, and John R. Ronchetto, "Navy Leadership Lessons from Operation Desert Storm: Effective Combat Leader Behaviors," draft Technical Report 92-005 (Orlando, FL: Naval Training Systems Center, January 1992).

17. Heifetz, *Leadership Without Easy Answers*, note 64, pp. 304–305, citing Bernard M. Bass, "Stress and Leadership," in *Bass and Stogdill's Handbook of Leadership*, 3rd ed. (New York: The Free Press, 1990), chapter 29.

18. Willner, *The Spellbinders*, pp. 14–15.

19. Zaleznik and Kets de Vries, *Power and the Corporate Mind*, pp. 242–243; and Bernard M. Bass, *Leadership and Performance Beyond Expectations* (New York: The Free Press, 1985), p. 170.

20. Bernard M. Bass, "Evolving Perspectives on Charismatic Leadership," in Conger et al., *Charismatic Leadership*.

21. Francis J. Yammarino and Bernard M. Bass, "Long-Term Forecasting of Transformational Leadership and Its Effects Among Naval Officers: Some Preliminary Findings," in Kenneth E. Clark and Miriam B. Clark, eds., *Measures of Leadership* (West Orange, NJ: Leadership Library of America, Inc., for the Center for Creative Leadership, 1990), p. 151.

22. Burns, James M., *Leadership* (New York: Harper & Row), pp. 240–244.

23. Noel M. Tichy and Mary Anne Devanna, *The Transformational Leader*, 2nd ed. (New York: John Wiley & Sons, 1990).

24. Peter M. Senge, *The Fifth Discipline: The Art and Practice of the Learning Organization* (New York: Doubleday, 1990), pp. 9, 205–232; and Peter M. Senge, *The Fifth Discipline: Fieldbook Strategies and Tools for Building a Learning Organization* (New York: Doubleday, 1994), pp. 6, 78, 82, 297–347, 427, 437, 448.

25. Yammarino and Bass, "Long-Term Forecasting of Transformational Leadership," pp. 151–169.

26. Ronald J. Deluga, "The Relationship of Leader-Member Exchanges with Laissez-faire, Transactional, and Transformational Leadership in Naval Environments," in *Impact of Leadership*, Clark et al., pp. 237–247.

27. Wilfred H. Drath, *Why Managers Have Trouble Empowering: A Theoretical Perspective Based on Concepts of Adult Development* (Greensboro, NC: Center for Creative Leadership, June 1993).

28. Jane M. Howell, "Two Faces of Charisma: Socialized and Personalized Leadership in Organizations," in Conger et al., *Charismatic Leadership*, p. 215.

29. Wills, *Certain Trumpets*, pp. 102–112.

30. Karl Deutsch, "Social Mobilization and Political Development," *American Political Science Review*, 55, no. 3 (September 1961), pp. 497–499.

31. Wills, *Certain Trumpets*, p. 111.

32. Peter I. Berger, "Charisma and Religious Innovation: Social Location of the Israelite Prophecy," *American Sociolgical Review*, 28 (1963), pp. 940–950.

33. Gay Hammerman and Richard G. Sheridan, *The 88th Infantry Division in World War II: Factors Responsible for Its Excellence* (Fairfax, VA, 1982).

34. John H. Cushman, "Challenge and Response at the Operational Levels, 1914–45," in Allan R. Millett and Williamson Murray, eds., *The Second World War*, vol. 3 of *Military Effectiveness* (Boston: Allen and Unwin, 1988), pp. 326–330.

15

Leadership in Military Combat Units and Business Organizations: A Comparative Psychological Analysis

Micha Popper

Leadership is one of the most common and least understood phenomena in the world.
—James MacGregor Burns, Leadership, 1978

Thus Burns[1] begins his book on leadership. However, despite the lack of clarity from the research point of view, there seems to be agreement and understanding with regard to the nature of leadership in practice, at least on the intuitive level. As defined by Kotter,[2] a well-known researcher on the subject, leadership is "getting people to act without coercion." Similar definitions have been offered by the most prominent writers on leadership.[3,4] According to this view, as Mintzberg[5] points out, the manager (like the military commander) does many things: co-ordination, logistics, management of information, of budgets, and so forth. One of their roles is leadership: motivating people to perform tasks to the best of their ability.

Based on the definition by Kotter and the prominent researchers of leadership, I will attempt in this article to characterize leadership patterns and classify them, according to differential organizational psychology contexts, along a continuum of leadership behaviour.

Reprinted by permission from the *Journal of Managerial Psychology*, 11:1, pp. 15–23.

The analysis and discussion will focus more on military leadership because (as will be explained in the body of the article) on the suggested continuum military leadership constitutes a very clear and prominent reference point for comparative analysis of types of leadership in organizations.

The distinct character of military leadership in combat units was clearly demonstrated by Gabriel and Savage,[6] who dealt with the leadership crisis among US army officers in Vietnam. They compared military leaders with managers in the civilian business sector and their main argument was that the combat officers in Vietnam were overly influenced by the business management ethos. In fact, they behaved as "battle managers" but were not able to "provide the required military leadership." The comparative analysis of those researchers was done in structural functional terms. The present article aims to analyze the social psychological meaning and the dynamics underlying military leadership in comparison with leadership in civilian organizations, particularly business ones, which represent the other end of the same continuum.

The starting point for this discussion is the description of leadership as an interpersonal process, following an approach that views leadership as a central phenomenon in the social psychology of groups and organizations.[7] This perspective, focusing on the psychological interaction between leader and led, permits analysis of leadership in differential organizational and social contexts.

The Relationship Between Leader and Led

The relationship between the leader and the led is described in the literature from two different perspectives.[8,9] One perspective describes this relationship as a framework of exchange relations.[10] Leadership in this view is expressed in the leader ability to make his/her people aware of a link between effort and reward. The effective leader, according to the criteria of this approach, is a sensitive psychological diagnostician, who accurately discerns his/her subordinates' needs and expectations and responds to them accordingly. Many models have been developed (generally described in the literature as contingency models) in which the leader is portrayed as a transactional leader. A long series of researchers add variables whose essence is the mapping of factors that influence the effectiveness of the "motivational transaction" between leader and the led (see, for example, House).[11]

The second perspective describes the relationship between the leader and the led as essentially emotional. The leader in this perspective, who is described by images such as charismatic,[12] visionary,[13] and inspirational,[14] is a person who arouses emotions in his/her people that motivate them to act beyond the framework of what may be described as exchange relations of "give and take."[15] Writers discussing leadership in this perspective have attempted to describe the reasons, the processes, and the characteristics of leaders who succeed in arousing emotions that are sometimes so powerful that people are even willing to sacrifice their lives for the leader.

With some degree of generalization, I suggest several alternative and/or complementary psychological explanations for the emotional bond between the leader and the led.[16,17] These explanations are examined below.

Psychological Explanations for the Emotional Bond Between the Leader and the Led

The Psychoanalytic Explanation: Transference

Psychoanalytic theories claim that parents have a critical effect on their children's psychic processes, particularly in the early years, which are a formative period in personality development. Authority (the parents) and its dynamics are major psychological factors that are expressed through the process of transference. In other words, most people (except in extreme pathological cases) have a deep-rooted longing and yearning for the feeling of the small child who was protected by big, strong authority figures, letting him/her live in Paradise, while they took all the responsibility. According to this explanation, there is a constant inherent longing for leadership, a longing which is regressive in nature. Leaders are authority figures, and thus objects of transference (see, for example, Kets De Vries).[18]

Projective and Attributional Explanations

The notions "projection" and "attribution" are close in terms of their explaining the significance of the leader to the led. Projection is, on the one hand, a psychological defense mechanism in case of negative emotions (the pot calling the kettle black) and, on the other, a way of expressing desires that the individual cannot for some reason fulfill in reality and so he/she projects them on to someone else. Attribution theories claim that individuals make mental "attributions," that is, they naively and intuitively attribute assumptions of cause and result between factors existing in their surroundings.[19] With the help of these concepts of projection and attribution, we can describe three more types of explanation for the emotional bond between the leader and the led.

The projective explanation is where the leader is his/her people's "projected being," he/she is the expression of their desires and, as such, serves their "ego expansion." By projecting on to the leader, the led can feel stronger, more successful, more competent.

The attribution explanation is as follows. The assumption underlying attributional explanations relevant to leadership is that ambiguous situations are too hard to bear.[20] In this context, leadership as an attributional solution is an available and convenient response. People attribute to leaders knowledge of the goal, the direction, order of priorities; briefly, the ability to "make sense of things" in chaotic environments.

Another explanation that can be seen as attributional (although not in the original research sense) relates to arguments proposed by psychologists such as Frankl,[21] that people have a basic need for *meaning*. According to this approach, leaders are figures to whom people attribute the ability to give meaning. Through the use of symbols, expressions that show vision, and behaviour of symbolic value, leaders serve as catalysts giving new meanings to their people's feelings and actions. In other words, leaders may create affective impact by arousing what Shamir[22] calls the "worthiness motive." This is a component of self concept that is expressed, among other things, by the wish to belong to certain groups and collectives that dictate the criteria for doing "worthy things".[23] Leadership, in this sense, is a question of raising and strengthening the "worthiness motive," which is not related to the "usual instrumental" motivation but to something essentially different: "normative commitment".[24] The nature of normative commitment and the "worthy behaviour" motive is aptly summed up by President Kennedy's famous saying: "Ask not what your country can do for you, but what you can do for your country".[25] It appears, therefore, that part of the possible explanation for leaders' ability to create an emotional effect is related to their ability to express the essence of a collective symbol which "recruits" the normative commitment of the group's members. I shall now discuss the relevance of the explanations presented to the discussion on leadership in differential organizational contexts.

Leadership in Various Organizational Contexts

The literature on leadership deals extensively with the issue of the leader's influence in generalized and monolithic terms, focusing mainly on the leader's behaviour and style.[26] There is insufficient consideration of the psychological conditions—resulting from the organizational context—which significantly affect the leader's impact.[27] The key concepts underlying this argument are "needs" and "expectations." These concepts permit dynamic analysis of the leader's influences in his/her various spheres of activity. The point of departure for the argument presented is the claim of "hierarchy of needs" as expressed in the well-known needs theories of Maslow[28] and Alderfer.[29] According to these theories, the needs that motivate the individual's actions operate hierarchically in terms of the intensity of their effect on the individual's life and work. The assumption is that the need for security is central in accounting for the leader's influence. Thus, in a perceived ambiguous situation, the human consciousness tries to create categories and schemata which introduce some order in the perception of reality. Leadership is a possible and psychologically convenient answer to the need for security. This argument can apply to attributional as well as projective explanations. Ross and Andersen[30] describe a phenomenon they define as "the fundamental attribution error." This refers to people's tendency to attribute to "actors" in a given situation more causality than the circumstances warrant. For example, Calder[31] pointed out that many tended to attribute to various presidents of the USA prime importance in changes that occurred in the US market even when these changes occurred so close to the president's election that they could not have been influenced by him. Projection and transference serve the same function in stressful ambiguous situations.

With the help of the psychological categories discussed here, we can now characterize and classify leadership patterns in various organizations. The proposed classification is based on analysis of the "response patterns" of an organization's members and the means by which the various types of response are achieved. This division shows three ways of causing people to perform tasks. These are, first, formal authority; second, use of reinforcements (positive or negative); and third, emotional influence. These ways are used differentially in different organizations. In "total institutions" formal authority is the main, if not the sole, source for making members act. In business organizations people are motivated to act by educated use of social rewards, material benefits, prestige, and so forth. In organizations such as combat units (as will be elucidated below) the sources of motivation for action are mainly emotional.

Furthermore, the intensity of the individual's response will differ in the context of each of these sources. Formal authority will produce obedience, educated use of rewards will elicit performance conditional on instrumental rewards, while emotional influence may create willingness to do things that are above and beyond the expected routine tasks including, for example, the willingness to risk their lives. This argument can be summed up in Table 15.1.

We see that the military combat unit is in the third category and, as stated, this is a distinct and unique reference point for comparative analysis. From this point of view, the military example is an ideal type of the kind of leadership based on emotions, therefore I will expand on this example. This, in my opinion, will permit a degree of generalization on the axis of distance from the ideal type presented by leadership in military combat units. We will examine, therefore, the unique factors of military leadership in combat units.

TABLE 15.1   Types of Response Pattern, Means of Eliciting Response, Behavioral Manifestation of the Response, and Leadership Patterns in Various Organizations

Types of Response	Behavioral Manifestation Response	Means of Eliciting Response	Main Leadership Pattern	Example of Organizations
Obedience	Minimal level of activity, aimed at avoiding punishment or not losing privileges	Fear of punishment	Little room for leadership	Prisons
Instrumental-based response	Level of activity expressing effort, connected with material and social rewards, prestige or professional interest	Social, material, professional rewards	Transactional leadership	Business organizations
Commitment	Level of activity expressing effort or sacrifice not necessarily connected with material rewards or presitige	Emotional means rooted in projection, transference, attribution, symbolic expression	Emotion-rousing leadership	Select military units

Leadership in Combat Units

The essential difference between combat units and other, especially business, organizations lies in their members' "response relations," namely, the motivational base and the game rules in these organizations. Rohrlich,[32] an American psychiatrist who studied and counselled managers in the US sector, sees the work of management in business organizations as a type of theatre in which the main process is one of interaction between role identities. One of Rohrlich's clients describes the rules of the game:

> In my work I know exactly where we all stand, where everything belongs, we have specific role descriptions, certain ways to dress every day, we have names and titles on our office doors, we have clear identities. I am a vice president, 350 people who report to me all have a certain rank on the ladder. No personal relationship is close enough to blur the lines of authority. In fact, nothing is blurred by friendship or emotion. Everything is guided by doing business and making profits. This is a kind of theatre; if you learn your lines well you are all right.[33]

The exchange mechanism of "give and take" is the main ordering mechanism between the leader and the led in business organizations. The "stage" and the "scenery" in combat units are very different. In combat units, unlike business organizations, there is an additional element that is extremely powerful: the possibility of death. Physical (or mental) injury is a close companion. The overt, and even more, the suppressed level of anxiety, is incomparably higher than anything that can be described in most organizations. Psychological conditions such as these provide fertile soil for the formation and existence of regressive psychological processes and the growth of projections related to leaders. In other words, these conditions intensify the longing and desire for a leader who is capable of reassuring and relieving deep anxieties. The leader, or the longing for a leader, are always at the centre of the soldiers' script (even if they are not always aware of it) and, unlike the leader in business organizations, the leader in a combat unit has an inherent powerful affective function. He provides a response to deep emotional processes, and he himself generates emotional processes. Thus, in addition to being a task leader, he is also a "projection screen" and a focus of attributions which affect the expectations directed towards him. The image of the military leader in combat units is of a resolute and somewhat paternalistic figure, and this is by no means accidental, since its sources, as mentioned, are in projective processes.

Several studies conducted on outstanding battalion commanders illustrate this argument clearly. "The battalion is a *family* and the battalion commander is its head," said a company commander who was interviewed in one study.[34] He added in clarification, "I mention this in contrast to the atmosphere prevalent in civilian organizations, where people say 'I just work here.'" Junior officers were even more extreme. In their eyes:

> The battalion cannot be defined as just a place of work. It is a way of life, a shared tradition, there are people who grew up with us from the role of tank commanders. The battalion is a home that will be hard to leave.[35]

The soldiers interviewed in the study added vivid descriptions that clearly illustrated the family image and the commander's place in this analogy:

> The battalion is an Indian tribe, an Indian family, with the battalion commander and his deputy at the center. The battalion commander is the grandfather, the chief; his deputy is the grandmother; the company commanders are the parents; the soldiers are the children, and the staff are the uncles, some of them good, some not.[36]

It is interesting to note that this view was shared by commanders who were interviewed in a separate study without their subordinates present.

For example, the commander of an engineering battalion describes his concept of professionalism: "The professional part is very important because officers, too (including company commanders), are still *children* who need guidance."[37] The commander of another battalion said, "The battalion is like a home, a family, *I bring them up.*"

The task of "bringing up" is central in the perception of combat unit leaders, and is particularly prominent among the outstanding commanders. An outstanding tank battalion commander described it in a way typical of most of the commanders who were studied. "My life's ambition is to educate the next generation. We are the ones who mold them. It is a great privilege and I take it very seriously."[38] These self perceptions of commanders illustrate that, in addition to the parents' traditional roles of providing their children with security, they also have symbolic roles which are expressed in their educational perspectives. The underlying assumption of these family metaphors relates to the different sources of motivation and attachment to the leader. In business organizations rewards are the major, and sometimes the only means of obtaining the subordinates' co-operation, whereas co-operation in organizations like the army is also based on internalization of goals, and the subordinates are motivated by a force defined by Etzioni as "normative force."[39] Similarly, Popper and Lipshitz[40] refer to different types of commitment, distinguishing between instrumental commitment resulting from evaluation of the rewards perceived, and normative commitment rooted in the individual's personal values. The essential difference between these two types of commitment lies in the psychological processes involved. While instrumental commitment is the product of evaluating cost/benefit at a given time, normative commitment is not necessarily connected to the concept of reward. Furthermore, there is evidence indicating that normative commitment is strengthened in the absence of immediate rewards. (These findings are consistent with psychological explanations such as cognitive dissonance.[41] According to these kinds of argument, the greater the investment, the sacrifice and the price paid, the stronger the normative commitment, in order to resolve the dissonance and create cognitive consonance. This process is contradictory to instrumental logic but is consistent with the need to rationalize actions and decisions whose source is emotional.) Indeed, studies on soldiers in combat units found that they were characterized by extremely high normative commitment.[42] Thus, it is not accidental that commanders speak so much about "values," "idealism," "commitment," and so forth. The commander's role invests him with inherent symbolic influence, giving him the potential to recruit the collective motive by clearly symbolic effects. Indeed, combat units make extensive use of symbolic elements and rituals related to *esprit de corps* and the unit's behavioural codes, and devote a great deal of energy to inspiring the aforementioned "worthiness motive."

Evidence of the differences between what is required of leadership in combat units compared with business organizations can be found in studies on officers who embark on a second career.

Yariv,[43] who conducted such research, quotes one of the retired officers:

> The key to my successful integration in this business system is that soon after my release I convinced myself that I had to *completely forget* my past as an army officer and begin a completely *new* chapter. When the people around me were convinced that I had internalized this belief I began to be accepted here.[44]

The images of leadership internalized by commanders in combat units seem to be entirely different from what they, at least, attribute to leadership in business organizations. One of them described it in the following metaphor:

> Before I set out on a second career as a manager in a business firm I felt that I had spent 25 years of my life in an aquarium made of magnifying glass and now I am "ejected" into the sea (of business). The question is: are the gills I have developed (internalized images of military leadership) suitable for the big sea, or have I been thrown into an ocean in which I have no chance of survival?[45]

Empirical evidence supports this subjective impression. For example, Yariv[46] found that most of the Israel Defense Forces (IDF) retirees turned to the public sector as their first choice, and approximately two-thirds of those who were employed worked in the public sector. Of the respondents, 57 per cent reported that they had obtained their first job through friends. Galay[47] found that in the years 1983–1984, 32 per cent of the officers retiring from the IDF (all relatively young people aged 40–50) did not find employment in their first year of retirement. In 1984–1985, the percentage of retiring officers who did not find work was 38, while in 1985–1986 over half of those retiring (55.5 per cent) did not find work in their first year of retirement—and all of this in conditions of full employment in the economy. In recent years, there has been a certain improvement in the scope of employment of the retirees, but there does not appear to be a change in the image of the retiring officer as regards his ability to integrate successfully into civilian business management. Although many army officers were in charge of big formations which sometimes included thousands of people, many people regard the retired army officer as inadequate to hold leadership positions in business organizations.[48]

Thus, it seems that the move to the business sector, which, as described, lacks the attributional and projective aspect that characterizes the military, is a move to a different system of perceptions, values, and psychological needs, where the game rules do not match the combat officer's socialization and self concept as leader. This argument can lead to the conclusion that the "fundamental attribution error," whereby individuals attribute excessive importance to the leader compared with the context or the circumstances, applies to a large extent also to researchers who write on this subject. In other words, the comparison presented in the body of this article leads to the conclusion that leadership interaction is largely dictated by patterns derived from the organizational context or, more accurately, the psychological implications derived from this context. In other words, it is not so much a question of differences between actors as between stages, and even more between game rules, rules of which the actors are sometimes unaware, although they carry weight in determining the character of the interaction between leader and led, shaping the dynamics of attributions, projections and differential expectations in the various stages. The comparison of leadership in military combat units with leadership in business organizations probably reflects this principle more clearly than most possible comparisons.

Notes

1. Burns, J. M., *Leadership*, Harper & Row, New York, NY, 1978.

2. Kotter, J., "What do leaders really do?" *Harvard Business Review*, May-June 1990.

3. Bennis, W., and Nanus, B., *Leaders: The Strategies for Taking Charge*, Harper & Row, New York, NY, 1985.

4. Bass, B., *Leadership and Performance Beyond Expectations*, The Free Press, New York, NY, 1985.

5. Mintzberg, H., "The manager's job: Folklore and facts," *Harvard Business Review*, July-August 1975.

6. Gabriel, R. A., and Savage, P. L., *Crisis in Command* (Hebrew translation), Israel Ministry of Defense, 1981.

7. Chemers, M., "The social, organizational, and cultural context of effective leadership," in Kellerman, B. (Ed.), *Leadership: Multidisciplinary Perspectives*, Prentice-Hall, Englewood Cliffs, NJ, 1984, pp. 92–108.

8. Shamir, B., "The charismatic relationship: Alternative explanations and directions," *Leadership Quarterly*, Vol. 2, No. 2, 1991, pp. 81–104.

9. Popper, M., Landau, O., and Gluskinos, U., "The Israeli defense forces: An example of transformational leadership," *Leadership & Organization Development Journal*, Vol. 13, No. 1, 1992, pp. 3–8.

10. Hollander, E. P., *Leaders, Groups and Influence*, Oxford University Press, New York, NY, 1964.

11. House, R., "A path goal theory of leader effectiveness," *Administrative Science Quarterly*, Vol. 16, 1971, pp. 321–328.

12. Shamir, "The charismatic relationship."

13. Bennis and Nanus, *Leaders*.

14. Bass, *Leadership and Performance.*

15. Ibid.

16. Shamir, "The charismatic relationship."

17. Popper et al., "The Israeli defense forces."

18. Kets de Vries, M., *Prisoners of Leadership*, John Wiley & Sons, New York, NY, 1989.

19. Twersky, A., Kahneman, D., and Slovic, P. (Eds.), *Judgement Under Uncertainty: Heuristics and Biases*, Cambridge University Press, Cambridge, 1980.

20. Popper et al., "The Israeli defense forces."

21. Frankl, V., *Man's Search for Meaning*, Pocket Books, New York, NY, 1963.

22. Shamir, "The charismatic relationship."

23. Popper et al., "The Israeli defense forces."

24. Wiener, Y., "Commitment in organizations: A normative view," *Academy of Management Journal*, Vol. 7, 1982, p. 428.

25. Popper, M., and Liphshitz, R., "Ask not what your country can do for you. The normative basis of organizational commitment," *Journal of Vocational Behavior*, Vol. 41, 1992, pp. 1–12.

26. Shamir, "The charismatic relationship."

27. Popper et al., "The Israeli defense forces."

28. Maslow, A., *Motivation and Personality*, Harper & Row, New York, NY, 1970.

29. Alderfer, C., *Existence, Relatedness and Growth. Human Needs in Organizational Settings*, The Free Press, New York, NY, 1972.

30. Ross, L., and Andersen, C. "Shortcomings in the attribution process: On the origins and maintenance of erroneous social assessments," in Twersky et al., *Judgement Under Uncertainty*, pp. 51–86.

31. Calder, B., "An attribution theory of leadership," in Staw, B., and Salanick, G. (Eds.), *New Directions in Organizational Behavior*, St. Clair Press, Chicago, IL, 1977, pp. 179–204.

32. Rohrlich, J., *Work and Love*, New York, NY, 1980 (Hebrew translation, Reshafim Press, Tel Aviv, 1990), pp. 46–7.

33. Ibid.

34. Nave, E., "Transformational leadership in outstanding battalion commanders in the IDF," MA thesis, Tel Aviv University, 1991.

35. Ibid.

36. Ibid.

37. Ibid.

38. Zakkai, E., "Outstanding battalion commanders," Research paper, IDF Leadership Development School, 1992, p. 33.

39. Etzioni, A., *A Comparative Analysis of Complex Organizations*, The Free Press, New York, NY, 1975.

40. Popper and Liphshitz, "Ask not what your country can do for you."

41. Wicklund, R., and Brehm, J.W., *Perspectives on Cognitive Dissonance*, Lawrence Erlbaum, Hillsdale, NJ, 1976.

42. Popper and Liphschitz, "Ask not what your country can do for you."

43. Yariv, D., "Integration of senior IDF officers (retired) in the civilian economy and the compatibility of military and civilian careers," MA thesis (Hebrew), Tel Aviv University, 1980.

44. Ibid.

45. Galay, A., "IDF preparation for retirement," MA thesis (Hebrew), Tel Aviv University, 1989.

46. Yariv, "Integration of senior IDF officers (retired)."

47. Galay, "IDF preparation for retirement."

48. Popper, M., "Comparison of leadership in the IDF and in business organizations," in Shenhar, A., and Yarkoni, A. (Eds.), *Management Culture in Israel*, in press, 1994.

16

Leadership Between a Rock and a Hard Place

Maj. Lee E. DeRemer

Integrity requires the courage of sometimes saying no—or at least a persistent asking "why?"—from all of us to others of us who institute unexamined regulations that often require "no-win" solutions for both the system and personal integrity.
—Richard D. Miller, Chaplain, Colonel, USAF

What if an operational leader told you that he had such conflicting demands that he was in a "no-win" dilemma? He could satisfy either demand but not both—and to fail to satisfy either would exact great professional and personal cost. Most people would say something like, "Sure, there's a solution. You just haven't considered all your options. Innovate. Improvise." Whatever the words, the message would be the same: find a solution. We expect that; it's our culture.

Our mind-set envisions success in spite of external constraints. The overriding assumption is that solutions to dilemmas do exist and that these solutions will be honorable to all parties without sacrificing the mission. A further assumption is the existence of clearly right and wrong choices in such dilemmas.

Life is not always so tidy. High military rank is often accompanied by competing or even conflicting interests. Problems can arise for which no painless options exist. For example, an organization's integrity may conflict with constraints that diminish the unit's safety and mission accomplishment. If that is the case, these demands are mutually exclusive. Since we can't compromise integrity, we must find a solution to the dilemma by

Reprinted by permission from *Airpower Journal*, 10:3, pp. 87–94.

changing the constraints. If *that* isn't possible, then rather than compromise integrity, leaders must sacrifice themselves professionally to change the constraints in order to resolve the dilemma and preserve the mission and the safety of their people.

Consider operational leaders faced with the legitimate concern for the effectiveness and safety of people under their command and with externally imposed constraints that not only complicate the mission but also unnecessarily imperil their people. These leaders face two realities. First, they don't have a lot of options. Second, none of the options are attractive.

Gen. John D. Lavelle faced such a dilemma toward the close of the Vietnam War. As the commander of Seventh Air Force, he was responsible for conducting the air war in Southeast Asia. He was relieved of command on 6 April 1972. The problems he faced, the solution he chose, and the ramifications of his choices offer us lessons about decision making. This honorable officer would be retired as a major general rather than full general—the rank he held as commander of Seventh Air Force. Never before had such an action occurred in American military history.[1]

Dilemma

When General Lavelle assumed command of Seventh Air Force in Saigon, South Vietnam, on 1 August 1971, he inherited rules of engagement (ROE) that had evolved over three years. The ROE maintained the basic restrictions of a 1968 agreement by the Johnson administration[2] and consisted of directives, wires, and messages defining the conditions under which US aircraft could attack enemy aircraft or weapons systems. Seventh Air Force consolidated those directives into a manual of "operating authorities" and disseminated it to the units. Aircrews received briefings on the ROE prior to each mission.[3]

Essentially, aircrews could not fire unless they were threatened. Enemy surface-to-air missiles (SAM) or antiaircraft artillery (AAA) had to "activate against" aircrews before they could respond with a "protective reaction strike." Warning gear installed in the planes alerted aircrews that an enemy SAM firing site was tracking them.[4]

American aircrews lost this advantage late in 1971, when the North Vietnamese took several actions to vastly improve their tracking capability, the most important being the integration of their early warning, surveillance, and AAA radars with the SAM sites. This integrated system allowed the North Vietnamese to launch their missiles without being detected by the radar warning gear of US aircraft.

General Lavelle believed that because those mutually supporting radar systems transmitted tracking data to the firing sites, the SAM system was activated against US aircraft anytime they were over North Vietnam. He also learned, through the bitter experience of losing planes and crews on two occasions, that US aircraft were much less likely to evade SAMs when the radars were so netted. He later testified that this experience provided sufficient rationale for planned protective-reaction strikes, noting that "the system was constantly activated against us."[5]

The North Vietnamese also improved their tactics by using ground controlled intercept (GCI) radars to track US aircraft. Azimuth information developed by GCI surveillance was fed to fire-control radars. This netting effectively eliminated tracking with the Fan Song radar and allowed more than one missile site to be directed against a single US aircraft. General Lavelle later testified to Congress that he "alerted his superiors to the enemy's netting of his radars and advised them that the North Vietnamese now possessed the capability of firing with little or no warning."[6]

The air war had changed. General Lavelle made repeated and futile attempts to get the ROE changed to reflect the new threat to his aircrews and planes. However, not only did Washington refuse to change the ROE but the Joint Chiefs of Staff (JCS) severely criticized General Lavelle for a lack of aggressiveness in fighting the air war. He received a personal visit from the chairman of the JCS, who made it clear that he was to find ways of prosecuting the war more aggressively within the constraints of the ROE.[7] The general had a problem. What took priority: the ROE or the safety and effectiveness of his command?

He chose the latter, authorizing a strike on 7 November 1971—the first of 20 to 28 missions from that date to 9 March 1972. Regarding these missions, Lavelle stated that he "made interpretations of the ROE that were probably beyond the literal intention of the rules."[8] Each strike involved six to eight aircraft, for a total of 147 sorties out of approximately 25,000 flown during the period. Each mission attacked missile sites, missiles on transporters, airfields, 122 mm and 130 mm guns, or radars.[9]

In response to a JCS inquiry about Seventh Air Force's authority to strike a GCI site on 5 January 1972, General Lavelle replied that, since his aircraft were authorized to hit radars that controlled missiles or AAA, he believed they were also authorized to strike GCI radars that controlled enemy aircraft. He later received another JCS message that, although sympathetic, said he had no authority to strike a GCI radar and that he should order no such strike again.[10]

Although amended on 26 January 1972 to authorize strikes against primary GCI sites when airborne MiGs indicated hostile intent,[11] the ROE still didn't address the netted SAM threat. This amendment was as close as General Lavelle got to persuading the JCS to adopt satisfactory rules of engagement.

Consequences

On 8 March 1972, a senator forwarded to the Air Force chief of staff a letter written by an Air Force sergeant—an intelligence specialist in Seventh Air Force. It alleged ROE violations and ongoing falsification of daily reports on missions. The Air Force inspector general (IG) flew to Saigon to investigate the matter and confirmed that "irregularities existed in some of 7th Air Force's operational reports."[12] General Lavelle immediately stopped all strikes in question and assigned three men to find a way to continue the protective-reaction sorties but report them accurately. The conclusion was that this couldn't be done.[13]

On 23 March 1972, General Lavelle was offered reassignment at his permanent grade of major general or retirement. He opted for retirement, effective 7 April 1972.[14] Little did he know what lay ahead.

The Air Force, having already announced that General Lavelle retired for personal reasons, would be forced to admit on 15 May 1972, after congressional inquiry, that the general had not only retired but had also been relieved of command because of "irregularities in the conduct of his command."[15] This revelation led to hearings before the Armed Services Investigations Subcommittee of the House Committee on Armed Services.

In his statements before the committee, General Lavelle convincingly maintained that he did not order the falsification of any reports. Although he insisted throughout the investigations by the Air Force and Congress that he learned of the falsified reports only after the IG investigation, as commander, he accepted full responsibility for those reports.

Reports on four of the missions were found to contain falsehoods.[16] General Lavelle stated that he traced the probable cause of the false reporting to the first protective-reaction strike, which he had directed from the operations center. When his lead pilot reported by radio that the target had been destroyed and that they had encountered no enemy reaction, the general stated, "We cannot report 'no reaction.'" As General Lavelle explained, "I could report enemy reaction, because we were reacted upon all the time [with the existence of the upgraded radar]."[17] Unfortunately, since his instructions to the pilot were vague, aircrews made false statements on some subsequent operational reports.

Congress accepted General Lavelle's explanation of the confusion over his intent regarding the reporting of the protective-reaction strikes—but only after many months of inquiry. By that time, few people were interested in clearing his name; consequently, General Lavelle would be remembered as someone who disregarded the ROE, fought his own unauthorized war, and made everyone falsify reports to keep it secret.

Although none of these allegations appear to be true, General Lavelle did make mistakes. His first was failing to make clear that Seventh Air Force demanded absolute integrity of its people. Had he done so, there would have been no mistaking his intent concerning operational reports. Indeed, such action might have had the effect of curbing widespread practices—unknown at the time—that were compromising the military's integrity. Specifically, widespread disclosures were made of illegal bombing and falsification of official records of these illegal raids, which had been going on for years before General Lavelle even appeared on the scene. These revelations caused the chairman of the Senate Armed Services Committee to drop his probe in August 1973. According to the chairman, "Air Force and Defense witnesses gave us to believe that falsification was so rare and so contemptible that it was good cause to remove General Lavelle from his command and drum him out of the service because he had ordered documents falsified."[18] However, the chairman's decision didn't even merit publication in any of the papers or periodicals that had previously convicted the general in print.

His second mistake lay in choosing to work around the ROE to accomplish the mission yet keep his crews safe. That meant bending the unrealistic ROE, an action that produced both positive and negative results.

From a positive viewpoint, despite the vastly improved North Vietnamese air defenses, no American lives or aircraft were lost during the raids in question. To that extent, General Lavelle's decision had the desired effect. Ironically, the conditions for protective-reaction strikes—relaxed in January 1972, as mentioned above—were abolished in March 1972, but not before the issue of integrity in reporting would cost General Lavelle his command.

General Lavelle's actions also had negative effects that he had no way of foreseeing. Therein lies the danger of working around bad ROE rather than having them changed. His decision to "interpret the ROE liberally" had several ramifications.

It led to continuing decay of the command's integrity, which contributed to the falsification of operational reports, which led to the sergeant's letter to the senator, which led to the IG investigation, which led to Lavelle's being relieved of command, which the Air Force kept secret, which led to a congressional investigation. This phenomenon is now commonly referred to as the "slippery slope effect." That is, when a leader starts cutting corners in integrity (intentionally or unintentionally), that action can pervade the entire organization.

For General Lavelle, it would get much worse. By this time, he *really* had no control of events, and some of the ramifications of his actions could have had strategic implications for peace negotiations and the credibility of the armed services.

Specifically, at the same time General Lavelle began strikes on the newly integrated radar SAM/AAA network, Henry Kissinger was in Paris conducting secret peace talks with the North Vietnamese. General Lavelle had no way of knowing about the talks, and Kissinger didn't know about the bombing. But Le Duc Tho of North Vietnam knew about both. To him, Kissinger was either lying or very poorly informed. Shortly thereafter, the talks broke off abruptly.[19]

General Lavelle, as well as the Air Force, Army, and Navy, would feel shock waves from his operational decision: Lavelle was accused of criminal misconduct;[20] courtmartial charges were filed against him and 22 other officers;[21] the nomination of Gen Creighton Abrams as chief of staff of the Army was delayed for over four months;[22] the Senate Armed Services Committee conducted an extensive and critical look at the command and control structure of the Air Force;[23] General Lavelle's retirement rank was reduced to major general;[24] naval aviators said that they had been involved in protective-reaction raids not authorized by the ROE;[25] Department of Defense IGs now reported directly to the service secretaries rather than to their service chiefs;[26] and the Senate Armed Services Committee placed an indefinite hold on promotions for about 160 Air Force officers.[27] Amazingly, none of the threatened action against any of the affected officers came to fruition. Although the investigations were eventually dropped, they underscore the fact that operational decisions are not made in a vacuum and that negative effects, however unintentional, can be extensive.

Instead of choosing between continuing the missions under intolerable circumstances or obeying the poor ROE, General Lavelle could have averted the problems listed above by ceasing operations until authorities changed the ROE to reflect the reality of the threat. Doing so would have meant going outside the chain of command when his superiors were unresponsive—an action that almost surely would have cost him his command. The option existed, but he chose not to take it. As it turned out, he lost his command anyway. Had he lost his command while demanding proper ROE, he would have (1) forced a change in the rules instead of leaving them to chance, (2) provided an example of the importance of taking care of people under our command *and* maintaining integrity, and (3) avoided the personally and strategically undesirable outcomes he could not foresee.

Lessons Learned

Two important lessons should be clear for operational leaders. The first is understanding the importance of integrity at all levels of command. The second is accepting the fact that sometimes leaders may have to sacrifice themselves because it's the best thing for the organization, the people, and the country.

The first lesson isn't difficult to understand, but it's tough to apply because choices aren't always clear in positions of increased responsibility. Nevertheless, a commandwide climate of integrity is indispensable. To accept anything less than absolute integrity in personal and professional behavior is to invite breakdowns like the one described by the noncommissioned officer who broke the story on false reports in Seventh Air Force:

> We went through the normal debrief, and when I asked [the aircrew] if they'd received any AAA, they said, "No, but we have to report it." I went to my NCOIC and asked him what was going on. He told me to report what the crew told me to report. . . . The false information was used in preparing the operational reports and slides for the morning staff briefing. The true information was kept separate and used for the wing commander's private briefings.[28]

This speaks to the possibility of a wide problem. But in October 1972, the Air Force responded quickly and well to the challenge of reestablishing the standard by sending the following message to all units. It's as applicable today as it was then:

> Integrity—which includes full and accurate disclosure—is the keystone of military service. Integrity binds us together into an Air Force serving the country. Integrity in reporting, for example, is the link that connects each flight crew, each specialist and each administrator to the commander-in-chief. In any crisis, decisions and risks taken by the highest national authorities depend, in large part, on reported military capabilities and achievements. In the same way, every commander depends on accurate reporting from his forces. Unless he is positive of the integrity of his people, a commander cannot have confidence in his forces. Without integrity, the commander-in-chief cannot have confidence in us.
>
> Therefore, we may not compromise our integrity—our truthfulness. To do so is not only unlawful but also degrading. False reporting is a clear example of failure of integrity. Any order to compromise integrity is not a lawful order.
>
> Integrity is the most important responsibility of command. Commanders are dependent on the integrity of those reporting to them in every decision they make. Integrity can be ordered, but it can only be achieved by encouragement and example.
>
> I expect these points to be disseminated to every individual in the Air Force—every individual. I trust they help to clarify a standard we can continue to expect, and will receive, from one another.[29]

That's the kind of message each commander needs to make clear from the outset—the kind of standard people should demand from each other. Still, a valid question remains: "Who can maintain absolute integrity? Not me and not you, so how useful or realistic is such a demand?" The answer begins with other questions. Without such a standard, how would you introduce yourself to your unit? By telling them you expect "really good integrity," "their best effort," "what suits each person"? The point is that the standard for integrity is just that—a standard. None of us will attain it every day, but we gain much by holding it before the unit. Consider this: if the standard doesn't apply fully and continuously, then what good is it as a core value? Its value exists precisely in its utility.

The second lesson is more difficult to discuss because the object of the lesson—sacrificing one's career if circumstances require it—is rather unpalatable. Indeed, people are often ridiculed for taking such a stand. Yet, history places some people in circumstances that require them to choose either to do the right thing or keep their careers intact. As the Stoic philosopher Epictetus tells us in *Enchiridion,* "Remember, you are an actor in a drama of such sort as the Author chooses—if short, then in a short one; if long, then in a long one. If it be His pleasure that you should enact a poor man, or a cripple, or a ruler, see that you act it well. For this is your business—to act well the given part, but to choose it belongs to Another."[30]

Furthermore, we must recognize that playing the part can exact a great price. Doing the right thing doesn't always result in accolades. The Book of Ecclesiastes has a simple, timeless message: "I returned and saw that the race is not always to the swift nor the battle to the strong, neither yet bread to the wise nor riches to men of understanding, nor favors to men of skill, but time and chance happeneth to them all" (9:11). The Book of Job is even more blunt: Job learns that life isn't always fair and that bad things happen to good people. Despite this realization, people must lead—and they must lead within the roles in which history places them.

Conclusion

Abraham Lincoln once remarked that "if you once forfeit the confidence of your fellow citizens, you can never regain their respect and esteem." Indeed, as unpleasant as the realization might be, sometimes leaders face dilemmas for which no comfortable solution exists. It's not entirely fair for me to criticize General Lavelle for his decisions, since I didn't experience his dilemma. Indeed, if I had to choose between the alternatives he considered, I probably would have made the same choice.

Nevertheless, the fact remains that even if leaders are faced only with gray areas that offer no clear choice, that still does not absolve them from the dilemma. There is a better choice: demand change. If the issue is important enough, the decision maker should demand resolution of unsatisfactory constraints (in this case, the ROE). Even though this option will likely cost the leaders their careers, it is the best decision for the institution and for the people under their command.

This article represents just the first half of the effort. The follow-up work must be an assessment of command ethics. Once we agree that a climate of integrity is a critical leadership issue, we'll want to measure that climate. Such an assessment must identify valid, reliable indicators of the ethical health of a command. It should highlight positive signs as well as warning flags of behavior that need to be addressed before a problem arises. That, it seems to me, is the key: having enough situational awareness in the command to foresee a problem—or at least to recognize one as it is developing—rather than seeing it only in hindsight.

Each commander can accept this challenge informally while preparing for new levels of leadership. Measuring how well the challenge is met might not be possible. That is, ethical lapses might still occur, and we have no way of knowing whether they would be more severe or more frequent in the absence of such an effort. What is certain, however, is that this examination—both before assuming command and during command—can ultimately groom more professional people and produce more effective units.

Notes

1. "New Chief for 7th Air Force," *New York Times,* 17 May 1971.

2. House Committee on Armed Services, Investigations Subcommittee, *Hearing on H.R. 201, Unauthorized Bombing of Military Targets in North Vietnam,* 92d Cong., 2d sess., 1972, 31–32.

3. House Committee on Armed Services, Investigations Subcommittee, *Report on H.R. 201, Unauthorized Bombing of Military Targets in North Vietnam,* 92d Cong., 2d sess., 1972, 2.

4. Ibid., 8–9.

5. Ibid.

6. Ibid., 4.

7. Seymour M. Hersh, *The Price of Power: Kissinger in the Nixon White House* (New York: Summit Books, 1983), 504–7.

8. House, *Hearing on H.R. 201,* 7.

9. Ibid., 8.

10. Ibid., 41.

11. House, *Report on H.R. 201,* 9.

12. Ibid.

13. Ibid., 6.

14. House, *Hearing on H.R. 201,* 4.

15. *Congressional Record,* 92d Cong., 2d sess., 1972, 20761.

16. House, *Hearing on H.R. 201,* 22.

17. House, *Report on H.R. 201,* 5.

18. "Hughes Drops Lavelle Probe," *Air Force Times,* 29 September 1973.

19. Seymour M. Hersh, "General Bombed in North before President's Order," *New York Times,* 11 June 1972.

20. Seymour M. Hersh, "Young Air Officer Formally Accuses Lavelle of Misconduct for Raids on North," *New York Times*, 22 June 1972.

21. Seymour M. Hersh, "New Charges Filed by Airman against Lavelle and 22 Others," *New York Times*, 4 November 1972.

22. Seymour M. Hersh, "Confronted with New Testimony, Stennis Orders Full Hearing on Lavelle," *New York Times*, 29 June 1972.

23. "Senate Inquiry Set Into the Air Force," *New York Times*, 30 August 1972.

24. Seymour M. Hersh, "Abrams Approved as Chief of Army by Senate Panel," *New York Times*, 7 October 1972.

25. Seymour M. Hersh, "Five Pilots Say Their Group Flew Unauthorized Raids," *New York Times*, 10 October 1972.

26. "Shakeup of IGs on Way," *Air Force Times*, 3 January 1973.

27. Bob Horowitz and George Foster, "Shock Waves from Lavelle," *Air Force Times*, 21 March 1973.

28. Senate Committee on Armed Services, *Hearings before the Committee on Armed Services*, 92d Cong., 2d sess., 1972, 168–69.

29. Message, chief of staff, US Air Force, to US Air Force personnel, 13 October 1972.

30. Quoted in James B. Stockdale, *Thoughts of a Philosophical Fighter Pilot* (Stanford, Calif.: Hoover Institution Press, 1995), 189.

17

Once a Leader,
Always a Leader?

David Stauffer

Would you like to cap your business career by heading a college or arts agency? Does that career Army officer seem to offer everything you need in a No. 2–except corporate experience? Do you wonder whether the talents and experience that boosted you to the top in a manufacturing firm would be relevant if you jumped to a service business?

Military to business. Business to academia. Consumer goods to financial service—and so forth. To what extent, if any, does success as a leader in one arena predict or contribute to similar achievement in a different arena—or even an entirely different sort of organization?

The experts of whom I asked these questions agree: The answer depends on what qualities you list as leadership attributes and on the width of the division between the areas that a leader wishes to leap across. "The successful Catholic cardinal or bishop probably would not do too well as football coach at Notre Dame," notes University of Southern California management professor Warren Bennis, author of *Organizing Genius: The Secrets of Creative Collaboration* (Perseus). "And Lou Holtz or the other great Notre Dame football coaches probably would not do too well heading General Motors. But the good news is that there are more than a few leaders who have demonstrated that success is transportable, provided the chasm they attempt to cross is not too wide."

The Bridgeable Chasm

What width can be bridged? Feedback from the real world seems confusing, to say the least. AT&T Corp. carefully groomed John R. Walter, previ-

---

Reprinted by permission from *Across the Board* (April 1999), pp. 14–19.

ously chairman, president, and CEO of commercial printer R.R. Donnelley & Sons Co., for its top job—then cast him out of the running after nine turbulent months. A board member claimed Walter lacked "intellectual leadership." But just a few months later, C. Michael Armstrong—former head of Hughes Electronics Corp—took the job, making an inter-industry leap that has been as spectacular as Walter's was disappointing.

In the realm of business-to-government shuffles, current Treasury Secretary and former Wall Street investment banker Robert E. Rubin is generally given high marks in both arenas. Not faring nearly so well, at least in current assessments, is Robert S. McNamara, who went from Ford Motor "whiz kid" to defense secretary under presidents Kennedy and Johnson to head of the quasi-governmental World Bank. "He was not terribly impressive in any one of the organizations he headed," says James O'Toole, managing director of the Booz Allen & Hamilton Leadership Center.

Kevin Cashman, CEO of LeaderSource, an international executive coaching firm based in Minneapolis, clarifies this muddled picture somewhat by pointing out that, "while the transferability issue might be judged in the marketplace, it's created internally. Most of us are surprised that, someone like, [former college and pro football star] Roger Staubach became a successful real-estate executive. That's because we all tend to limit our thoughts about people to the arena in which we got to know them. We defined Staubach as 'athlete.' But *he* didn't. And he, unlike us, probably was not surprised by his success."

Cashman says we can change a too-restrictive view of our own chances of making a successful move to a new arena. "A public official in the upper levels of state government told me he couldn't make the major career change to the private sector he wanted, because everyone would see him as only another government bureaucrat. I urged him to look at himself in terms of his contribution rather than his role. In that light, he was all about service. When he internalized this and went into the marketplace as a successful service executive, he landed the upper-level job with a software company that he wanted."

In contrast with Cashman's focus on what's inside is the view O'Toole offers: "In theory, if someone is a good leader in one calling, he ought to be a good leader in others, because characteristics of successful leadership transcend role or occupation. But we don't find nearly as many instances of this as we should."

"The reason has less to do with the leaders than the followers. People in groups tend to resist those they perceive as outsiders. They tend to think special qualities are required in their domains. So they put up all sorts of barriers. I know of a recent case where a military leader moved to the private sector. I think he's a very impressive man, but he's meeting with great resistance."

More dramatic and sadder, O'Toole says, was the 1979 move of the late Rene C. McPherson from CEO of Dana Corp. to dean of the Stanford Business School. "He tried to change things, but the faculty dug in and resisted. They made his life an absolute hell. He was literally carried out on a stretcher." McPherson was involved in a serious auto accident two months after his Stanford appointment, but he kept his new post until 1983. According to *The New York Times*, "He said he stepped down primarily for health reasons."

Long Odds Against the Soldier

Former Marine Brent Filson, founder of the Williamstown, Mass.-based Filson Leadership Group Inc., believes the chasm between organization types grows wider the longer one stays put in one area—at least where military experience is the issue. "A great way to begin to learn leadership is as a squad or company leader in the military," he contends. "But once you go higher, or stay with the military past age 30, you've stayed too long. A move later to the corporate world isn't nearly as likely to work out, because you've lost the face-to-face interaction on the small-unit level. Instead, you become ingrained in the culture of the military. I believe this is one reason the corporate headhunters aren't beating down the doors for career military people."

Another former marine shares that view. "Maybe the career military guy isn't leaving just any organization, but one of the most close-knit brotherhoods in the world," says Dan Carrison, co-author of *Semper Fi: Business Leadership the Marine Corps Way* (AMACOM). "In the Marines, everyone shares everything they know; they support and promote one another. That's how they survive. In the corporate environment, there are secrets; people play their cards close to the vest; they compete for recognition and promotions. That can result in long odds against the soldier who switches."

Filson's opinion is supported by executive search consultant Millington F. McCoy, managing director of New York search firm Gould, McCoy & Chadick Inc. "If you look at the top of the top in the corporate world, you can find a few—very few—cases where the military-to-business transfer worked well. When you look farther down, however, you find that young military officers are a wonderful pool of talent. I think that's because they've learned leadership and management, and in most cases, realized maturity very quickly and under pressure. Ross Perot at EDS discovered this many years ago. More recently, Citicorp [now part of Citigroup Inc.] launched an effort to recruit the best young military achievers."

McCoy says she's personally found successful candidates among career military officers when her client's situation virtually dictated that source. She found the COO of a swimming-pool company—a U.S. Army Corps of

Engineers early retiree—because the small firm couldn't afford to pay the going private-industry salary. When a telecommunications company needed a new assistant VP with "state-of-the-art expertise" in earth-station technology, "the only place it existed was in the Navy. He later became the firm's COO."

But these are the infrequent instances of success, McCoy contends. "It's not done routinely, because the common outcome isn't so favorable." She isn't much more enthusiastic about transfers across industries within the corporate world. "I had experience recruiting the first wave of marketing people for the banking industry, which of course had no one" when banks were first permitted to enter non-traditional, competitive markets. "We went to top people in consumer packaged goods—where competition has been fierce all along. I learned that something more than a cultural fit was required." More specifically, she explains, the recruits who worked out had some familiarity with finance or math, even if only as a college undergraduate, as well as personalities that allowed them to deal with the rapidly changing pace of the industry.

History certainly teaches that military and civilian leadership are not the same. Civil War General Ulysses S. Grant is generally regarded as a prime example of a stunningly successful military leader who just as stunningly failed as president.

But Grant chronicler Al Kaltman sees his subject not as a failed president but as one who "mismanaged" the nation's highest office in a number of crucial ways. Therein lie timeless management lessons for all managers, says Kaltman, author of *Cigars, Whiskey, and Winning: Leadership Lessons from General Ulysses S. Grant* (Prentice-Hall).

Kaltman claims that Grant's shift from the military to politics "shows you always have to understand what business you're in."

"For example, he clearly understood the necessity of gaining allies in war. He was one of few Army generals in history who cultivated and worked effectively with naval leaders. But he came into the presidency saying he was above identification with any political party, alienating the power structure of the Republican Party—the people who helped him gain his office. He clearly didn't understand, at first, that the presidency is a political office."

Kaltman—senior executive VP at MBNA America Bank in Wilmington, Del.—says that planning is another managerial skill that Grant abundantly displayed in war but not in political office. "One of Grant's key objectives as president was to achieve greater racial equality. But, unlike his performance in the Civil War, he articulated the goal without articulating concrete plans to accomplish it. Instead, he reacted to spreading racial violence by stopping its worst excesses, winning a battle here and there, but in the end losing the war."

The key to this disappointing outcome, Kaltman contends, "is Grant's failing to understand that his role as president extended to pushing his favored policies, not just recommending them."

The third managerial skill that Kaltman sees in Grant's command in the military but not in his presidency is "surrounding himself with good people and getting them to work together as a team. Gen. Grant was closely acquainted with the men who served under him; President Grant was not. He acknowledged in his final State of the Union address that the people he had previously appointed were almost all unknown by him." Continuing scandals involving many of those appointees dogged his presidency.

Kaltman sums up the military Grant as "a hands-on manager; a master of detail, who got out and saw for himself what was happening in the units under his command. President Grant thought of himself as a purely administrative officer, more like a presiding magistrate than a manager."

Look Inside to Cross the Chasm

For San Diego leadership consultant Janet E. Lapp, "two points argue against the transferability of leadership success." The first, she says, is that strong leadership qualities "emerge at critical junctures in their organization's history," and that not many leaders are on hand at such times in the lives of two or more different organizations. The second is that "a sense of life-or-death urgency and great passion for the cause" are essential to leadership success, and few people demonstrate such feelings in two widely differing arenas. "We saw urgency and passion in Colin Powell's leading the military and Gandhi's leading India to independence. But I'm not sure we'd see them in Powell as a politician or in Gandhi as head of Chrysler."

Filson, author most recently of *Results! Results! Results! Getting More Faster* (Williamstown), also suggests difficulties in transferring leadership qualities that matter to new arenas. There's no question that leading by "ordering people to go from point A to point B" will have about the same effect at one organization as at another. "But leadership that is effective and ultimately successful isn't a matter of ordering people to do things—it's motivating them to want to find their own way to do the things that need to be done. More succinctly, true leadership is motivating others to lead others to get results. The would-be leader who grasps this essential trust, who can develop teams that get results, can write his or her own ticket in life in any chosen field."

Kevin Cashman also says that there's no problem assessing transferability of leadership when it is viewed simplistically. "If you look at a competency model of leadership—it consists of external manifestations such as vision, judgment, drive, creativity, and so forth—then you just look at the competencies that make up the model, see if a candidate has them, and see if the new role you might give a person requires them. Steps one, two, three, and done. That tells you whether leadership is transferable."

But Cashman, who wrote *Leadership from the Inside Out* (Executive Excellence), admits the competency model is demonstrably misleading. "Every leader shows up a little differently in terms of competencies. This one excels at creativity, that one at interpersonal relations, and another at communication. That shouldn't happen if there is a defined list of competencies required to be a leader. So leadership must be something different, something deeper and more fundamental."

That something is what Cashman calls "authentic self-expression that creates value." Self-expression is a characteristic that allows for different competencies from one leader to another, he asserts. "For example, one may be very charismatic, one very introverted—but both can be very successful leaders." The key to transporting leadership success under this construct is to "free yourself of being too tied up in what's on a résumé." Don't accept the definition of the marketplace, which sees you in a role.

"Look deeper, to what's inside," Cashman urges. "Transferability comes when we manage our careers from the inside out—figuring out what our contribution is—how we add value to our organizations or units or teams."

Warren Bennis, too, finds the key to a leader's successful chasm-crossing within. "I think we can identify the critical element using Daniel Goleman's term *emotional intelligence*. Those who lead successfully in all circumstances have certain qualities in common: They know who they are, they're good diagnosticians, their egos don't get in the way of learning a new organization. In other words, they have enough emotional intelligence to deal with the jump—the uncertainties, the personalities, and the doubters."

As a leading example of such a "chasm crosser," Bennis nominates Harold M. Williams, whom he calls "a great success story, maybe the greatest, considering the vastly different spheres of the groups he's headed."

Since Bennis made that assertion only a few months back, Williams has added yet another post—as counsel to super-lawyers Skadden, Arps, Slate, Meagher & Flom. This position brings him full circle, in a sense, because his wide-ranging work life began with practicing law at what was then called Hunt Foods, where he later ascended to chairmanship. He chucked it in 1970 to become dean of UCLA's Graduate School of Management, crossed the continent in 1977 to head the Securities and Exchange Commission, and then, beginning in 1981, spent 17 years as president of the J. Paul Getty Trust—spectacularly capping his tenure with last year's opening of the Getty Center. He remains linked with the trust as president emeritus.

What possesses an executive—or, more accurately, what does he possess—to repeatedly depart the relatively safe haven of one organization and risk a roll of the dice with another far removed? "I never went into anything that didn't turn me on," says Williams. "Nor did I take any new job without at least a hypothesis on how it might be done better. When I went from Norton Simon to UCLA, I had ideas for turning the school around in certain ways, because I had hired many MBAs and seen blind spots in their worldview."

"This isn't to say I came in and announced, 'Here's what I am going to do.' I knew I couldn't do anything alone. But I had learned by talking to faculty members before I took the job that many of them agreed with some of the changes I thought might be needed."

In all of his varied posts, Williams says, "I saw myself in essentially the same way. I am a manager of people. They know their subject matter better than I. They have their own vision. And they have what I call the big motors' that drive them toward that vision. I realized, early on, that good leadership means giving such people plenty of room. That made trust the most important attribute required of me in any of those jobs. Trust that they'll do what's right and best, and that they'll be straight with me."

Williams also points to possessing "a good bit of self-confidence," which allows him "to learn from the people I manage." There is within him, too, "a fair degree of humility—enough to give people the room they need to make me look good."

Despite the solid groundwork of research and consultations he lays down before accepting any new post, Williams acknowledges that, "It was impossible to remove all the risk of making a change. And I wouldn't want to. If there were no risk, why would anyone want to make a change?"

PART 4

The Changing Context

Make the most of yourself, for that is all there is to you.
—Ralph Waldo Emerson

Over the past few years, the military mission has become more ambiguous and complex with increasing combat assignments and peacekeeping responsibilities. Reduced budgets have led to changes in the retirement contract with active duty personnel as well as to downsizing, recruitment pressures, and a variety of directives that change the operating environment on short notice. Flexibility and responsiveness have become more important, yet the military is a vast organization, and frustrations occur with ever-changing expectations. The once cohesive and unified culture is stressed and strained as our country copes with the realities of constantly changing multinational forces and multiple missions.

Recognizing the problem becomes more difficult as fewer members of Congress come with any military experience. On the one hand, this reduces the possibilities of emotional commitments to the military; on the other hand, there is a waning empathy for those in the service in terms of how they can meet all of the growing expectations and achieve an acceptable quality of life. There are serious concerns whether political leaders truly understand military life and the accompanying issues.

Active duty forces are no longer able to handle the ongoing commitments directed to the military beyond peacekeeping. Reserve and National Guard units are called up more frequently for limited combat operations. No one argues that the part-time forces are not competent. However, leadership is tested in different ways when the career culture clashes with the culture of limited service and engagement.

Military leadership is global in scope. A variety of multicultural and cross-cultural issues must be addressed. This diversity is an organizational imperative that adds new dimensions to leadership. Effective leadership is dependent upon the contributions of people regardless of their heritage, characteristics, and values. The organization's success depends upon each person doing his or her share with commitment and expertise.

Military organizations now have to deal with constant social and technological change as well as the process of anticipating and adapting to that change. Airborne weapons launched from 30,000 feet can be targeted to a small building amid urban sprawl, but when the maps are old, the technology fails us in the accomplishment of the mission. The context changes and therefore so does much of the organizational culture. More than ever, we must analyze and anticipate.

At the same time, information technologies are both resources and constraints. Influence is based upon our ability to access, analyze, and disseminate information. Telecommunications technologies give us instant access to the world and what it knows. We are able (and do) collect more data than ever before; yet leaders and commanders face a critical problem: They are overloaded with data and starved for meaningful information. The result is often delay in awaiting for yet more information prior to making decisions.

Those aspiring to leadership roles must anticipate change in internal and external environments while presenting acceptable responses to those changes. Some focus on the short-run effectiveness for unit efficiency, and others expect a commitment to the long view for mission accomplishment. The leader of tomorrow must give full attention to both. Past and current actions of the leader are given close scrutiny by friend and foe. Performance standards increase, and we do not support those who fall short.

Effective leaders understand that intuition is a valuable guide. *Intuition* is our education and experience as we have learned from it. Synthesizing what we know sometimes confounds logic; the data say one thing but we really "know" something else. The temptation is to go with the data because the logic of the decision is documented. Effective leaders have learned when to go with their intuition because, in many respects, it is based upon information, not data. Military legend is replete with examples of how true leadership occurred when the leader acted on intuition. The risks are high because the defense of a mistake is personal. We must examine our accountability measures carefully to ensure that in the future we do not penalize taking risks in unimportant decisions, because by reducing the willingness to take risks we will reduce our effectiveness as leaders and be unable to effectively handle change.

Tomorrow's leader must have a sense of timing. Our pace of life accelerates, and important decisions must be made with immediacy. For each of these real-time decisions, we find that there are long-term consequences. Hence, the quality of information is increasingly important. Leaders are conflicted with demands for timely decisions and the need to consult with others to address the complexity of their task. Consultation takes time and, despite our innovations in communications, is often set aside to get the job done. Finding balance will be the challenge of the future.

Projecting Leadership

The harsh reality of military downsizing is the topic of "Our Military Condition" (Chapter 18), by John Lehman. He notes that we need deterrence. Yet he suggests that the absence of a strong military leads to its more frequent use, and he cites the fact that in the first five years of President Clinton's term the U.S. military had been engaged some fifty times. The military has a mission to fight wars, and Lehman believes that the many peacekeeping missions have been a grave error. Using the military for social intervention and the separation of the military from our civil society casts an unclear image of the military and war-fighting culture. He summarizes the steps that need to be taken to restore the military to its mission of fighting wars.

In Chapter 19, "Ineffective Leadership and Military Retention," Capts. Derek T. Hasty and Robert M. Weber posit that escalating problems with retention in the armed forces are a direct result of poor military leadership, not monetary rewards. According to the authors, ineffective leadership results in a dysfunctional organizational culture, a lack of focus, and an absence of trust in senior military leaders, which cause career junior officers to leave the service. Hasty and Weber discuss the implications of these problems for the development of future senior military leaders.

Polly LaBarre presents a description of the leadership style of United States Navy Commander D. Michael Abrashoff in Chapter 20, "The Agenda—Grassroots Leadership." Commander Abrashoff is the captain of a guided-missile destroyer, USS *Benfold*, which in 1998 had the best combat-readiness in the U.S. Pacific Fleet. Underlying Commander Abrashoff's model of leadership is his belief that innovative practices combined with true empowerment produce phenomenal results. The performance of the *Benfold* validates that philosophy. LaBarre's chapter demonstrates the importance of a leader's ability to translate theory into action and the positive effect of the leader "walking the talk."

We close with Chapter 21, "Military Leadership into the 21st Century: Another 'Bridge Too Far?'" In this thoughtful essay, Walter F. Ulmer Jr. carefully documents the many new challenges for military leadership, but he points out that there is no strategic design to change the culture. In comparing "best practices" for leadership development, Ulmer contends that the military still provides early opportunities for development, is mixed in articulating values for leader behavior, and failing in providing feedback and mentoring. He suggests some remedies that are consistent with the importance of continuing education in the military. General Ulmer's charge is that the challenge to the military is not defining what is expected of leaders; rather it is developing and sustaining effective leadership.

18

Our Military Condition

John Lehman

Will Rogers once said that "if you want to know when the next war might be coming you just watch the United States and see when it starts cutting down its defenses. It's the surest barometer in the world."

The history of this country is one of great reluctance to resort to arms, ferocious prosecution once engaged, and euphoric disarmament following victory. After every war we have disarmed, and by the heedlessness of those disarmaments we have usually sown the seeds of the next war. Recent American policy following the historic victory in the Cold War has been no exception to this historical pattern. In his legendary lectures at the University of Pennsylvania, Robert Strausz-Hupé used to say that while history doesn't repeat itself, patterns in history do. While we are not repeating exactly what happened after World War II and after World War I, the recent example of our inability to deter Saddam Hussein suggests certain parallels. We have in fact a relatively high level of spending in defense today, but spending does not necessarily produce capabilities. Given the vast global breadth of our vital interests, obligations, and entanglements, our interdependence of trade, commerce, and resources, we have steeply reduced the capabilities of our forces.

While the cataclysmic perils of the Cold War are gone, the world remains a very dangerous place. We now have only one superpower but no accepted order. The world is a virtual petri-dish of despots, disturbers of the peace and fundamentalist ethnic and economic rivalries not possible under the bipolar discipline of the Cold War. This disorder flourishes along with a proliferation of horrendous weapons of mass destruction.

We now know that Saddam Hussein has used biological and chemical

Reprinted by permission from *The American Spectator*, 21:11, pp. 25–27.

agents, and continues to strive for nuclear capability even as he gives the U.S. and the U.N. loud raspberries. Irrational, utterly unpredictable rogue states such as North Korea and Libya are developing access to nuclear weapons, biological agents and chemical weapons, and the means to deliver them. Iran has reportedly obtained contraband tactical nuclear weapons. The arsenal of the former Soviet Union remains partially unaccounted for. In the nuclear states of India and Pakistan, ethnic passions can overwhelm caution.

This is not a world in which to indulge euphoria, or to resume the American tradition of drastic disarmament.

What We Need

We need deterrence. We all hope that diplomacy works against Saddam, the Iranian terrorist-supporting state, and against all those ethnic conflicts that are disrupting the orderly pattern of peace that we thought we had won in the Cold War. But a strong diplomacy requires a strong defense. Our credibility in dissuading those rogues from attacking our interests, from developing and then using nuclear, chemical, and biological weapons, is diminishing before our eyes and the eyes of the world. Lobbing $100 million worth of unmanned cruise missiles into Sudan and Afghanistan while otherwise continuing diplomacy as usual suggests to the world that America no longer has the forces or the will to deal effectively with our enemies.

Ironically, the lack of a strong military leads only to its more frequent use. The Reagan administration sent forces abroad eighteen times to tamp down crises; the Bush administration, fourteen times. So far in the Clinton administration, only five years old, forces have been deployed some fifty times. These are costly deployments. Haiti alone cost $2 billion. Bosnia is well over $9 billion per year by the most conservative accounting and still climbing. Many have become virtually permanent, like "Operation Constant Vigil," in northern Iraq.

In order to deter our enemies, America needs forces that are recruited, trained, and directed to do not social services, not international welfare, not peacekeeping, not drug interdiction, but to rain fire and destruction on our enemies if they break the peace and seek to attack us and our close allies. The armed services are not just another branch of the civil service.

Our forces must be trained and equipped to exploit the huge technological advantage that we as a free and innovative technological society have over every other potential adversary in the world. We must infuse our armed forces with the same constant innovation, constant velocity of change in the use and development and application of technology and information that has characterized the tremendous renaissance of American productivity over the last decade.

We need forces that are representative of society, drawn from all social levels and welded into forces that are in the tradition of this country's founding fathers; of the Cincinnatus of the west, George Washington; of the citizen soldiers, and citizen sailors. The military must not be an employment agency of last resort, nor a closed self-perpetuating corps of janissaries remote from the rest of society.

What Is Wrong

There are some glaring things wrong with our defense preparedness. First, the mission of our armed forces is to fight wars. It is to deliver violence and destruction on our enemies when our security demands it. Only with such certain capability, and the undoubted will to use it justly, can wars be prevented.

One grave error has been the excessive use of American troops for peacekeeping. Those 241 marines killed in the bombing of their barracks in Lebanon in 1983 died because—despite the express opposition of the Marine Commandant—they had been turned into diplomats. Used as place holders between warring ethnic factions, and saddled with rules of engagement that guaranteed that they could not fight back, they were inevitably targeted by those who wished to drive us out of Lebanon in humiliation. The lesson has not been learned. Increasingly the way to rise in the armed forces is by serving as a "peacekeeper" in civic action in Bosnia or some other ethnic trouble spot, and in mollifying and mediating disputes among warring factions. Such duty demands very different skills from fighting in a war, and the time devoted to training units for the one directly reduces our capability for the other.

Using the armed forces for drug interdiction is yet another serious mistake. By accepting that new (and I believe unconstitutional) mission, the services have become de facto police. To involve the services in domestic law enforcement is to cross a dangerous line in the separation of powers. Thomas Jefferson would be horrified. Moreover, trying to seal our borders against drug smuggling is hopeless, and actually aggravates the problem by giving politicians an easy substitute for effective action. Like peacekeeping, drug interdiction also distracts from the cultivation of war-fighting skills.

Perhaps the most debilitating disorder afflicting the services today is the primacy of social engineering. We have changed the recruitment, training, and promotion systems of our armed services to make them more socially acceptable, more politically correct, and more gender-conscious. In so doing, we have weakened the ability of our forces to face down, deter, and if necessary smash the Saddam Husseins and Osama bin Ladens of the world.

The political crusade to achieve gender equality is undermining the services' ethical integrity through mandated (though unspoken) quotas, de facto double standards, and McCarthy-style blacklists such as those that followed Tailhook. This administration has required everyone from young recruits to four-star generals to pretend that up is down and day is night, and to parrot statements that clash with what they see with their own eyes every day.

Another serious problem area, emerging in the last decade, has been civil-military relations. Almost unnoticed, the historic concept of the citizen-soldier that George Washington gave to us is disappearing. Today's armed forces are a special caste of highly skilled professionals.

Recruiting norms are set to favor those who will commit to career service. Psychological profiles have been developed to be able to select and give priority for admissions to service academies' officer programs, and technical enlisted programs to those who are most likely to serve a full career. If they don't fit that profile no matter how otherwise talented, they are not desired. It is very hard, except in the Army, to get a two-year enlistment; six years is what the Air Force and Navy try to sell to every recruit. Those who wish to serve for a period between high school and college with no apparent intent to stay permanently are not encouraged. Anyone who puts his papers in to go from the regulars to the reserves is treated as a defector.

As a result the military does not include anything like a cross-section of our society. This is already reflected in the last class to enter Congress with only 15 percent of its members having had any military exposure at all. And for the first time in history we have a presidential cabinet completely devoid of military experience (the only arguable exception being Vice-President Gore). The rising generation of corporate, professional, and educational leaders is similarly unfamiliar with the military, its virtues and peculiar limitations. Nor is the average American any longer familiar, either directly or through relatives, with our armed forces.

The broader result has been the gradual separation of our military from the society it serves, and a growing feeling of contempt in the career forces for the society that they defend. A recent book by Thomas Ricks, *Making the Corps*, offers a thoroughly researched insight into the trend. Ricks quotes officers who believe that "American society is showing signs of serious decay," and who predict that "'the next war we fight is very likely to be here on American soil.'"

"The subject of domestic peacekeeping," Ricks reports, "is now a hot topic in all of the command and staff college courses in the country. And indeed there are quite a few officers vocally arguing for giving the military the powers to detain suspects, confiscate weapons, and conduct searches without warrants as they do on occasion in the drug interdiction campaign."

The last of the serious disorders I see afflicting our services is the de facto unilateral disarmament underway in our defense procurement policies. As we have cut the forces 40 percent over the last five years, the bureaucracy has not been cut at all. There are currently 130,000 civilian bureaucrats, about 5,000 more than there were when the Cold War ended, in the Department of Defense inside the Beltway. Not one even carries a pistol. It is just as bad in each of the services. For every Captain or Colonel in operational command, there are nine in staff jobs. As fighting units have been almost halved, joint staffs have ballooned.

Remedy the Disorders

The first priority should be to restore the war-fighting culture of the forces. We should do our part in international peacekeeping with the United Nations or with regional alliances, but our contribution should never be forces on the ground. As the only superpower, our ground forces are inevitably targets and there are many other non-controversial nations quite willing and able to provide ground peacekeepers. We should be providing what no one else can: the C-5s, the satellite intelligence, the communications, the aircraft carriers, the 24-hour-a-day air cover.

With respect to social engineering, the solution is simple: no double standards. Women should be allowed into every specialty in which they can compete and win that rating or win that job against all comers. Certainly there are women who have the talent and desire to be attack bombardiers or commandos skilled in hand-to-hand combat. But they should not be artificially pushed into quotas or allowed lower standards of physical capacity and training than men. They must meet standards appropriate to their profession and specialty.

We must also come to grips with the double standard in the draft. Every 18-year-old male has to register for the draft today, but no woman has to. Although it is highly unlikely that we will ever need more troops than the all-volunteer force can provide, this disparity is an intellectual and a moral fissure running right through this ideology of gender equality in the services. Congressmen should either require the drafting of their constituents' daughters into the infantry or drop the registration of males.

As for the civil-military balance, we must increase the importance of the National Guard and Reserves, changing the way we train and pay them in order to give them a real share in the burdens of peacetime deterrence. Under Reagan and Bush, the Guard and Reserve fought in Desert Storm and all of the other conflicts and crises that brought victory in the Cold War. Now they have been cut out of all proportion in order to preserve the bureaucracy. The Navy, for instance, has cut back from over seventy drilling reserve ships to only four. We should offer ROTC service academy graduates the option of performing their obligated service with a long commitment in the drilling reserves.

Increase Procurement

We must have armed forces that are sustainable in cost. One of the great dividends of defeating the Soviet Union is that we now spend only slightly more than 2 percent of the GDP, down from 6 to 8 percent during most of the Cold War. That has helped us to eliminate the annual budget deficit, and has freed up much technical and engineering talent for commercial and civilian technological development. I, for one, do not believe that we need to go beyond the current percent of GDP spent for defense. This should not be an issue of throwing more money at the problem.

Secretary of Defense Cohen just came out with what I think is the best program of reforms that I have seen in the postwar period. Whether they can be carried out in this bureaucracy-loving administration I don't know, but they are targeted on exactly the right things: Cut the bureaucracy by a third. Reorganize and reduce the Office of the Secretary of Defense, the military departments, all the defense agencies, all of the bureaucrats, civilian and military, the staff of the Chairman of the Joint Chiefs, and the proliferating unified command staffs. Push out into the private sector much that is being done in those last pockets of real socialism and statement ownership, the industrial facilities of the armed forces like the Naval Weapons Centers and the Army arsenals and naval shipyards. The tremendous savings to be gained by those measures should be plowed back into new equipment and new research and development.

We need to reduce the pork. It has of course been a part of our system since the U.S.S. *Constitution*, in the first days of our Navy, when the original six frigates were built in different cities. That's part of democracy. But the scarcity of people in Congress with any military experience has meant that pork barrel runs wild and is grotesquely distorting procurement and the use of the scarce dollars appropriated to the services. When you see liberal Democrats in the northeast pushing through a nuclear submarine that the Navy didn't want, you know that we have got a serious problem of distortion.

All of these afflictions that now degrade and debauch our forces flow from one cardinal sin. The president charged with the sacred duty of protecting the forces under his command, from the braying political mob of partisan hacks, feminazis, porkers, and contract seekers, has instead delivered them over to these enemies who have had their way with them unimpeded. The Republicans in Congress have acted at best like the cowardly neighbors of Kitty Genovese, averting their eyes from a murder, while many have simply joined in the despoliation. The measures of rehabilitation as suggested above, or others like them, can flow only from a single cardinal virtue, the assertion of leadership.

19

Ineffective Leadership
and Military Retention

Captain Derek T. Hasty and
Captain Robert M. Weber

Picking up a newspaper or magazine these days might lead you to believe that "duty, honor, country" has given way to "show me the money."[1] Contrary to popular belief, problems with retention in the military are a direct result of poor military leadership, not monetary issues. Poor leadership results in a dysfunctional organizational culture, a lack of focus, and a lack of trust in senior leadership that has driven many people to make the decision to leave the service. Thus far, Congress and senior military officers have attempted to increase pay in order to improve retention. However, most departing service members have clearly stated that lack of financial satisfaction is not the driving force behind their decision to leave. It's not the money; it's the leadership.

Many have been quick to point the finger at pay and benefits, but money is not the only issue on the minds of service members leaving the armed forces. Issues such as political correctness, the use of the military as a social proving ground, decreasing emphasis on good order and discipline, eroding retirement benefits, and decreasing societal recognition of honorable service have an impact on job satisfaction. All of these issues must be addressed with the same level of attention that is given to issues of compensation, for seeing officer retention as a purely economic issue ignores the struggles that military people face today.[2]

The military is responding to its retention problems. Compensation packages, retirement benefits, and quality-of-life issues are being addressed. The Army chief of staff, General Dennis J. Reimer, told Congress in January 1999, "We do not have to wait for people to leave the force to recognize that we cannot keep the world's best soldiers unless we compensate them adequately for their service and sacrifice."[3] It is not the lure of easy money that causes military people to resign. In fact, many exiting service members take a pay cut when they leave the military. Instead, most service members believe that the long-term overall improvement in quality of life is worth the short-term pay cut.[4] Furthermore, most exiting service members do not see leaving the "certainty" of the military for the unknown of the civilian world as a major concern, but instead they view staying in as a far greater unknown with which to be concerned.[5] One can argue, and argue well, that all of these issues play an important part in why so many are getting out. However, the one driving issue behind all of these other issues is ineffective leadership.

Dysfunctional Culture

Ineffective military leadership leads to a dysfunctional military culture, a lack of focus, and a lack of trust in senior officers. First, problems with retention are a direct result of the current dysfunctional organizational culture in the military. According to Captain E. Tyler Wooldridge, III, U.S. Navy, "Some might argue that our problems could be eased by money— more money yields better training, better equipment, greater job satisfaction, more ships, more port visits, and better retention—but hefty budgets only mask the real issues."[6] It's not the money, it's our culture that needs repair. Give good junior officers opportunities to have fun, in a culture willing to confront problems and take care of its own, and they will stay.[7]

An organization with a culture that encourages its people to confront problems should thrive on candor. Many departing service members feel as though the military, in the midst of downsizing and budget cuts, has become a zero-defect environment. In this environment with no room for error, the emphasis is on looking good rather than actually being good. The zero-defect environment seems to have spread throughout the military over the past decade. Whether it is a perception or a reality, it is clearly not conducive to leaders' making an accurate assessment of the situation and making an honest effort to improve it.

Major Jon Hull, U.S. Marine Corps, argues in a recent article that lack of candor is by far the greatest factor contributing to the exodus of quality junior ground officers from the Marine Corps. He states:

> As unwavering as our expectation of integrity is, however, junior officers perceive a void between integrity and its relationship with candor. Too often candor is met with hostility, overreaction, is perceived as "malcontent," or interpreted as questioning a commander's decision. In actuality, candor should be not only encouraged but expected—if not demanded. It must be an integral part of any staff planning evolution and most important present as a com-

mander formulates his decision. Once the commander makes his decision and puts it into action, continued candor remains vital—although it is never a means of justifying less than full and vigorous support of the commander. Integrity without candor, the "if you have nothing good to say, say nothing at all" approach, in no way prepares us for or wins wars. Its absence often leads to a "politically correct" interpretation of actions or events, facilitates the perpetuation of a flawed effort, or allows a reinfestation of micromanagement within the ranks. We are all quick to jump on the "people must be allowed to make mistakes" bandwagon, but too often we quietly caveat this with the thought, "As long as they're not my people."[8]

This zero-defect, anticandor environment leads into another phenomenon among military professionals called careerism. All the armed services have suffered from careerism to some extent. This "ticket-punching" mentality clearly becomes more threatening during peacetime, when bureaucratic skills are paramount and where combat skills are less obvious and less valued. Many senior leaders are reluctant to criticize the present system because it has served them well. According to Captain Wooldridge, a third-generation Naval Academy graduate, "We had command and made captain, so it can't be too bad, right? Sure, we lost some good officers along the way, but isn't this business all about survival of the fittest?"[9] Unfortunately for the military, it may be the best careerists that are surviving, not the best war fighters. A young officer in today's military must start mapping career milestones early in his or her career to get the good jobs and make the tough cut promotions. The good jobs like joint duty, war colleges, Washington staff assignments, and aide and executive assignments do not allow time for jobs that are fun, nor do they allow for a second chance after a rough start, an opportunity Wooldridge says that he certainly had. This focus on ticket punching over at-sea experience and reduced command opportunity have made the careerist's values part of the culture. "'What have you done to make me look good?' hardly ranks with 'Don't give up the ship!' but that is what today's SWO [surface warfare officer] is most likely to hear as she searches for words of inspiration."[10] The desire to achieve the next career milestone drives many officers' daily thoughts and decisions. Furthermore, most careerists have no real love of the military, the units, or the followers they command or will command. As Wooldridge puts it, "Sea duty done 'right'—don't take risks, play the system, take the right jobs, look good—is just part of playing the game." Ultimately, "careerism fosters a culture that is not receptive to bad news, covers up problems, and emphasizes style over substance."[11]

The careerist culture shifts the focus from organizational success to individual success. In the past, the military sought and rewarded organizational, not individual, success. The careerist culture, however, encourages individual over organizational success. In the military today, just as in the corporate world, it is far more accepted that successful individuals will not remain with the same organization for very long. In fact, some employment specialists say that in today's rapidly changing environment, if you are not seeking or preparing yourself for your next position after just a few years with a company, you are well behind the power curve.[12]

Lack of Focus

Against the backdrop of this dysfunctional culture that favors careerism over candor, senior officers' inability to provide focus for more junior officers results in increased frustration among lower-ranking officers. Ultimately these experienced midlevel officers opt to leave the service. Currently the military is called upon to perform almost any type of mission, from saving sea turtles entangled in fishing nets to stopping ethnic cleansing in Kosovo. The gamut of missions required of the military is the primary driver behind what makes it so difficult for leaders to articulate a clear focus for their followers. Lieutenant Lewellyn D. Lewis, U.S. Navy, remarks in a recent article that "in spite of our nearly perpetual engagement overseas, the inability of our national leadership to establish a role and promulgate a sense of mission for the military has those in uniform feeling left in the lurch." If we have a military where "entire services search to establish new roles and missions, is it a surprise that individual officers are wondering about their personal purpose in the grand scheme?"[13]

Because the gamut of missions is not clearly prioritized by senior officers, in reality none are a priority. Captain Wooldridge maintains that except for the interesting interludes provided by Saddam Hussein, surface warfare in the 1990s can be a life of drudgery. He explains how numerous nontraditional missions such as preserving marine life, humanitarian operations, maritime interdiction operations, and the sheer monotony of managing gender integration, plastic waste disposal, liberty behavior, and other "hot" issues keep today's surface warfare officer extremely busy. These nontraditional missions do not provide today's service members with the same excitement or sense of pride and accomplishment that traditional military missions had in the past.[14]

Because of these numerous nontraditional "priority" missions, it has become common for many military leaders to lose track of what is really important. For example, "there are division officers, department heads, and executive officers who prioritize as if dental readiness were as vital to combat readiness as firefighting capability."[15] The good leaders, Wooldridge says, "routinely de-emphasize certain areas to dedicate resources to big-ticket items, but the sum of all the requirements we place on our officers is staggering, and what frequently goes away is time and enthusiasm for good SWO training and professional development."[16]

The military, like any other organization, cannot be superior at everything. Something has to give. Because leaders cannot or do not clearly set priorities for followers, we compromise our standards—and our integrity—in things that are vital to readiness, such as status of readiness and training reports, maintenance reports, and personnel qualification standards.[17] In the end, "these measures of readiness simply become figures to be manipulated in our drive to do it all, and to look good doing it."[18] Wooldridge provides the following example:

> During one of my recent tours, an experienced, competent junior officer brought me the results for an exam that ships self-administer prior to a Propulsion Examining Board visit. I was impressed by the tremendously high scores, even for personnel who had recently reported aboard. When I questioned the validity of the results the officer readily admitted that he had altered the scores, in accordance with existing practice. He was stunned when I directed him to record the actual grades, and he made it clear that he viewed my action as naive. He, like many of his peers who shade the truth to deliver the product that superiors demand, had lost respect for our system and was just playing the game.[19]

In fact the junior officer described here was doing much more than just playing the game. In an effort to study the effects of such an organizational culture, the Army has enlisted the efforts of the Army Research Institute, which issued a command climate assessment to over 20,000 Army and civilian personnel. The report revealed that the Army's state of ethical conduct is widely viewed as abysmal. Commanders have fallen prey to turning their backs on integrity because of this zero-defects mentality on the part of their superiors. It has been proven to be more detrimental to an officer's career to tell the truth about a deficiency than it is to get caught covering one up. As a result, many officers are placed into a position of ethical compromise.[20]

Since the military cannot do everything well, leaders must manage risk. Managing risk is like juggling. Some of the balls are made of rubber and some are made of glass. You may have to drop some of the rubber ones, but just make sure you don't drop the glass ones. In a 1998 interview, *Air Force Times* asked General Henry "Hugh" Shelton, the chairman of the Joint Chiefs of Staff, what his biggest single worry was in preparing for the twenty-first century. His response was: "We try to balance modernization and quality of life and readiness, we manage the risk in such a way that the force that's the first to deploy, the ones that are forward deployed, are fully capable and ready to go on a moment's notice."[21] When asked why he didn't mention money as a problem, he responded: "Money ties into that.

It's all resource driven. I can modernize as rapidly as industry can crank it out, and I can keep the highest state of readiness in the world if I've got enough in the budget. But balancing all of that is accepting some level of risk there in order to ensure that you're continuing to modernize and getting ready to have a trained and ready force for the future. It's the balance. And that's what keeps you awake at night."[22]

This balancing act that keeps the chairman of the Joint Chiefs awake at night also has a significant impact on the midlevel officers of the military. These people are the muddy-boots leaders of the military. They are the ones who must inspire soldiers, sailors, and airmen to fight and die for their country. They are the ones who constitute the backbone of the military force. They are experienced professionals who want to do well. Retention of these midlevel officers is key to the success of the military now and particularly in the future. The loss of military personnel from the ranks is not the real problem. It is the loss of high-quality, experienced, professional military leaders that should concern us. Providing a clear focus for midlevel officers would help decrease the frustration that has led to the exodus of so many of these talented military professionals.

Lack of Trust

The third major factor of poor leadership that leads to retention problems is the lack of trust the midlevel leaders have in the senior military officers. In a 1998 article Commander John R. Hatten and Lieutenant Commander Ronald Horton describe how the perception that general officers are mostly concerned with politically correct solutions rather than the morally correct solutions has created a lack of faith in senior leaders. Many junior and midgrade officers think that senior leaders are out of touch with the realities of day-to-day operations at their level. Throughout history, the greatest challenge of command has been the ability "to reconcile the big picture held by those at the top with the detailed knowledge available only at the scene."[23] This is especially true today, as there seems to be a vast communication gap between the midlevel and senior officers. Understandably, midlevel and junior officers do not fully comprehend the multitude of factors that go into the decision-making process of the senior officers. However, it is now time for the senior officers to take action and improve communication in order to generate a better understanding up and down the chain of command.[24]

Because of the rapidly changing environment of the military, senior leaders are not always knowledgeable on what it takes to fix the problems. According to a recent article in *Air Force Times*, "Senior Air Force leadership and Congress have no clue what the real issues are—or ignore them when surveys tell them what they are . . . and that no one is really thinking through problems beyond throwing money at pilots."[25] Many service members have been saying all along that money is not the big issue driving them out of active military service. The lack of trust in the senior military leaders manifests itself in a perceived low quality of leadership and a perceived low level of leader competence. A recent Army Research Institute Survey reveals that only 70 percent of officers are satisfied with the quality of leadership at their place of duty and the level of competence of their supervisors.[26]

Another condition that results in a lack of trust in senior military officers has evolved out of the aforementioned dysfunctional culture: Mentorship has nearly disappeared among the ranks of military officers. Mentoring has a long history throughout the military and has always held an important role in the development of high-quality junior officers into fine commanders and senior-level leaders. This heritage is so strong that despite its relative absence today it is still desired and valued. Many junior officers are seeking role models who will coach them the way they have heard it was done in the past. Junior officers want to hear what areas they should sustain and what areas they should improve.

Mentorship cannot be delegated and should not be confused with sponsorship. Often the responsibility of mentoring is delegated to the lowest level possible. To use an Army example, a battalion commander (O-5), who senior rates a platoon leader (O-1), delegates his or her mentorship responsibility to the company commander (O-3), who rates the platoon leader. Ironically, the members of a promotion board focus primarily on the senior rater's evaluation of the officer. By delegating mentorship responsibility, the battalion commander deprives the platoon leader of valuable feedback and advice that only an officer of his or her experience level can provide. A recent Army Research Institute survey revealed that only 65 percent of officers are satisfied that their performance is evaluated fairly and that their accomplishments are recognized to an appropriate degree.[27] However, feedback from the senior rater on a regular basis throughout the rating period would provide the platoon leader the opportunity to improve his or her performance and result in a fairer and more accurate evaluation. Another form of delegating mentorship is through permanent sponsorship programs. Sponsorship is the practice of assigning an incoming officer a peer sponsor who assists his or her transition into the new unit. In some cases, a permanent sponsorship program is used as a substitute for mentorship. In this instance, the senior rater who justifies a reduced role in mentoring is just checking the block by creating the appearance that officers are developed through a strong sponsorship program. In reality, leaders who delegate their mentorship responsibility are not mentoring at all.

Despite its tremendous significance, however, mentorship is not occurring throughout the military today. The military is becoming more technically oriented, and the focus has been taken off of professional development. The same technology that is used as an excuse for not developing lower-level officers can be used to enhance professional development. For example, mentors can use Internet resources, e-mail, video teleconferencing, and distance learning to enhance the mentoring process. Because of this technology the mentoring process does not necessarily end once the parties are geographically separated as a result of reassignments.

Many junior officers have heard their commanders and some senior officers attest to the belief that today young officers are required and expected to be far more competent than the junior officer of their era. Many junior officers sense an aura of competition as these leaders compare themselves as young officers to those of today and realize that they would fall short. It appears that senior leaders are insecure and perhaps feel threatened or challenged by the subordinate officer's potential to eventually surpass the senior officer professionally. Young officers may be especially threatening to senior officers in the area of technology. For example, senior officers may be reluctant to ask lower-ranking officers for assistance in understanding new equipment.

The communication involved in mentorship not only benefits the protégé but also brings to the surface insights and feedback that the senior officer may find very useful in improving his or her current command climate and leadership ability. This process will also provide senior officers an opportunity to learn more about themselves. Mentorship requires strong, confident senior leaders. Leaders must have the confidence to be brutally honest in assessing their followers' performance and potential, and they must have the moral courage to communicate the assessment to their followers.

Because of the potential benefits of mentoring, it is vitally important that senior officers undertake this mission of cultivating lower-level leaders. Today's junior officers are tomorrow's senior leaders of the Armed Forces. The mentoring process entails short- and long-term professional development, coaching, and guidance. As a result, this effort benefits the follower, the leader, and the institution.[28]

As evidenced by their focus on pay and benefits to solve the retention problems, many senior officers have not identified the real issues. They have implemented the right solutions for the wrong problems. Often the solutions that they implement are designed to treat the symptoms rather than cure the disease. The symptoms are relatively easy to fix, and positive results are generated quickly. The disease is much more complicated to identify, and it requires a lengthy and often unpleasant implementation process. If senior officers only made an effort to identify and fix the real issues for the long term, more officers would stay. Lieutenant Lewis has noted, "More than once, I have heard a fellow junior officer state that he would stay 'if the Navy just made an effort.'"[29] Moreover, the military should utilize the talents and ideas of its junior officers when attempting to resolve its current problems. Most officers truly care about the future of the military. Unfortunately, the perception exists that senior officers are not interested in the opinions and thoughts of junior officers, who are often most affected by current policies. For example, when a junior officer asked about a recent widely circulating e-mail message that expressed the opinion of a disgruntled Navy officer, a squadron commander remarked, "You weren't supposed to read that!"[30] The idea that junior officers cannot engage in critical thinking or do not possess the necessary military experience to contemplate such "high-level" subjects is degrading and leads to an environment of mistrust. There is a tremendous amount of energy, talent, and intellectual ability in the ranks of our junior officers, and military leaders can choose either to employ it in helping address this situation or to idly stand by while it moves to the civilian world.[31]

Implications for Leadership

The Army is facing an alarming rate of attrition among its soldiers, especially its junior officers. The deputy chief of staff for personnel, has stated that the Army's number one issue is the extreme shortage of personnel.[32] Air Force and Navy pilots are fleeing the military and taking jobs with major airlines that offer better pay and a more stable family life, free of disruptions from frequent and dangerous deployments. The Air Force is more than 850 pilots short of its required strength as its retention problem worsens. At the current rate of decline, the Air Force will find itself short 2,000 pilots by fiscal year 2000. Furthermore, midgrade officers and petty officers, the Navy's future instructors and trainers, are leaving the service at alarming rates. This trend is worsened by the absence of a steady supply of recruits to replenish the vacancies.[33] Many of those who have chosen to remain in the military realize the predicament the military is facing with its retention problems, and worse, they are forced to deal with the manpower shortages while still accomplishing the same missions. An Army Research Institute survey shows that only 25 percent of officers are satisfied with the number of people available to do work.[34] Eventually, carrying this tremendous burden will take its toll on even the most loyal and dedicated officers, as they are likely to become frustrated and disgruntled over being forced to do so much with so little. No organization, including the military, can sustain a more-with-less mindset for an indefinite period. As in any organization, more with less will eventually turn into less with less, no matter how high the level of expertise or dedication.

What does the retention crisis mean for future military leaders? Perhaps the greatest implication of the retention crisis for current and future leaders is that retention problems have created an ethical dilemma for commanders between improving retention statistics in their units and maintaining a high-quality force. *Air Force Times* recently reported that Lieutenant General Michael McGinty, the deputy chief of staff for personnel, sent a memorandum to commanders stating that "the policy governing separations for 'miscellaneous reasons' will be adjusted soon. He called first term attrition a 'significant leadership concern' that needs to be addressed so the Air Force does not continue to lose one in three airmen before they complete their first term."[35] Furthermore, McGinty wrote, "Commanders and first sergeants should make every effort to identify airmen who exhibit a likelihood for early separation and improve their chances for retention through counseling, remedial training and other corrective steps before initiating involuntary separation action."[36] Ironically, recipients of these types of corrective measures may view them as punishment rather than development, thus worsening the situation by driving them from the service at an even greater rate. But he added that commanders should not hesitate to force out airmen "who do not demonstrate potential for further military service" in order to "avoid negative mission impact associated with keeping the wrong people."[37]

McGinty's memorandum outlines personnel management guidance that pushes the retention burden down to the lowest levels. Commanders will now have to choose between keeping poor performers in order to improve their retention statistics and eliminating poor performers in order to maintain a high-quality force. The ethical dilemma inevitably occurs when commanders cannot do both and must choose which is more important. What is the specific guidance for this situation? One or the other must give. Which one is the priority? Given the current seriousness of the retention problems, the conditions stated in McGinty's memorandum force commanders into an ethical dilemma, a delicate balance between meeting retention requirements and maintaining a quality force.

As the number of highly talented midlevel leaders leaving the military increases, the quality of future senior military leaders decreases.[38] Personnel shortages are a harbinger that readiness among deployed and nondeployed forces is suffering. Senior military officers have been reluctant to admit that the military is returning to the days of the hollow force experienced in the post–Vietnam War era of the 1970s; however, the current condition of the armed services is quickly approaching that low point. The chief of naval operations, Admiral Jay Johnson, told Congress, "Recruiting and retention are inseparable from readiness. If we are unable to reverse the Navy's personnel trends, the hollow force will be unavoidable."[39]

Whatever happens with the current retention problems in the military, it won't happen overnight. As General Richard Hawley, commander of the Air Combat Command, said, "You can't turn it around quickly. It's like the Titanic. . . . We can apply a lot of rudder to the force today, and it's going to take time before those trends begin to stabilize and we can reverse them."[40]

Notes

1. Bryant, Jordan. "Still Punching Out." *Air Force Times,* March 9, 1998, 3.

2. Lewis, Lewellyn D., Lieutenant, U.S. Navy. "Where Have All the O-3s Gone?" *U.S. Naval Institute Proceedings,* February 1998, 25–26.

3. Slabodkin, Gregory. "Coming Up Short." *Military Training Technology,* Volume 4, Issue 2, 4.

4. Lewis, "Where Have All the O-3s Gone," 25–26.

5. Hull, Jon P., Major, U.S. Marine Corps. "When It's Time to Pay Their Dues . . . " *U.S. Naval Institute Proceedings,* September 1998, 45.

6. Wooldridge, E. Tyler, III, Captain, U.S. Navy. "Five and Out?" *U.S. Naval Institute Proceedings,* August 1998, 28.

7. Ibid.

8. Hull, "When It's Time to Pay Their Dues," 46.

9. Wooldridge, "Five and Out," 26.

10. Ibid.

11. Ibid.

12. Hull, "When It's Time to Pay Their Dues," 45.

13. Lewis, "Where Have All the O-3s Gone," 25.

14. Wooldridge, "Five and Out," 26.

15. Ibid.

16. Ibid.

17. Ibid.

18. Ibid.

19. Ibid.

20. Reimer, Dennis J., General, U.S. Army. Congressional testimony before the Budgetary Subcommittee, U.S. House of Representatives, 1st Sess., 106th Cong., February 26, 1999.

21. Weible, Jack, and Wilson, George C. "Interview with Army Gen. Henry 'Hugh' Shelton, the Chairman of the Joint Chiefs of Staff on Feb. 18, 1998." *Air Force Times,* March 9, 1998, 29.

22. Ibid.

23. Hatten, John R., Commander, U.S. Navy, and Horton, Ronald, Lieutenant Commander, U.S. Navy. "Is Anyone Listening?" *U.S. Naval Institute Proceedings,* February 1998, 80.

24. Ibid., 77.

25. Bryant, "Still Punching Out," 3.

26. Army Research Institute. "Quality of Life and Job Satisfaction Survey," 1998.

27. Ibid.

28. Fast, Barbara G., Lieutenant Colonel (P), U.S. Army. "Mentorship: A Personal and Force Multiplier." *Military Intelligence,* July-September 1996, 34.

29. Lewis, "Where Have All the O-3s Gone," 26.

30. Ibid.

31. Ibid.

32. Meek, Jeffrey A., Captain, U.S. Army. "Personnel Leader's Conference Summary." *Deputy Chief of Staff Personnel,* March 16, 1999, 1.

33. Slabodkin, "Coming Up Short," 4.

34. Army Research Institute, "Quality of Life and Job Satisfaction Survey."

35. Bird, Julie. "Hey, Not So Fast!" *Air Force Times,* May 25, 1998, 3.

36. Ibid.

37. Ibid.

38. Hatten and Horton, "Is Anyone Listening," 77.

39. Slabodkin, "Coming Up Short," 4.

40. Pulley, John. "Running on Empty: Air Force Leaders Are Still at a Loss to Fix Retention Problems." *Air Force Times,* March 16, 1998, 3.

20

The Agenda—
Grassroots Leadership

Polly LaBarre

You expect to be awed by the view from the deck of the USS Benfold. The
$1 billion warship is one of the U.S. Navy's most modern, most lethal fight-
ing machines: 8,300 tons of steel armed with the world's most advanced
computer-controlled combat system; revolutionary radar technology; a
stock of missiles capable of taking out precise targets on land, sea, or air;
and a crack crew of 300 highly skilled, totally committed sailors. In 1997, a
year and a half after its commission in the Pacific fleet, the guided-missile
destroyer spearheaded some of the most critical missions in a confrontation
with Iraq. Now tethered to a dock on San Diego's sprawling naval base, the
Benfold gleams with power. When eating up the sea at full throttle, she generates a plume of froth that's two-stories high.

What you don't expect to find on board the Benfold is a model of leadership as progressive as any celebrated within the business world. The man
behind that model is Commander D. Michael Abrashoff. His career includes a sterling service record, combat experience, and prestigious posts in
Washington, DC. He has won dozens of medals. He is also credited with
building the Benfold's reputation as the best ship in the Pacific fleet. Last
year, in fact, the ship won the prestigious Spokane Trophy for having the
best combat readiness in the fleet—the first time in at least 10 years that a
ship of its class had received that honor. Yet Abrashoff doesn't quite look
the part: Think of a military leader, and you may envision George C. Scott's
depiction of General George S. Patton. Abrashoff, however, has an easy
smile and electric-blue eyes.

Reprinted by permission from *Fast Company* magazine, 23 (April 1999), pp. 114 et seq.
© 1999 by *Fast Company*. All rights reserved. To subscribe, please call 800/688-1545.

Behind Abrashoff's relaxed confidence is his own brand of organizational zeal. Settling into his stateroom, Abrashoff, 38, props his feet on a coffee table, sips a soda, and says, "I divide the world into believers and infidels. What the infidels don't understand—and they far outnumber the believers—is that innovative practices combined with true empowerment produce phenomenal results."

That the ranks of the nonbelievers include most of his superiors and fellow commanding officers doesn't deter Abrashoff one bit. "I'm lucky," he says. "All I ever wanted to do in the navy was to command a ship. I don't care if I ever get promoted again. And that attitude has enabled me to do the right things for my people instead of doing the right things for my career. In the process, I ended up with the best ship in the navy—and I got the best evaluation of my career. The unintended benefit? My promotion is guaranteed!" After completing his 20-month tour of duty as commander of the Benfold this past January, Abrashoff reported to a top post at the Space and Naval Warfare Systems Command.

Abrashoff continues to see his mission as nothing less than the reorientation of a famously rigid 200-year-old hierarchy. His aim: to focus on purpose rather than on chain of command. When you shift your organizing principle from obedience to performance, says Abrashoff, the highest boss is no longer the guy with the most stripes—it's the sailor who does the work. "There's nothing magical about it," he says from his stateroom on the Benfold. "In most organizations today, ideas still come from the top. Soon after arriving at this command, I realized that the young folks on this ship are smart and talented. And I realized that my job was to listen aggressively—to pick up all of the ideas that they had for improving how we operate. The most important thing that a captain can do is to see the ship from the eyes of the crew."

That perspective provided Abrashoff with two insights about change: First, there's always a better way to do things. In the first few months of his command, Abrashoff took apart every process on board and examined how each one helped the crew to maintain operational readiness. "I pulled the string on everything we did, and I asked the people responsible for—or affected by—each department or program, 'Is there a better way to do things?'" Most of the time, he discovered that there was.

Abrashoff's second insight about change: The more people enjoy the process the better the results. Spending 35 days under way in the Persian Gulf is anything but enjoyable—but Abrashoff managed to lead his sailors through their missions and to have fun in the process. An ingenious supply officer procured pumpkins—not an easy task in the Middle East—thereby allowing the Benfold to sponsor a pumpkin-carving contest for the fleet in October 1997. During replenishments alongside supply tankers, the Benfold's crew became known throughout the Gulf for projecting music videos onto the side of the ship. The crew took its entertainment detail a step further during Christmastime, when K.C. Marshall, the ship's highly skilled Elvis impersonator (and chief navigator), serenaded the admiral's ship with a rendition of "Blue Christmas."

Abrashoff first developed his inclination to skirt standard operating procedure during his post as military assistant to then-Secretary of Defense William Perry, in 1994. He sat beside Perry during the arduous implementation and assessment of the Defense Acquisition Reform Initiative, and he took every opportunity to apply lessons from that initiative on the Benfold. For example, in purchasing food for the ship, Abrashoff switched from high-cost naval provisions to cheaper, better-quality name-brand food. With the money he saved, Abrashoff sent 5 of the Benfold's 13 cooks to culinary school—and as a result made the ship a favorite lunchtime destination for crews across the San Diego waterfront.

Abrashoff's leadership formula produces benefits that are both financial and operational. In fiscal year 1998, the Benfold returned $600,000 of its $2.4 million maintenance budget and $800,000 of its $3 million repair budget. Abrashoff notes that because any surplus goes back to the navy's top line, "there's no rational reason for saving that money—except that we've created an environment in which people want to do well." The navy's bean counters slashed the ship's maintenance budget this year by exactly $600,000—yet Abrashoff expects the ship to return 10% of its reduced allotment.

At the same time, the Benfold's performance has set new standards. For the past two years, the ship's "readiness indicators" have featured the lowest count of "mission degrading" equipment failures and the highest gunnery score in the Pacific fleet. The crew also completed the navy's predeployment training cycle in record time. That process normally requires 22 days in port and 30 days under way. The Benfold's crew required 5 days in port and 14 days under way to complete the cycle—and to earn coveted shore leave.

Another critical performance measure is a ship's retention rate. The Benfold's rate is off the charts. On average, only 54% of sailors remain in the navy after their second tour of duty. Under Abrashoff's command, 100% of the Benfold's career sailors signed on for an additional tour. Given that recruiting and training costs come to a minimum of $100,000 per sailor, Abrashoff estimates that the Benfold's retention rate saved the navy $1.6 million in personnel-related costs in 1998.

Yet the most compelling sign of Abrashoff's success may be the smooth interaction that now exists among the ship's company. The Benfold's experienced department heads, its divisional officers (most of them fresh out of the naval academy or ROTC), and its enlisted sailors all show a deep appreciation of the ship's relaxed discipline, its creativity, and its pride in performance. Commander Abrashoff walked Fast Company through six principles that have made the USS Benfold a working example of grassroots leadership.

Don't Just Take Command— Communicate Purpose

The Benfold is a warship. Our bottom line is combat readiness—not just in terms of equipment but also in every facet of training and organization. But the military is an organization of young people. Many of them go into the military to get away from bad situations at home. Many have been involved with drugs or gangs. Although they know what they don't want, they don't quite know what they do want. Getting them to contribute in a meaningful way to each life-or-death mission isn't just a matter of training and discipline. It's a matter of knowing who they are and where they're coming from—and linking that knowledge to our purpose.

Within two days of when new crew members arrive, I sit down with them face-to-face. I try to learn something about each of them: Why did they join the navy? What's their family situation like? What are their goals while they're in the navy—and beyond? How can I help them chart a course through life? Ultimately, I consider it my job to improve my little 300-person piece of society. And that's as much a part of the bottom line as operational readiness is.

Leaders Listen Without Prejudice

Most people in this organization are in "transmit mode"—meaning that they don't "receive" very well. But it's amazing what you discover when you listen to them. When I first took charge of the Benfold, I was having trouble learning the names of everyone in the crew, so I decided to interview five people a day. Along with Master Chief Bob Scheeler, the senior enlisted guy on the ship, I met with each person individually and asked three simple questions: What do you like most about the Benfold? What do you like least? What would you change if you could? Most of these sailors had never been in a CO's cabin before. But once they saw that the invitation was sincere, they gave me suggestions for change that made life easier for the whole crew and also increased our combat-readiness ratings.

From those conversations, I drew up a list of every practice on the ship and divided those practices into non-value-added chores and mission-critical tasks. I tackled the most demoralizing things first—like chipping-and-painting. Because ships sit in salt water and rust, chipping-and-painting has always been a standard task for sailors. So every couple of months, my youngest sailors—the ones I most want to connect with—were spending entire days sanding down rust and repainting the ship. It was a huge waste of physical effort. A quick investigation revealed that everything — from the stanchions and metal plates to the nuts and bolts used topside—were made of ferrous material, which rusts. I had every nut and bolt replaced with stainless steel hardware. Then I found a commercial firm in town that uses a new process that involves baking metal, flame-spraying it with a rust inhibitor and with paint, and then powder-coating it with more paint. The entire process cost just $25,000, and that paint job is good for 30 years. The kids haven't picked up a paintbrush since. And they've had a lot more time to learn their jobs. As a result, we've seen a huge increase in every readiness indicator that I can think of.

I not only know the names of my crew members—I also know where they're from, as well as a little bit about their families; I know what they aim to do in life. I learned from the interviews that a lot of them wanted to go to college. But most of them had never gotten a chance to take the SAT. So I posted a sign-up sheet to see how many would take the test if I could arrange it. Forty-five sailors signed up. I then found an SAT administrator through our base in Bahrain and flew him out to the ship to give the test. That was a simple step for me to take, but it was a big deal for morale.

Practice Discipline
Without Formalism

In many units—and in many businesses—a lot of time and effort are spent on supporting the guy on top. Anyone on my ship will tell you that I'm a low-maintenance CO. It's not about me; it's about my crew. Those initial interviews set the tone: In my chain of command, high performance is the boss. That means that people don't tell me what I want to hear; they tell me the truth about what's going on in the ship. It also means that they don't wait for an official inspection or run every action up and down the chain of command before they do things—they just do them.

Lieutenant Jason Michal, my engineering-department head, recently had to prepare for engineering certification. That's one of the most critical and stressful inspections on the ship, but I kept away until he asked me to come down to review his work. What I saw blew my mind. He had been tweaking procedures for months and had implemented about 40 changes in the operating system. Of course, he aced the inspection. When the people who do the work know that they—not the manual or policy—have the last word, you get real innovation in every area.

One of our duties during the 1997 Gulf crisis was to board every ship going to or coming from Iraq and to inspect it for contraband. This inspection was a laborious process that involved filling out a time-consuming four-page report each time a ship made a crossing. One of my petty officers created a database to store information about each ship and to generate reports automatically. I gave a copy of the database to another CO, who showed it to the admiral. Now that database method is policy throughout our battle group.

None of this means that we've sacrificed discipline or cohesion on the ship. When I walk down the passageway, people call attention on deck and hit the bulkhead. They respect the office but understand that I don't care about the fluff—I want the substance. And the substance is combat readiness. The substance is having people feel good about what they do. The substance is treating people with respect and dignity. We gain a lot of ground and save a lot of money by keeping our focus on substance rather than on extraneous stuff.

The Best Captains
Hand Out Responsibility—
Not Orders

Companies complain about turnover, but a ship's company isn't a static population. Not counting dropouts and other separations, about 35% of a ship's crew transfers out every year. That means that I must be constantly vigilant about cultivating new experts. After improving the food on this ship, my next priorities were to advance my people and to train my junior officers, who are called on repeatedly to make life-and-death decisions.

I not only have to train new folks; I also have to prepare higher-level people to step into leadership roles. If all you do is give orders, then all you'll get are order takers. We need real decision makers—people who don't just sleepwalk through the manual. That means that we have to allow space for learning. Removing many of the nonreadiness aspects of the job—from chipping-and-painting to cleaning—lets us spend more time on learning how to use all of the sophisticated technology in our combat-information center and on running through war scenarios on our computer system.

And because we're more interested in improving performance than we are in pomp, we can create learning experiences at every turn. When something goes wrong on a ship, the traditional attitude is "Hurry up and fix it, or we'll look bad." Well, if you don't care about getting promoted, you'll give a sailor time to learn how to do the job right—even if you run the risk of having the admiral stop by before the problem is fixed.

As a result, we have the most proficient training teams on the waterfront and a promotion rate that's over the top. In the last advancement cycle (that's the process that determines base pay, housing allowance, and sea pay), Benfold sailors got promoted at a rate that was twice as high as the navy average. I advanced 86 sailors in 1998. That amounts to a huge chunk of change and a lot of esteem for roughly one-third of my crew.

Successful Crews
Perform with Devotion

At a conference for commanding officers that I attended recently, more than half of the officers there argued that paying attention to quality of life (QOL, as we call it) interferes with mission accomplishment. That's ridiculous. It doesn't make sense to treat these young folks as expendable. The navy came up 7,000 people short of its 52,000-person recruitment goal in 1998, and it expects to be 12,000 people short of its goal in 1999. In every branch of the military, one-third of all recruits never complete their first term of enlistment. We've got to provide reasons for people to join, to stay—and to perform. The leader's job is to provide an environment in which people are not only able to do well but want to do well.

I looked at what usually happens when new 18- or 19-year-old recruits check in: They fly in from boot camp on a Friday night. They feel intimidated and friendless. They stow their gear in their berths and immediately get lost in San Diego. To change all of that, we've created a welcoming plan: Now, when new recruits come on board, their bunks are assigned, their linen and blankets are there, and we match them with a hand-picked sponsor who shows them the ropes. They can even call home—on my nickel—to tell Mom and Dad that they've made it.

The biggest complaint when we're out to sea for weeks on end is military-issue entertainment. When we pulled into Dubai—one of the better liberty ports in the Persian Gulf—a sailor took me aside to tell me that the crew members were frustrated because their tour-bus drivers didn't speak English and wouldn't deviate from assigned routes. On the spot, I rented 15 10-passenger minivans. I told the crew to divide into groups, and I assigned a senior petty officer to serve as a monitor on each bus.

Now, that wasn't strictly legal, but it helped morale so much that it has become a popular procedure for ships throughout the Gulf. A more serious issue for crew members at sea involves time away from their families. Most ships report several family problems during every deployment, and most of those problems result from lack of communication. I created an AOL account for the ship and set up a system for sending messages daily through a commercial satellite. That way, sailors can check in with their families, take part in important decisions, and get a little peace of mind.

Back in port, the top frustration for the crew involves 24-hour shipboard duty between deployments. The standard practice is to divide the crew into four sections that stand duty in rotation—with each section serving a 24-

hour shift every 4 days and getting only 1 weekend off each month. That's criminal! So I suggested an eight-section duty rotation, which would require a 24-hour shift every 8 days while providing 2 weekends off each month. In order to maximize flexibility, I cross-trained all of the sailors to perform every function of their duty section. The system has worked so well that many ships on the waterfront are now copying it.

Maintaining "quality of life" is simply a matter of paying attention to what causes dissatisfaction among the crew. You do what you can to remove those "dissatisfiers" while increasing the "satisfiers." Increasing satisfaction may be as simple as recognizing that everybody loves music and then setting up a great sound system or buying a karaoke machine. "Quality of life" is also a matter of creating an environment in which everyone is treated with respect and dignity. The Benfold is one of the first ships in the navy that was built from the keel up to accommodate women. It's no secret that the military has had problems with sexual harassment and with prejudice in general. Yet when we do equal-opportunity surveys for the Benfold, we get stunning results: Only 3% of minorities on board reported any type of racial prejudice, and only 3% of women reported any form of sexual harassment.

That's not because I give long lectures on prejudice or sexual harassment—it's because I talk about the effects of community and about the need to cultivate unity and teamwork with as much care as we give to maintaining our equipment.

True Change Is Permanent

Ships in the navy tend to take on the personality of their commanding officers. But neither my crew nor I worry about what will happen now that I've moved on. We've set up a virtuous circle that lets people know that their contribution counts. This crew has produced phenomenal results, and now it's motivated to do even better. My attitude is, once you start perestroika, you can't really stop it. The people on this ship know that they are part owners of this organization. They know what results they get when they play an active role. And they now have the courage to raise their hands and to get heard. That's almost irreversible.

Sidebar

During engagements in hot spots like the Persian Gulf, the navy hands out its toughest assignments to the USS Benfold. That's because the Benfold has the highest level of training, the best gunnery record, and the highest morale in the fleet. According to D. Michael Abrashoff, who until recently was the ship's commander, its stellar performance reflects a powerful way of leading a ship's company. Here are some of the principles behind his leadership agenda.

1. **Interview your crew.** Benfold crew members learned that when they had something to say, Abrashoff would listen. From initial interviews with new recruits to meal evaluations, the commander constantly dug for new information about his people. Inspired by reports of a discrepancy between the navy's housing allowance and the cost of coastal real estate, Abrashoff conducted a "financial wellness" survey of the crew. He learned that it was credit-card debt, not housing, that was plaguing the ship's sailors. He arranged for financial counselors to provide needed advice.

2. **Don't stop at SOP.** On most ships, standard operating procedure rules. On the Benfold, sailors know that "It's in the manual" doesn't hold water. "This captain is always asking, 'Why?'" says Jason Michal, engineering-department head, referring to Abrashoff. "He assumes that there's a better way." That attitude ripples down through the ranks.

3. **Don't wait for an SOS to send a message.** Listening is one thing; showing that you've heard what someone has said is quite another. Abrashoff made a habit of broadcasting ideas over the ship's loud-speakers. Under his command, sailors would make a suggestion one week and see it instituted the next. One example: Crew members are required to practice operating small arms—pistols and rifles—but they often find it hard to secure range time while they're on base. So one sailor suggested instituting target practice at sea. Abrashoff agreed with the suggestion and implemented the idea immediately.

4. **Cultivate QOL (quality of life).** The Benfold has transformed morale boosting into an art. First, Abrashoff instituted a monthly karaoke happy hour during deployments. Then the crew decided to provide entertainment in the Persian Gulf by projecting music videos onto the side of the ship. Finally, there was Elvis: K.C. Marshall, the ship's navigator and a true singing talent, managed to find a spangly white pantsuit in Dubai and then staged a Christmas Eve rendition of "Blue Christmas." The result: At a time when most navy ships are perilously understaffed, the Benfold expects to be fully staffed for the next year, and it has attracted a flood of transfer requests from sailors throughout the fleet.

5. **Grassroots leaders aren't looking for promotions.** Abrashoff says that because he wasn't looking for a promotion, he was free to ignore the career pressures that traditionally affect naval officers. In-

stead, he could focus on doing the job his way. "I don't care if I ever get promoted again," he says. "And that's enabled me to do the right things for my people." And yet, notes Abrashoff, this un-career-conscious approach helped him earn the best evaluation of his life as well as a promotion to a post at the Space and Naval Warfare Systems Command.

21

Military Leadership into the 21st Century: Another "Bridge Too Far?"

Walter F. Ulmer, Jr.

On 15 September 1997, after a 19-hour flight from Fort Bragg, North Carolina, 620 members of the 82d Airborne Division parachuted into Shymkent, Kazakhstan. Genghis Khan would have been impressed. En route to the drop zone the C-17s might have passed over American soldiers on the ground in Senegal or Uganda or Bosnia or Macedonia. While this military exercise involving armies of the former Soviet Union received some notice in the press, there was little expressed amazement. The American people took it for granted that our armed forces were up to the task.

Fighting forest fires in Colorado, operating medical clinics in Latin America, retrieving Soviet nuclear weapons, policing Haiti or Bosnia, keeping the North Koreans at bay—all seem equally unremarkable. Effectiveness with Hurricane Andrew recovery, with flood relief in Bangladesh, and with the Saudi National Guard was not unexpected. Even in the midst of headlines in 1997 describing appalling behavior on the part of cadre at Aberdeen Proving Ground, Maryland, opinion polls continued to show strong support for the American military. Perhaps most remarkably, heroic actions of soldiers from Panama to the Gulf to Mogadishu confirmed that the tradition of courage under fire has not been lost.

Reprinted by permission from *Parameters: Journal of the U.S. Army War College* (Washington, D.C.: Government Printing Office), 28:1 (Spring 1988), pp. 4–25. Reprinted by permission of the author.

Adventures in peacekeeping, warfighting training, drug interdiction, Olympic Games protection, and technological adaptation took place amid a force reduction of monumental proportions. In a drawdown of more than one-third strength in five years, with massive personnel turbulence, a notoriously high pace of activities, and an austere operating budget, admirable pride prevailed. In 1996, Army operational deployments averaged 35,000 soldiers per day among 70 countries. Many soldiers stationed in the United States spent more than 130 days away from home station that year. Much of the warrior spirit has somehow survived the influx from a supposedly self-centered generation. West Point cadets still compete for assignments in the combat arms.[1] "Exciting but demanding times," some soldiers have said. Our most robust corporations might—just might—have withstood the trauma to which the Army has responded so well in the 1990s. Performance of assigned, tangible missions in the last decade represents one of the finest examples of institutional stamina, commitment, and versatility in military history.

The Army also has been working diligently, in conjunction with the other military services, to anticipate and prepare for the future. The new series of war games at the Army War College, for example, seeks the insights needed to identify force structure and materiel changes that might take place in the second decade of the 21st century. Much is written and discussed about changing technology, especially in communications and automation. Through it all, we continue to profess that the Army is first and foremost the people who serve in it. Still, there appears to be a growing unease among informed observers regarding the capacity of the US armed forces to sustain operational excellence in the decades ahead.

Erosion amid Success

In an August 1997 press conference, the Chairman of the Joint Chiefs of Staff acknowledged that there were "cracks" in unit readiness. Strong anecdotal evidence to the same point has been emerging for several years. Some service members indicate they no longer recommend that their children enter the armed forces. Talented young officers appear to be leaving in disproportionately high numbers, although documentation for this is absent. The exodus of Army helicopter pilots has been described as a "hemorrhage."[2] Consider:

- A 1997 survey of several thousand soldiers conducted as part of the investigation of abuse of authority at Aberdeen Proving Ground and elsewhere reported that less than half the respondents replied positively to questions of confidence in their leaders.

- A survey sponsored by the Army Command and General Staff College in 1995 found some concerns about leadership and the command climate strikingly similar to those reported in the 1970 Army War College *Study on Military Professionalism.*[3]
- Articles in military journals increasingly include comments to the effect that innovation is being crowded out by fear of failure ("Fear of Mistakes Throttles Initiative in the Ranks," says one headline.) Thoughtful pieces in *Army* magazine argue that both personality and systemic factors undercut aspects of professionalism in the officer corps.[4]
- A House National Security Committee notes its concern that senior officials may not be admitting degradations in combat readiness.
- Many senior service college students in recent classes seem to display more than typical student skepticism about the quality of senior leaders they have observed.[5] Anecdotes about poor leadership, particularly at the field grade and general officer levels, are too persistent to ignore.

It is noteworthy that much of the data revealing troublesome trends have come not from a tabloid reporter's notes, but from Army surveys and analyses that have been made available for public scrutiny. It is also noteworthy that the same phenomenon revealed in the 1970 Army War College *Study on Military Professionalism* and the 1971 Army War College study on *Leadership for the 1970s* is present today: dramatically different climates exist simultaneously within the Army. While a generalized high level of stress is clearly present today, enthusiasm and trust reside in one unit, frustration and anxiety in another. Good leadership may not be able to compensate for incoherence in the web of strategic policies. But clear differences in morale and esprit among units of the same type provide another validation of the crucial role of organizational leadership.

The most optimistic reading of collective quantitative and anecdotal information on the current state of morale is discomforting. Measures of trust, commitment, and morale have shown localized problems over many years. The confluence of organizational and environmental pressures at this moment, however, presents institutional response challenges of a different order of magnitude. A healthy job market for officers who leave the service, the lack of a clear military threat to the United States, the higher expectations for a "decent family life," and less tolerance among capable young people for poor leadership climates create a potent mixture. The crux of the matter seems clear. It is a tale of dedication and commitment that has produced local miracles while in effect neglecting and hazarding the future of the institution. The Army's culture promotes vigorous response to policy initiatives without regard for the collective long-term consequences of such response. Inordinate focus on the immediate (non-tactical) mission along with institutional systems that cater to conspicuous short-term results represent major challenges to both current and future leadership.

Leadership in the 21st-Century Army

In any Army, in any time, the purpose of "leadership" is to get the job done. Competent military leaders develop trust, focus effort, clarify objectives, inspire confidence, build teams, set the example, keep hope alive, and rationalize sacrifice. For this century or the next, there is little mystery about requisite leader competencies or behaviors. Desirable qualities and skills may vary a bit, but the basic formula for leader success has changed little in 2,000 years. However, the method for routinely inculcating, supporting, and sustaining the desired leader behaviors has yet to be determined. The link between concept and practice is the heart of the matter. Certainly, progress in human systems design has been outpaced by technological advance. Also, during the last 30 years, higher expectations about what constitutes appropriate leader behavior have evolved in all sectors of American society.

Studies have listed the essential competencies for 21st-century leaders in different societal sectors.[6] They have typically included an ability to deal with cognitive complexity, tolerance of ambiguity, intellectual flexibility, a meaningful level of self-awareness, and an enhanced understanding of the relationships among organizational sub-systems that collectively construct the prevailing "climate." These would supplement timeless leader qualities: integrity, high energy, courage, and commitment to institutional values.

A 1982 report from the Walter Reed Army Institute for Research noted that leaders must sustain "intellectual and cognitive effort" when future warfare will have a pace, intensity, and technological complexity of unprecedented dimensions. The report's author is particularly insightful in discussing the need for leaders to be able to "not only maximize the probability of successfully completing their current mission, but to conserve what [human] resources they can for the mission that will surely follow."[7] The basic cognitive and emotional demands of the future battlefield as we now describe it in Army After Next (AAN) documents have been recognized for decades. However, strong conclusions about required competencies and behaviors have rarely produced powerful and integrated new policies designed to support the development of the heralded attributes. A discussion of "best practice" in critical human resources development matters appears later in this article.

In an interview reported in the 30 June 1997 *Army Times*, the departing Chairman of the Joint Chiefs of Staff noted that future leadership demands would be marked by the "unprecedented stress," "isolated battles," and "dispersion" of the battlefield. At his confirmation hearing the incoming Chairman said, "People are more important than hardware. We cannot allow the quality of the force to suffer." A 1996 symposium on "Leadership Challenges of the 21st Century" included thoughtful descriptions of leader competencies relevant to those battlefield stresses and doctrines. A 1997 draft of a new Army manual on leadership included attention to the future requirement for leaders' continuous learning and introduced a major conceptual breakthrough. This was the distinction between a leader's need to "operate" or achieve well-defined short-term goals, and the need to "improve" the workings of the system and thereby sustain the institution over the long term. The fact that replacement of the earlier edition of FM 22-100 appears to be a slow and tortuous process may indicate that the Army comes to grips more easily with operational and structural change than with modification of leadership doctrine.

In a September 1993 issue of *Army Focus* magazine, then Army Chief of Staff General Gordon R. Sullivan noted thoughtfully and persuasively that "The times we live in are times of profound change . . . political, ideological, and technical. We must adapt to that change and we must grow." Such "growth" of course would have to entail new perspectives, new learning, and new behaviors on the part of many senior officers. Since they initiate and exemplify organizational change, their performance as part of any change strategy is crucial. Yet in this 42-page magazine describing future demands on the Army and its response to those demands, one-half page is devoted to leader development. Further, nothing is mentioned about the task of building and sustaining climates that undergird any "learning organization."[8]

The July 1997 *Annual Report on The Army After Next Project to the Chief of Staff of the Army* used less than one of its 60 pages to discuss human issues. The leadership issues that were addressed were unrefined, unexplained, and unexplored. Relatively cavalier coverage of human dynamics is typical of brochures describing the Army After Next and the Revolution in Military Affairs. Earl H. Tilford, Jr., in *The Revolution In Military Affairs: Prospects and Cautions*, a 23 July 1995 Strategic Studies Institute report, concludes that "Discussions of the . . . RMA . . . often develop along technological lines . . . [W]hat is lost . . . is the nature of war, which remains a complex interaction of political objectives, human emotions, cultural and ethnic factors, and military skills." In the overview of Future Land Warfare in the Autumn 1997 issue of *Parameters*, Paul Van Riper and Robert H. Scales, Jr., note how technology will likely compound the stress on battle decisionmakers, and that "leadership far more than technology will determine who wins and who loses."[9] And the current Army Chief of Staff remarked after the Advanced Warfighting Experiment at the National Training Center in the Spring of 1997 that the experiment "is not necessarily about technology, although that's an important part of it. It's about changing an Army . . . [and] most of all changing the culture."[10]

Changing the culture of any organization is a leadership task, yet there appears to be no strategic design for how to change Army culture.[11] Immediate crises in Washington and the field, combined with a mixed appreciation of the need for "cultural change" among serving Army general officers, seem to have colluded to put non-technical macro issues on the back burner. The robust agility that characterizes a progressive and adaptable organization, one that can handle the Haitis, the Bosnias, and the Koreas across decades—does not derive from structure or weaponry alone. Development of technological applications and operational procedures continues to capture a disproportionate share of the Army's creative energy even though we acknowledge that soldiers—not machines or structures—ultimately determine the outcome of battle.

Searching for Contemporary "Best Practice"

Large, complex organizations of every type are more alike than different regarding the challenges of attracting, developing, and retaining talented people. The greatest similarities in requisite leadership competencies are at the upper organizational levels. Of course there are fundamental differences between the civilian and military sectors that directly affect leader selection and development. First, there is only one American Army. One cannot transfer out of that army without also leaving the institution. The executive who is unhappy at GM might find employment of a similar nature at Ford. But the Army officer who becomes frustrated in his job must either bear up or exit the profession. Second, an employment contract with Sears or GE does not carry with it the implicit duty to risk one's life to meet corporate goals. There are no unlimited liability contracts in commercial organizations. Third, the military leader-follower relationship is supported by law and tradition as well as by local policies. Fourth, all senior military leaders have been promoted from within the ranks of the organization.

To these basic differences we add the warrior ethos essential to an effective fighting force. Philosophical orientation and common endurance of hardship in the military form interpersonal bonds rarely seen in the commercial world. There are, however, two sides to tight bonding within a strong culture. One side produces wonderful team efforts toward the mission; the other maintains a conservative approach to institutional change. While few institutions revitalize themselves without enormous external pressures, strong authoritarian cultures have the potential for dramatic directional change if the collective leadership is so inclined. Integration of minority members into the US Army is one example of such change.[12]

The quest for insight into leader development brings us to the concept of "best practice." In some professions, "best practice" is routinely updated and clarified if not codified. Optimal designs for nuclear power plants or current techniques for removing plaque with balloon angioplasty are relatively specific. What is "best" in human systems design remains a more open question. Still, from the human resources criteria in the Baldridge Award to the broad discourses in relevant academic journals, we can discern evolving patterns of organizational practice that have gained reasonably high agreement among both scholars and practitioners as worthy of serious consideration. Given the differences between civilian and military organizations, but also aware of the similar aspects of all large, complex human organizations, it seems worthwhile to make some comparisons.

Three assumptions are relevant to the following comparisons of "best practice" in the Army and in US corporate structures. One is that a supportive, rational organizational climate is essential to attract, motivate, and develop high-quality people. Another is that such organizational climates are greatly influenced—for better or worse—by the values, insights, skills, and behaviors of the senior leadership of the organization.[13] Last is the reality that competition for high-quality people in business and industry as well as in the armed services is becoming increasingly stiff. Meanwhile, social mores (the acceptability of short-term employment relationships) and organizational change (the attending anxiety of instability and downsizing) conspire to undermine long-term commitment to any organization.

Early opportunities for varied responsibilities can support leader development. Here the Army is ahead of everybody. No institution does it better. Most lieutenants have opportunities to lead groups of significant size in performing challenging tasks. They are exposed to command and staff relationships and resource management early on. Young people in the corporate world often wait five to ten years for opportunities to head a project team or be responsible for an office of 20–40 people.

It's true, of course, that early opportunities for platoon and company leadership may not present a "level playing field" for the late bloomers, or for those who through no fault of their own miss the opportunity for command at company level. It is quite possible that spectacular early success or failure may create expectations or reputations that follow the individual too closely.

Produce and articulate precepts for leader behavior. This comparison is mixed, although the Army's doctrinal materials, the traditional warrior ethic, and pre-commissioning and professional education reinforce leadership concepts in ways unequaled in any sector of our society. Codes, princi-

ples, proscriptions, and good examples are plentiful in the Army. Companies increasingly are formulating explicit standards for leader behavior, seg-
mented for different echelons in the organization. Generally, in both commercial and military organizations, the higher the echelon, the less clear
leadership precepts become. The Army does not enforce guidelines about
leadership style except at the extreme edge of the acceptable behavior enve-
lope. Our monitoring system reacts promptly to selected misbehaviors such
as driving under the influence or misusing a government sedan. But our sen-
sors and mechanisms for responding to arrogant, abusive leaders who have
not created a public spectacle are less well developed. Perhaps reluctance to
inhibit subordinate initiative has prevented the required surveillance of
leadership techniques. No doubt the lack of reliable information about the
prevailing relationships between senior and subordinate one or two levels
down the chain of command has precluded timely interventions by senior
officers whose keen interest in good leadership is unquestioned. Whatever
the cause, the dearth of practical guidelines and, more important, the lack
of systematic monitoring permit a potentially unhealthy range of leader behaviors. Nonproductive behaviors may be seen by peers and subordinates
as institutionally acceptable if not condoned.

Most military doctrine at the operational and strategic levels is directly
devoted to structure and force employment, albeit within the context of
traditional values. There presently are no highly visible, heavily resourced
efforts to define, inculcate, and monitor the creation and sustainment of organizational climates that challenge, inspire, and motivate all ranks. This
remains the case even after highly visible fractures in organizational climates have generated public concern and surely alienated many commis-
sioned and noncommissioned officers over the past two years.

Doctrinal ambiguity does not apply to Army values, which have been
traditionally clear in their essence. The recently announced value set is consistent with the past and reinforces Army interest in such matters: *Duty,
Loyalty, Selfless Service, Honor, Courage, Respect, and Integrity* represent
the core of a noble tradition. Announcing them is necessary but insufficient,
however, for shaping leader behavior and for demonstrating what the Army
considers "best practice" in this respect.

The best companies are serious about recrafting their leadership selection
and development programs. The present level of interest in executive standards and style, feedback techniques, mentoring, and measurement of leadership results would have been difficult to find in the corporate world 20
years ago.[14]

Use developmental feedback and mentoring. "Best practice" in this area
has left the Army behind. Army feedback and mentoring programs are
most robust at the NCO and junior officer levels. The Officer Efficiency Report, even when the prescribed counseling is conducted, has been a crude

instrument for commenting usefully on individual strengths and weaknesses. The complex task of giving developmental feedback to subordinates is not taught in the Army school system. The Army War College has included some behavioral feedback in its program in recent years, but it is unlikely that there is the essential follow-up in the students' next organization to exploit the process.

Increasing numbers of large civilian organizations require mid-level (field grade equivalent) managers to participate in laboratory exercises that include structured, instrumented feedback from peers and subordinates. Programs for senior executives (general officer equivalent) which incorporate behavioral feedback from observers at the work site are increasingly popular.[15]

The reason for higher acceptance of developmental feedback in the for-profit world is no secret. Too many executives were and are failing, at great cost to the organizations. It is not possible to determine exact "failure" rates at the general manager and higher levels, but estimates made over the past decade range from 30 to 60 percent. There are no known sources of hard data about Army leaders' success rates. In both cases the definition of "failure" is imprecise. If one were to query serving officers about the percentage of battalion, brigade, division, and corps commanders who were seen as unsatisfactory leaders by a plurality of their subordinates and by many of their peers, I suspect the figure would be between 15 and 25 percent. Actually, there have been enough informal surveys, anecdotal reports, and ancillary studies over the past 20 years to make this more than a "suspicion."[16]

It does seem that the Army has a lower failure rate in perceived leadership effectiveness at mid and senior levels than does corporate America. Possibly, Army systems are somehow more tolerant of some non-ethical varieties of marginal performance. Or perhaps Army selection and development systems are simply more reliable. Regardless, the ranges of estimated failure rates in both sectors are alarming. One out of five selected commanders who cannot gain the trust and confidence of subordinates is intolerable over the long term. Selection errors have an extraordinarily debilitating effect on both the commercial and governmental sectors. The larger institutional sin is that the majority of today's leader selection mistakes are preventable.

Some percentage of individuals seems to have been immunized against significant adult learning, either by genetic happenstance or by early developmental neglect. But leader success rates can be improved by a combination of conceptual training, developmental feedback, environmental support for continuous learning, a performance appraisal system that attends to both development and selection, and a system for promoting leaders based on more than written reports from superiors in the organization.

A program of formal mentoring can assist in the developmental process and in assignment and selection. Mentoring and coaching have long been in the Army lexicon, but their routine use is a localized phenomenon, highly dependent on the interests and skills of unit leaders. There is no meaningful institutional motivation for being a good coach, yet that skill is highly prized by subordinates at every level. Mentoring is done more routinely at junior levels than with field grade and general officers. Most formal mentoring practices in corporations are pairings of a junior and a senior. Even in this design the senior as well as the junior typically learns because of the relationship. Where all leaders must seek and identify one or more mentors from among their peers, superiors, subordinates, or out-siders, and then record their insights over time, even more learning takes place. While there are potential downsides to a formal mentoring pro-gram, including perceptions of favoritism or cronyism and some diversions of energy from the immediate task, the consensus is that mentoring pro-grams pay their way.[17]

The Army introduced an improved Officer Evaluation Report late in 1997; it reemphasizes the need for coaching or counseling as part of the of-ficer evaluation process. Junior officers will be well served by this increased emphasis if counseling becomes increasingly important in the evaluation process. Suggestions regarding style and effects of leadership may continue to be excluded from most counseling of officers above the company-grade level. Junior officers will benefit also from an innovative administrative pol-icy that will keep OERs of their lieutenant years out of the hands of selec-tion boards for promotions above the grade of captain. Here we have a fine example of a breakthrough policy that reinforces in practice the pro-nouncements about providing opportunities to learn without penalty. Con-versely, the new OER may compromise its potential as a developmental tool by highlighting a competition for simplistic numerical ratings. It will unfortunately be administered at least initially in a climate that is viewed as ever more competitive and unforgiving.

Broad performance feedback at the organizational level is uncommon in both the military and corporate cultures. The Army's after-action review process for exploring the inner workings of tactical unit performance is a model of structured feedback not replicated routinely in the business world. That review process, however, is often omitted from the Army's non-tactical activities.[18] J. F. C. Fuller had it right in 1936 when he commented on the role of tactical critiques for teaching senior officers what they really should know: "Tactical exercises set to bring out ... *tactical* lessons are not worth the setting. What an exercise should bring out *is the personality and common sense of the generals.*"[19]

The Harvard Business School may use more case studies on recent mili-tary management and leadership than do the military schools. And while significant numbers of commanders of brigades, divisions, and corps have strong reputations for great success or awful failure, the Army does not have a useful protocol for collecting and using the rich lessons that could be distilled from their command experiences. There is no comprehensive, structured after-action review at the conclusion of a command tour. Wouldn't the Schwarzkopf-Franks controversy hold productive lessons about wartime relationships among senior commanders?[20]

There are methods to tap into these cases that would compromise neither unit nor individual privacy. The collective capacity of mid- and top-level executives to learn about themselves and their profession is the critical factor in organizational learning.

Measure organizational climate. The Army is behind corporate "best practice" in this initiative. Progressive commercial organizations routinely use climate surveys to articulate organizational values, sense strong and weak aspects of the environment, coach managers, and sometimes contribute to assignment or promotion decisions.[21] Some elements of the Army—such as parts of the Army Material Command in recent years—have completed extensive organizational surveys along with instruments that provide feedback on leader behavior. Usually these are the products of a particular commander who has knowledge of the potential of these questionnaires. But while there is no regularly administered Army survey to measure important elements of a command climate, crises sometimes bring on special surveys such as the recent look at sexual harassment and abuse of authority.[22] Morale, mission focus, clarity of priorities, effectiveness of communication, trust in leaders, confidence to perform mission-essential tasks, perceived level of discipline, support for initiative and innovation, and fair treatment of all personnel are not systematically recorded. Had a climate survey been routinely administered, many of the derogatory headlines of 1997 might have been avoided, or the severity of the problems attenuated by timely command intervention.

In other respects, the Army forcefully and frequently collects data on equipment and financial readiness (the outmoded and simplistic monthly Unit Readiness Report, for example). The absence of a parallel reporting emphasis on the state of the human component relegates that aspect of combat readiness de facto to a secondary position. Recent interest in measuring unit operating tempo is a positive move in this area. Another innovation with considerable potential is the *Ethical Climate Assessment Survey* that was gently introduced in draft form in 1997. That survey provides a structure, and perhaps more important a rationale, for assessing in useful terms the character of the organizational climate. It was designed for informal, optimal use by commanders in the field. If supported by the Army's professional education system and appreciated by commanders, it could lead to generalized improvement.

Educate leaders in techniques for assessing the effectiveness of individuals and groups.   Neither military nor corporate organizations do this well. Methods for measuring unit or individual efficiency and effectiveness are the most neglected element in managerial education, and both kinds of organizations assume leader competence to perform these delicate and important tasks. Army doctrine does not cover methods of personal or unit evaluation except in domains of individual soldier skills and small-unit tactical operations. At the Army's Combat Training Centers, officers assigned as Observer Controllers develop unique competence in critiquing tactical actions. Critique of leader behavior has been less formal, slipped into debriefings or informal conversations at the Centers. This approach appears in vogue also at the Battle Command Training Program.

The Army and many corporations have used assessment center technology in one form or another for leader development, and in a few cases for leader selection and assignment. Assessment center methodology was first used in the United States by the OSS in World War II. The reliability of OSS operatives who passed the assessment screening was mixed; lessons from that experiment, while significant, were mostly disregarded. But assessment and other executive training programs clearly have been useful in raising the self-awareness of participants. They most likely produce other salutary developmental outcomes, including improved competencies for performance evaluation by the individuals who monitor the exercises. Army Recruiting Command and the Admissions Office at the US Military Academy are among the Army entities that have used assessment center concepts. Their findings reinforce the utility of these techniques in enhancing the assessment skills of the staff members who conducted the exercises.[23]

When executives participate in a simulation designed to hone their personnel selections skills, results (similar to those obtained from long-range studies done at AT&T and elsewhere) show that experienced leaders can enhance the reliability of their assignment and promotion decisions through targeted training.[24]

The Army does not address the very complex task of how to evaluate the performance of a subordinate on the job, how to apply available technologies to assist in this process, how to take advantage of research in this field, or how to take the temperature of the unit climate and exploit the results to enhance unit effectiveness. Remarkably, many commanders are doing it right anyway. But "many" is not enough. Interestingly, the 1983 version of FM 22-100, *Military Leadership*, advised its readers to "avoid using statistics as a major method of evaluating units and motivating subordinates." But this wise guidance—supported clearly by pronouncements from the current and prior Army Chiefs of Staff—has not been translated into the coordinated institutional system required for its generalized implementation.

Use multiple sources of input as the basis for promotion decisions.   The leading American corporations are ahead of the Army in using "best practice" in making promotion decisions. Many companies have evolved a system of multiple sources of information to support promotion decisions. And while scholarly literature has urged this approach for years, only in the last decade has the practice become routine in any but the most adventuresome work settings.[25] The evaluation of people for either development or selection, but especially for selection, by anybody but the boss has long been considered intolerable. Such action was thought to undermine authority, to be susceptible to fostering a "popularity contest," and to be hostage to the softer interpersonal standards hostile to productivity criteria. Yet the more closely we scrutinize either theory or practice, the more inadequate the exclusively top-down assessment of performance and potential appear.

"Transformational" leaders have been identified in both military and commercial settings as more effective than are leaders who rely heavily on transactional or management-by-exception leadership styles.[26] (This finding is being reconfirmed at junior levels by an ongoing Army Research Institute study of platoon leader and platoon sergeant behavior.) Some of the critical characteristics and behaviors of the transformational leader are often undisclosed to the boss but are glaringly evident to subordinates and frequently clear to peers. What the boss measures most reliably are immediate task accomplishment, structural decisions, and adherence to prescribed strategy. Perhaps this is why the Army has probably produced the most effective cadre of managers of short-term results—in addition to large numbers of true leaders—on the planet. Meanwhile, transformational behaviors, such as articulating a motivational vision, providing intellectual challenge, inspiring teamwork, considering subordinates as individuals, being open to ideas, demonstrating moral courage, and setting the example of subordinating self to mission, are unreliably observed by seniors even though they require just that information for their evaluation of subordinates.

Peer and subordinate evaluations have been used by commanders especially interested in leader development in some Army schools, in selected pre-commissioning programs, in some special training situations, and in a few units. And while they are apparently used routinely in the military services of some other nations, they appear to remain broadly unacceptable to the US Army general officer corps. It is difficult to dispute the reality that in order to promote individuals who are in fact good leaders we must somehow measure their style of leadership. Only the led know for certain the leader's moral courage, consideration for others, and commitment to unit above self. This is the indisputably crucial element in leader assessment and development systems. If in fact we prize these values and want to ensure that we promote those who have routinely demonstrated them, some form of input from subordinates is required. Again, the concept and technology are available to handle such inputs without organizationally dysfunctional side effects.

Provide systemic support for continuous learning. Corporate America is struggling with this issue, and the Army has approached it in piecemeal fashion. Adult learning has the attention of the business world because of global competition. While there is a need to deal with the rapid obsolescence of technical subject matter, that is not the central challenge. The pragmatic pedagogical issue is not "what to learn," but "how to learn."

No corporation in the world equals the Army's commitment to continuing formal education. The Army also leads the way in broad education of its leaders among the military services, and a recent Army conference on professional military education noted the importance of the neglected "how to learn" issue.[27] This is another area where conceptual thinking in the Army is advanced but application of the knowledge is slow. The pace of application is dramatically different from the aggressive exploitation of digital information technologies that is driving the Advanced Warfighting Experiment. Are we buying hardware at the expense of those who must train and lead our Army in its use?

Few institutions provide reliable support for the kind of learning or the kind of creativity and innovation essential in a rapidly changing and stressful environment.[28] The question, then, is how do we marshal our intellectual and operational resources to facilitate learning from our individual and collective experience? Workshops tailored specifically to "learning on the job" or "learning from experience" have been one method some corporations have put in place. Such workshops are conceptually similar in attempting to separate skill learning (which the Army does particularly well) from cognitive process awareness (which the Army and most corporations have not come to grips with). Workshops typically involve exercises that require the executives to examine carefully "how" they made specific significant decisions, good and bad. Journals, reflective thinking, work with concepts of adult learning and the emotional hurdles accompanying that process, and ideas on use of mentors comprise the usual curriculum. The challenge is to implant methods for raising awareness about the cognitive and emotional processes that result in decisions. The core of the "learning" issue may be illustrated by a battalion commander's learning from a training incident where the advancing forces moved beyond the range of supporting mortars. One lesson might be "I learned to displace the mortars more frequently so they can provide continuous coverage to the advancing troops." A deeper learning might be "I learned that I need to change my behavior and approach to the staff so that they can interrupt me if necessary to get timely approval to displace the mortars. Or, perhaps I should delegate that authority to my operations officer or fire support officer."[29]

In many respects the Army's attention to human factors is unmatched by other sectors. Building on sincere traditional concerns for compassion as well as for operational competence, many units are notably well led today even as they remain overcommitted. Additionally, the Army has at its disposal a vast but scattered knowledge base that covers the full spectrum of the behavioral, cognitive, social, and biological sciences.

Special Aspects Delineating Military Leaders

In addition to the military's unlimited liability contract, two other factors contribute to the current status of the military institution. These combined aspects militate against too strong an analogy between civilian and military leaders.

The general officer personality factor. The Army's ability to cope with the challenges of the 21st century will be determined largely by the collective values and abilities of its general officers. They will set and exemplify standards and create policies and climates. Personality and behavioral data on corporate executives and Army brigadier generals have been collected for two decades. Most of these data have come from behavioral questionnaires completed by the participants and from people who have worked with and for them. Other insights were collected as the generals participated in leaderless group exercises with their civilian classmates. Because most of the data are collected using standard psychological tests, many of the generals' results can be compared with that of groups in other sectors. As with all data comparisons there are inherent limitations, but the findings have been reported in both academic and popular journals. There were originally presented by Dr. David Campbell in a 1987 paper.[30]

> General officers that we have now are outstanding—they are bright, well educated, experienced, responsible and well indoctrinated into democratic ways. Further, in the few ways we have to evaluate them in comparison with civilian leaders, generals come across as more impressive. In that regard, we are a fortunate society.

Dr. Campbell concludes also that the data (which have changed little since the data collection began in the late 1970s, although today's generals have been observed as somewhat more open and less insulated than those of a decade ago) are sufficient to identify a personality syndrome that he describes as "the aggressive adventurer." His description of that personality would be: "dominant, competitive, action-oriented patriotic men who are drawn naturally to physically adventuresome militaristic activities." Tests show reasonably high needs for "control," tendencies toward "dominance" well above the level of a typical manager, greater comfort with data than with intuition, and a high "achievement through conformity" orientation. (Their executive counterparts in the corporate world have test scores only a bit closer to the population norm.) This set of personality characteristics is highly desirable in many situations. Campbell continued: "Despite my few misgivings, I am impressed by most of the officers that I have been working with. . . . The other civilians in our courses who have worked with them for a week have been almost informally impressed by their intelligence, capabilities, and dedication to this country."

The foregoing notwithstanding, there is substantial evidence—summarized in the "aggressive adventurer" description—of a typical personality type whose strengths and weaknesses should be carefully noted as we move into the next century. Research shows convincingly how strengths that served well to accomplish the tactical tasks of early managerial years can become dysfunctional when individuals move to the strategic level. Work by T. O. Jacobs and others in the military community show similar patterns of differential effects of competencies as officers move up in rank.[31] It seems unlikely that the "below the zone" battalion commander will have the inherent inclination to review the suitability of his style for higher command.[32] Again, the issue is that certain characteristics which are invaluable in a strong leader in any organization, and especially prized in the military—such as self-confidence, willingness to accept responsibility, a thirst for facts and hard data, and respect for the status quo—all have possible downsides. Army policy formulation must take into consideration the typical senior officer personality, safeguarding the collective strengths as it consciously attempts to ameliorate the weaknesses.[33]

The essential but potentially disruptive warrior ethic. Douglas MacArthur was right in 1962 in his parting address at West Point when he said that the mission of Army officers was to "win our wars." If we lose sight of that reality, nothing else will matter in the 21st century. Our Army will become irrelevant at best and disavowed at worst. The issue here is how to sustain the warrior spirit while enhancing those aspects of the leader personality that will embrace change, agility, creativity, and self-awareness when the need for those attributes is paramount.[34]

The "can do" attitude toward military tasks that we rightly prize, when coupled with the typical personality of our colonels and generals, has a downside. Of all the services, the Army epitomizes the loyal servant mentality. It complains less in public about its resource levels, a cultural artifact that has been noted in several studies. Carl Builder said in a 1987 talk, "The object of the Army's worship is the country . . . The Navy worships at the altar of tradition . . . The Air Force worships at the fountain of technology."[35] Samuel Huntington wrote in 1957, "The Army developed an image of itself as the governments' obedient handyman performing without question or hesitation the jobs assigned to it." And in a fascinating 1996 dissertation, Stephen Scroggs concluded that the Army is less effective in its relations with Congress than are the other services because of the Army's sense of unseemliness in operating aggressively outside its institutional boundaries.[36]

The warrior ethic does more than set expectations for heroic competence on the battlefield. It also sets the stage for leader behaviors. The primary positive behavior, at the heart of the professional tradition, is the concept of self-sacrifice. This value, remarkably alive amid a professed self-centered society, distinguishes the soldier and supports tactical success. Because obedience is correctly entwined with sacrifice and loyal commitment, and because warfare demands discipline, the need for a hierarchical organization persists even in the shadow of technological change. Arguments to the contrary have not been confirmed in practice.

The impediment to optimal organizational functioning arises from failure to recognize that the efficacy and de facto legitimacy of the authoritarian mode differ dramatically depending on the situation. There really are only two "different situations" the leader must confront. As mentioned earlier, there is the situation where immediate action and centralized control are the guiding parameters. This is the "operating" situation, requiring standard procedures and crew "drills," with expectations for prompt, discernible, measurable results. The linkage between cause and effect is clear. Hard data are usually available for decisionmaking. Reflection or contemplation is out of place. The typical general officer or CEO personality fits well into this situation. Any tendency of personality toward immediate action is reinforced in the junior leadership years when prompt, aggressive control of the tactical situation represents laudatory behavior.

The other type of situation gives the general officer or CEO personality more trouble. It requires contemplation before action, patience with ambiguity, and an appreciation for broad participation in the decisionmaking process. This is the "building" or "improving" situation. Its focus is on sustaining or improving the strategic situation, on protecting institutional values, on reconfiguring organizational systems, on investing in basic research and education, on taking time to coach and mentor. There are tenuous links here between cause and effect; results—even when discernible—are difficult to quantify. Often there are incomplete or conflicting data from multiple sources. Skilled, self-aware leaders are able to recognize and discriminate between the behaviors suitable for these two situations.

More important, senior leaders in particular must be able to shift from one set of leader behaviors to another. Army performance appraisal rewards the "operating" mode. This bias is reinforced by such behavior modifiers as the monthly "readiness" reporting juggernaut that highlights the measurable and not necessarily the important. Then we compound the problem by allowing relatively limited time in any one assignment, making it difficult for a leader to gain trust and to make seminal contributions. In effect, everything about the current system moves leadership style relentlessly toward the "operating" end of the spectrum.

The warrior ethic, essential as the distinctive characteristic of the profession of arms, can rationalize leader behaviors that are situationally inappropriate. The classic example is the authoritarian leader whose penchant for centralized control results in poor decisions because his style denies him essential information. An idea long enunciated by many respected senior Army leaders—disagreement is not disloyalty—has not permeated the fabric of the institution.[37] The absolute authority essential in battle can be a spawning ground for abuse of power. This is especially true if behavioral guidelines for the exercise of authority are sketchy. Fortunately, many aggressive, mission-oriented officers are also self-restrained, sensitive to the situation, respectful of others, tolerant of ambiguity, open to ideas, and generally comfortable with themselves.

There are no indications that the environment of the 21st century will be less challenging for leaders than that of the 20th century. As military operations become ever more complex, and their environments more exacting, the boundaries of acceptable and productive leader behavior in different situations will become more restrictive.

Systemic Adjustments to Support Army Leader Development

Adjustments in the educational system. The first adjustment—the shift from what to learn to how to learn—has been identified or at least rediscovered in recent Army discussions. Curriculum changes at the Army War College and the Industrial College of the Armed Forces lately have focused more attention on "thinking skills" in their introductory courses. This modification can be conducted throughout the Army's professional educational system without distracting from mastery of essential technical skills. We need close scrutiny of student research papers, greater use of analysis of prevailing procedures and doctrine, and creation in the classroom of a skeptical—if respectful—mindset. Case studies in leadership and management need to substitute for some of the repetitious tactical scenarios. Excellent tactics will not compensate for lack of perceptive leadership in either preparing or employing military units.

The second adjustment has been under consideration for years and implemented primarily in basic skill training where it has received mixed reviews. This is the move at staff and war college levels from a *selection and attendance* mode of education to a more *individualized and competence-based* mode. Instruction should be tailored to individual students. Length of residence would depend on a careful assessment of student needs, experience, and expectations. Student achievement should be based on demonstrated competence in written and oral examinations given when the student feels prepared for the individualized tests leading to a diploma. Some students may take two years to complete a course at one of the service war colleges; others could be finished in six months. There might be some minimum number of months in residence to gain the insights that come from residential membership in an academic setting. Significant credits toward graduation could be earned through prior "distance learning." Structured coaching in leader behavior and standards should continue in post-schooling assignments.

Adjustments in unit readiness reporting.   Unit readiness and its reporting should be redefined to include assessments of cohesion, morale, and discipline in addition to the traditional measurements of equipment status and personnel fill.[38] Reporting intervals for major units should be changed from monthly to quarterly. This simple step would reduce the significant administrative effort now expended on a reporting process that is in disrepute at lower organizational levels. More important, this revision would provide a mild sense of liberation and empowerment to unit commanders, and a step in the direction of cultural change to strengthen mutual trust within the chain of command.

A separate but related action would require periodic assessments of the organizational climate in a more comprehensive manner than through the quarterly readiness reports. There are techniques available for this purpose; they would have to be explained to all interested audiences and taught in the professional education system. The Army would have to decide how the results of the surveys should be compiled and distributed, and be candid regarding their potential effects on commanders' records and reputations. The best model for climate surveys for the early years of their implementation is to provide unit results only to unit commanders, with higher headquarters receiving only consolidated reports. After a few years other modes of distribution of results should be considered. The questionnaires themselves would constitute a tutorial on Army expectations about organizational leadership.

Adjustments on how to learn leadership on the job.   The issue here is feedback. It should come from two sources: a formal mentoring program and a supplement to the Officer Evaluation Report. Each field-grade and general officer should be required to select two formal mentors. The specifics of "mentoring" should be broadly defined, with the professional education system once again responsible for teaching the selection and roles of mentors along with techniques for receiving and providing behavioral feedback. Mentors could be active or retired military, or civilian; they could offer intimate and non-threatening feedback, and they could provide a confidential repository that the chain of command simply cannot.

At the end of a battalion-level command assignment, there would be a comprehensive analysis of the leadership strengths and weaknesses of the outgoing commander. This should be an off-the-record procedure designed to assist in leader development, and it should be formalized by Army regulation. Lessons learned from the mentorship program would be provided to the Army's professional education system. These analytical feedback sessions should be conducted by a specialized team outside the local chain of command, with participation from that chain of command, and from mentors, and scheduled well after all evaluation reports have been completed.

There should also be developmental feedback to the rated officer from peers and subordinates as well as from superiors. (Where this is being done in industry, there have been no reports that the chain of command has been ruptured as a result.) Information on behaviors, collected by a suitable questionnaire, should be provided initially only to the officer concerned. There are modalities for keeping feedback somewhat confidential as to actual source (using a minimum of five or six individuals who are not specifically identified, for example) and the feedback does not have to derive exclusively from current peers or subordinates.

If in fact leadership is important, we need to develop more effective ways to measure it than we now possess. We have found no way to verify the presence or absence of some crucial leader behaviors other than to query the followers. If the institution cannot come to grips with this fact, it will never reduce significantly the error rate in leader selection. The need to enhance the retention of high-quality personnel in the competitive decades ahead will reduce even further the acceptable level of mistakes in military leader selection.

Adjustments in the promotion system. Revisions of career field groupings envisaged by the new officer personnel management system can provide a giant first step in adjusting the Army officer promotion system.[39] The proposed de facto compartmentalized promotion quotas will limit competition to within career groups; it will thereby eliminate the system that now abandons most combat arms officers who are not selected for battalion command.

The promotion process itself requires major adjustments. Selection boards for promotions to the grade of lieutenant colonel and higher need a broader base of information than is now available. In addition to whatever evaluation reports are in the file, there should be an application from the officer himself, indicating the positions for which he feels qualified and interested, and outlining the special skills he has amassed over the years.[40] The selection board also should be provided the results of a canvass of peers and subordinates attesting to the leadership side of the personality. There should be a fresh query of former superiors, some selected by the applicant, who would indicate on some scale the relative readiness for particular assignments of the individual being considered. The main point is to expand the useful information available to the boards. This protocol can be designed in a manner that does not subvert command authority. The judgment of selection board members would still reign supreme.

Selection of brigade-level commanders should be similar to the promotion scheme outlined above. Again, officers should apply for brigade command. They should have an opportunity to explain their career goals. This procedure would also offer an opportunity for quiet avoidance of the command selection process for those officers who have concluded that other options are more realistic or comfortable for them.

The Essential Task Is Not How to Define Requisite Leadership, But How to Develop and Sustain It

Leadership principles and lists of traits and descriptions of required situational behaviors will continue to flood the market, even though the basics of leadership that derive from timeless human needs and aspirations have changed little in all of recorded history. While studies and the deductions therefrom will shed light, our challenge is to move into the 21st century with a good record of practice, not just a solid platform of theory. It is the record of practice to date that should give all of us who have participated some feelings of satisfaction along with profound concern and resolve to do better. Our Amy has recovered from several low points over the last hundred years. The revitalization between 1970 and 1990 is a monument to collective institutional commitment supported by creative Army leadership and an understanding public. Were we to sink again to a real low, there could be a serious question regarding the national capacity to restore the institution to what it must be. Bold initiatives now can ensure the future. "Good leadership" is essential not only as the ultimate battlefield force-multiplier but also as the primary guardian of the institution.

Notes

1. A recent study showed high levels of patriotism and "warriorism" among West Point cadets. See Volker C. Franke, "Warriors for Peace: The Next Generation of U.S. Military Leaders," *Armed Forces & Society*, 24 (Fall 1997), 33–57.

2. A number of such assertions can be found in the popular press. The 1997 issues of *Army Times,* articles in the *Wall Street Journal,* an item in the 22 September 1997 *U.S. News and World Report,* commentary in service journals, and other evidence would be unconvincing singularly. However, comments from the House National Security Committee as reported in the 14 July issue of *Army Times* and the findings from the recent large survey associated with sexual harassment, confirming

other recent survey data, leave little doubt that there are more than superficial problems with elements of the climate of the Army. Other studies going back more than a decade (HQDA, "Longitudinal Research on Officer Careers," and the 1985 "Professional Development of Officers Study," among others) found substantial levels of dissatisfaction.

3. From a presentation by then-Brigadier General David H. Ohle on "1995 Leadership & Professionalism Assessment Study Trends," at a conference on military ethics, Cantigny, 13 March 1996.

4. See Major General John C. Faith, USA Ret., "The Overcontrolling Leader: The Issue Is Trust," *Army*, June 1997.

5. Personal discussions and informal surveys by the author.

6. A representative collection of papers describing future leader demands was presented at the "Leadership Challenges of the 21st Century Army Symposium," 18 March 1996, prepared by the Institute for Management and Leadership Research of Texas Tech University. A similar set of required leader behaviors was mentioned by several speakers at the 9–10 December 1997 conference, "The Impact of High Technology on the Physiological and Psychological Dimensions of Warfare," held in Atlanta.

7. This 1982 publication, *The Future Battlefield: Human Dimensions and Implications for Doctrine and Research* (Washington, D.C.: Walter Reed Army Institute of Research, 1982), has relevance for 21st-century leadership.

8. General Gordon R. Sullivan, USA Ret., is not naive about concepts of "learning organizations." His book *Hope Is Not a Method* (1996) provides broad insights on the subject. But the institution struggles with the link between concept and practice.

9. Paul Van Riper and Robert H. Scales, Jr., "Preparing for War in the 21st Century," *Parameters*, 27 (Autumn 1997), 9–10.

10. General Dennis Reimer's quote in the 31 March 1997 issue of *Army Times* is consistent with his other comments on AWE implications. He has shown a keen awareness of the potential effects of the downsizing and high optempo on the organizational climate, and of Army After Next leadership challenges.

11. An excellent article on the subject is Major Donald E. Vandergriff, "Toward a New Institutional Culture: Creating the Officer Corps of the Future to Execute Force XXI Blitzkrieg," *Armor* (March-April 1997).

12. See Charles C. Moskos and John Sibley Butler, *All That We Can Be* (New York: Basic Books, 1996).

13. The effect of "climate" on trust, cohesion, and unit effectiveness has been validated in many studies. One good reference is the *ARI Newsletter*, Vol. 9 (June 1992), which relates leadership to small-unit effectiveness. An ongoing ARI-sponsored study led by Dr. B. M. Bass will revisit some of these issues. Another important work on climate and trust is Major J. A. Simonsen, Captain H. L. Frandsen, and Captain D. S. Hoopengardner, *Excellence in the Combat Arms* (Claremont, Calif.: Naval Postgraduate School, December 1984).

14. One of many overviews of issues and programs in the corporate world is Leonard R. Sayles, *The Working Leader: The Triumph of High Performance over Conventional Management* (New York: The Free Press, 1993). The Peters, Bennis, Waterman, and Drucker books have much the same kind of information.

15. A most convenient reference for 360-degree feedback and enhancement of self-awareness is the Summer and Fall 1993 Special Issue (Vol. 32, Nos. 2 & 3) of *Human Resource Management*. An officer's first deep insight in this issue may come from the Leadership Development Program conducted by the Center for Creative Leadership (CCL) that is available to brigadier general selectees.

16. An Army War College Military Studies Project authored by Tilden Reid dated 5 June 1983 and titled "Performance of Successful Brigade Commanders Who Were Selected to BG as Viewed by Their Former Battalion Commanders," concluded that 28 percent of those brigadier generals should not have been selected.

17. For a convenient overview of mentoring programs, see Christina A. Douglas, *Formal Mentoring Programs in Organizations: An Annotated Bibliography* (Greensboro, N.C.: Center for Creative Leadership, 1997).

18. Two exceptions were the 1986 *Fort Hood Leadership Study* prepared for HQDA-HRL by the Essex Corporation; and the September 1987 report on the formation of the 7th Infantry Division (Light) prepared by Walter Reed Army Institute of Research as Technical Report No. 5. (The effect of these organizational analyses is unknown.)

19. J. F. C. Fuller, *Generalship: Its Diseases and Their Cure* (1936: rpt. Harrisburg, Pa.: Military Service Publishing Co., 1984), p. 76.

20. Tom Clancy with General Fred Franks, Jr., USA Ret., *Into the Storm: A Study in Command* (New York: G. P. Putnam's Sons, 1997), should stimulate professional discussion on issues of authority, style, and relationships.

21. The Army has considerable experience with a variety of surveys. There was once, and perhaps still is, an HQDA Pamphlet (600-69, 1 October 1986) that provided a convenient "Unit Climate Profile" format. One summary of corporate use can be found in Daniel R. Denison, "Bringing Corporate Culture to the Bottom Line," *Organizational Dynamics* (1984). It is use of data, not the gathering of data, that has been the primary flaw in the Army's survey efforts.

22. In late 1997 the Army distributed a special survey ("Army 1998 Survey") that queried a sample of officers, NCOs, and DA civilians on the six Army imperatives: Quality People, Effective Doctrine, Force Mix, Challenging Training, Modern Equipment, and Leader Development. This survey has potential for deriving important insights on perceptions in these areas. Something of this genre is needed on a routine basis, with considerable discussion about distribution and use of the results.

23. The Fort Benning Field Unit of the Army Research Institute and various offices at the U.S. Military Academy have conducted in-house research on assessment centers.

24. A. Howard and D. W. Bray, *Managerial Lives in Transition: Advancing Age and Changing Times* (New York: The Guilford Press, 1988), is a definitive, exhaustive work that supports the thesis that we can do better.

25. For a discussion of the issues of the use of peer and subordinate feedback in organizations, see David W. Bracken et al., *Should 360-Degree Feedback Be Used Only for Developmental Purposes?* (Greensboro, N.C.: Center for Creative Leadership, 1997).

26. Bass and Avolio, eds., *Improving Organizational Effectiveness Through Transformational Leadership* (1994) has since been updated with more support for

the general thesis: transformational leadership produces productivity that is unequaled by other styles in the full range of leader behaviors.

27. *Professional Military Education: An Asset for Peace and Progress,* Panel Report (Washington, D.C.: Center for Strategic and International Studies, March 1997).

28. See Morgan W. McCall, Jr., et al., *The Lessons of Experience: How Successful Executives Develop on the Job* (Lexington, Mass.: Lexington Books, 1988). This is about the best book around on this subject.

29. There has been a lot of good material produced in the past several years on the challenges "successful" adults have with their growth and continued learning. See, for example, Robert E. Kaplan et al., *Beyond Ambition: How Driven Managers Can Lead Better and Live Better* (San Francisco: Jossey-Bass, 1991); and Gilbert Brim, *Ambition: How We Manage Success and Failure Throughout Our Lives* (New York: Basic Books, 1992).

30. David Campbell, "The Psychological Test Profiles of Brigadier Generals: Warmongers or Decisive Warriors?" invited address, Division 14, American Psychological Association, New York City, 30 August 1987. The study data were updated at the Center for Creative Leadership in 1996 with no significant changes in the collective test scores of the general officers participating in CCL programs.

31. Dr. T. O. Jacobs, formerly with ARI and now on the faculty of ICAF, has studied general officer capacities and competencies for three decades. His briefings on senior officer requirements have described, particularly in the cognitive domain, most of the requisites we now discuss as essential for leadership in the 21st century.

32. Data are scarce on whether the selectees for the critical battalion command positions have more of the desired characteristics of senior leaders than do the non-selected. Some preliminary analysis of comparisons between battalion command selectees and their non-selected peers conducted at the USAWC and the Industrial College of the Armed Forces appears to find few differences in many of the attributes normally associated with successful performance at strategic levels. Contributors to this research include Colonel (Ret.) M. L. McGee, Dr. T. O. Jacobs, Dr. R. N. Kilcullen of ARI, and Dr. H. R. Barber of the Army War College.

33. An excellent discussion of personality and the senior leader is found in "Executive Assessment," in *Strategic Leadership and Decision Making* (Washington, D.C.: Industrial College of the Armed Forces, National Defense University Press, 1997).

34. One good recent publication that mentions the challenge of selecting warriors from a peacetime force is a Naval Doctrine Command paper by Dr. James J. Titten titled "Navy Combat Leadership for Tomorrow: Where Will We Get Such Men and Women?" (July 1995).

35. Carl H. Builder (RAND staff member), "Mirrors to the Service's Personalities," luncheon presentation to a conference on "The Air Force in the 21st Century," 28 March 1987.

36. Stephen K. Scroggs, "Army Relations with Congress," Ph.D. diss. Department of Political Science, Duke University, 1996.

37. Part of the problem must rest on the shoulders of followers, albeit a small part. See Ira Chaleff, *The Courageous Follower: Standing up and for Our Leaders* (San Francisco: Berrett-Koehler Publishers, 1995).

38. The *Report of the Defense Science Board Task Force on Readiness*, June 1994, contains some good advice in the "Personnel" section. It mentions "demonstration of a real commitment to 'people first' programs" and "careful management of OPTEMPO," pp. 12–13.

39. The task force led by Major General David Ohle has constructed a rearrangement of Army career paths and promotion alternatives that, if implemented, can have a significant positive effect on the culture.

40. The Army's new Officer Evaluation Report (a better name than the previous Officer Efficiency Report) includes a section for the rater to note "unique professional skills" which could assist in this process.